THE EPISTEMOLOGY OF READING AND INTERPRETATION

Reading and textual interpretation are ordinary human activities, performed inside as well as outside academia, but precisely how they function as unique sources of knowledge is not well understood. In this book, René van Woudenberg explores the nature of reading and how it is distinct from perception and (attending to) testimony, which are two widely acknowledged knowledge sources. After distinguishing seven accounts of interpretation, van Woudenberg discusses the question of whether all reading inevitably involves interpretation, and shows that although reading and interpretation often go together, they are distinct activities. He goes on to argue that both reading and interpretation can be paths to realistically conceived truth, and explains the conditions under which we are justified in believing that they do indeed lead us to the truth. Along the way, he offers clear and novel analyses of reading, meaning, interpretation, and interpretative knowledge.

RENÉ VAN WOUDENBERG is Professor of Philosophy at Vrije Universiteit Amsterdam and Director of the Abraham Kuyper Center for Science and the Big Questions. He is Co-editor of *The Cambridge Companion to Common-Sense Philosophy* (with Rik Peels, Cambridge University Press, 2020) and *Scientism: Prospects and Problems* (with Rik Peels and Jeroen de Ridder, 2018).

THE EPISTEMOLOGY OF READING AND INTERPRETATION

RENÉ VAN WOUDENBERG
Vrije Universiteit Amsterdam

Shaftesbury Road, Cambridge CB2 8EA, United Kingdom
One Liberty Plaza, 20th Floor, New York, NY 10006, USA
477 Williamstown Road, Port Melbourne, VIC 3207, Australia
314–321, 3rd Floor, Plot 3, Splendor Forum, Jasola District Centre, New Delhi – 110025, India
103 Penang Road, #05–06/07, Visioncrest Commercial, Singapore 238467

Cambridge University Press is part of Cambridge University Press & Assessment, a department of the University of Cambridge.

We share the University's mission to contribute to society through the pursuit of education, learning and research at the highest international levels of excellence.

www.cambridge.org
Information on this title: www.cambridge.org/9781009016360

DOI: 10.1017/9781009025171

First published 2021
First paperback edition 2023

A catalogue record for this publication is available from the British Library

Library of Congress Cataloging-in-Publication data
NAMES: Woudenberg, René van, author.
TITLE: The epistemology of reading and interpretation / René van Woudenberg.
DESCRIPTION: Cambridge, United Kingdom ; New York, NY, USA : Cambridge University Press, 2021. | Includes bibliographical references and index.
IDENTIFIERS: LCCN 2021026879 (print) | LCCN 2021026880 (ebook) | ISBN 9781316516799 (hardback) | ISBN 9781009016360 (paperback) | ISBN 9781009025171 (epub)
SUBJECTS: LCSH: Reading, Psychology of. | Hermeneutics. | BISAC: PHILOSOPHY / Epistemology
CLASSIFICATION: LCC BF456.R2 W68 2021 (print) | LCC BF456.R2 (ebook) | DDC 220.601–dc23
LC record available at https://lccn.loc.gov/2021026879
LC ebook record available at https://lccn.loc.gov/2021026880

ISBN 978-1-316-51679-9 Hardback
ISBN 978-1-009-01636-0 Paperback

Contents

Acknowledgments

This book is an outcome of the large-scale research project "The Epistemic Responsibilities of the University," which was executed in the theoretical-philosophy section of the Department of Philosophy of the Vrije Universiteit Amsterdam. Theoretical philosophy at the Vrije Universiteit Amsterdam is a very lively affair, with much discussion going on, many conferences being hosted, and many guests and visiting scholars making their appearance.

Over the years, I have profited greatly from discussions with numerous colleagues in the Netherlands and abroad. I mention Bill Alston, Valentin Arts, Lieke Asma, Michael Bergman, Wout Bisschop, Roland den Boef, Bram Bos, Lex Bouter, Gijsbert van den Brink, Alexander Broadie, Kelly Clark, Terence Cuneo, Jonathan Dancy, Marian David, Lieven Decock, Igor Douven, Coos Engelsma, Hans van Eyghen, Richard Gaskin, Mikkel Gerken, Alvin Goldman, Wouter Goris, Gordon Graham, Sander Griffioen, Gerben Groenewoud, Dirk-Martin Grube, Annemie Halsema, Tamarinde Haven, Martin van Hees, Roger Henderson, Geertjan Holtrop, Daniel and Frances Howard-Snyder, Christoph Jäger, Everard de Jong, Klemens Kappel, Ian Kidd, Naomi Kloosterboer, Pieter van der Kolk, Kees van der Kooi, Hilary Kornblith, Edwin Koster, Anders Kraal, Klaas Kraay, Thirza Lagewaard, Brian Leftow, Noah Lemos, Kelvin McQueen, Trenton Merricks, Reinier Munk, Rob Nijhoff, Nicolaj Nottelmann, Tim O'Connor, Eric Olsen, Tim Pawl, Rik Peels, Jeanne Peijnenburg, Alvin Plantinga, Duncan Pritchard, Chris Ranalli, Michael Rea, Baron Reed, Henk de Regt, Jeroen de Ridder, Alex Rosenberg, Michael Ruse, Bruce Russell, Emanuel Rutten, Hans Schouten, Russ Shafer-Landau, Ernest Sosa, Michael Stenmark, Bob Sweetman, Richard Swinburne, Joeri Tijdink, Alan Torrance, Peter van Inwagen, Lies Wesseling, David Widerker, Jan-Willem Wieland, Tim Williamson, William Wood, Marritta van Woudenberg, Dean Zimmerman, and Lambert Zuidervaart. Many of these people have given written comments on drafts of parts of the book that is now in your hands.

I owe special debts, and words of great appreciation, to a few more people. Feeling apprehensive because of its novelty, I discussed the basic idea of this book with Nick Wolterstorff over lunch during a meeting of the American Philosophical Association (APA) in Chicago. Nick listened, asked questions, and enthusiastically urged me to pursue the idea. My indebtedness to him for this, as for so many other things, is great and heartfelt. A few days prior to that lunch, I gave a talk at the philosophy department of Northwestern University on material that found its way into this book. Jennifer Lackey, who was present, later saw me at the APA meeting, broke out of a conversation she was having, walked up to me and said, "I really think reading is a neglected but great epistemological topic – stay with it!" or words of similar intent, which meant a lot to me. Over the years, Robert Audi has taken a genuine interest in the gestation of the book, and he offered invaluable comments on early drafts of chapters. Special thanks are due to Stephen Grimm and another reader for Cambridge University Press, both of whom gave comments on an early draft of the book. I owe them much for their generous and critical commentaries, which have led to substantial rethinking and rewriting. I have already mentioned Jeroen de Ridder and Rik Peels, but I mention them again to thank them for the intellectually vigorous and open environment they helped create in our theoretical-philosophy group, for so many forms of happy collaboration, for their critical comments, and for so much good sense and humor.

Material that in some form or other found its way into this book has been presented at conferences and seminars of the European Epistemology Network and at Oxford University, the University of St. Andrews, the University of Notre Dame, and the University of Louvain. In revised form, various paragraphs of two papers of mine have found their way into this book: "Reading as a Source of Knowledge," published in *Synthese*, and "The Nature of the Humanities," published in *Philosophy*.

Final words of thanks are due to Hilary Gaskin from Cambridge University Press for her efficient and friendly way of overseeing the project. To Elisa Matse, who did so much on the logistic and administrative side to make the project "The Epistemic Responsibilities of the University" such a success. To Mathanja Berger, for her skillful copyediting of the manuscript. To Andrew Serazin, the president of the Templeton World Charity Foundation, for the grant that enabled me to write this book. (I add that the views developed in this book do not necessarily coincide with those of the foundation.) And to Annemiek van Woudenberg, for her unflagging love and for keeping up with an often-baffled epistemologist.

Introduction

Reading can and does expand our knowledge. When I read a newspaper article, for instance, I may come to know a variety of things. As an example, consider the following newspaper report that appeared in the Dutch newspaper *Trouw* in April 2019:[1]

> During the second national bee count this weekend, over 19,000 bees were counted, a considerably lower number than the 30,000 bees that were counted last year. But then, it was much warmer last year with temperatures measuring around 20 degrees Celsius at the time. In particular, bees able to endure the cold were spotted, with the honeybee, the bumblebee, and the red mason bee making up the top three. As many species failed to appear because of the cold, the count has been extended until 19 April. The count is an initiative of Nederland Zoemt.

Upon reading this article I may come to know all of the following facts (things I didn't know prior to reading the article): that a bee count was organized in the Netherlands; that this was the second one; that bees are sensitive to temperatures; that there is a bee species called the red mason bee; and that the bee count has been extended because of the cold weather. In addition, I may come to know that the article contains ninety words and four numerals, and that its first word is *during*. Whereas I can come to know the first five facts rather easily (given that I know the language of the article), I cannot as easily come to know the latter facts simply by reading. Still, I *can* come to know them through reading (plus perhaps something extra, such as counting).

What holds for reading newspaper articles obviously also holds for reading scientific and scholarly papers and books: we can and do expand our knowledge by reading them. What we may come to know, for instance, is the problem that the scientific paper addresses, the design of

[1] "Bijentelling enkele dagen verlengd" (Bee count extended by a few days). The translation is my own.

the experiment that has been conducted, the evidence that is taken into account, how the evidence was collected, the conclusions that are argued for, and the kinds of argument that have been used. We may also come to know things about authors: we may come to know some of the things they believe (expressed, for instance, in the discussion section that many scientific papers have) and what they have read (we can glean this from the reference list that is part of the paper).

What holds for newspapers articles as well as for scientific and scholarly papers and books also holds for works of fiction. By reading them, we may acquire knowledge of a variety of things. Consider, for instance, Aesop's fable of the fox and the crow (quoted from Goldsmith 1973, 6–7):

> A crow having taken a piece of cheese out of a cottage window, flew up into a high tree with it, in order to eat it. Which a Fox observing, came and sat underneath, and began to compliment the Crow upon the subject of her beauty. I protest, says he, I never observed it before, but your feathers are of a more delicate white than any that I ever saw in my life! Ah! what a fine shape and graceful turn of body is there! And I make no question but you have a tolerable voice. If it is but as fine as your complexion, I do not know a bird that can pretend to stand in competition with you. The Crow, tickled with this very civil language, nestled and wriggled about, and hardly knew where she was; but thinking the Fox a little dubious as to the particular of her voice, and having a mind to set him right on that matter, began to sing, and, in the same instant, let the cheese drop out of her mouth; – which the Fox presently chopt up, and then bade her remember that whatever he said of her beauty, he had spoken nothing yet of her brains.

Through reading this fictional work we may, first, acquire knowledge *of the work itself*, by which I mean that, for example, we may come to know the language it is in (English, even though that is not the fable's original language), its style, and its content (a story about a crow and a fox). Second, we may, by reading the fable, acquire knowledge *of the world*. The knowledge we may acquire, I suggest, is neatly summed up in the following quatrain (quoted from Goldsmith 1973, 6):

> *"It is a maxim in the schools,*
> *That* Flattery's the food of fools:"
> *And whoso likes such airy meat*
> *Will soon have nothing else to eat.*

Through reading the fable, one can only come to know that flattery is the food of fools – if it *is*, indeed, the food of fools. Here a qualm may arise. For one might think that it just isn't *true* that flattery is the food of fools, and that, since knowledge is factive, one simply cannot *know* this, just as no one can know that the earth has seven moons. If we take this qualm seriously, if only for the sake of argument, this is a reason to identify a third area of knowledge that can be acquired through reading, viz., knowledge of the author's beliefs, convictions, assumptions, and so forth. For if the maxim is indeed false, then through reading the fable we can at least come to know what the author believed to be true.

Through reading texts, then, we can acquire knowledge. But there are other epistemic benefits to be gained through reading. First, the reader can be reminded of things they knew but that were, somehow, not real or alive to them. Aesop's fable can be a reminder of something one already knew – through reading the fable, the truth of the maxim (for the sake of argument I now assume it is true) may come alive. Second, through reading we can obtain additional evidence for something we already believe so that the belief becomes stronger, or we may obtain counterevidence for things we believe so that the belief may become weaker. Reading is an immensely important way to acquire evidence and counterevidence for what we believe, and it is pertinent to the thoughts we entertain as well as to theories and hypotheses we consider. A third benefit is that through reading we may gain understanding or receive insights: we may come to see or sense how things hang together, which is an epistemic state that, many feel, goes beyond propositional knowledge.

To be sure, these epistemic benefits can also be gained in other ways. The facts about the bee count can also be known through a radio report. The maxim can also be known, or come alive, in other ways than through reading Aesop's fable – a real, live encounter with someone who lost his head through flattery may do it. And additional evidence or counter-evidence for something one already believes can also be obtained through perception or through conducting empirical experiments. But this just shows how complex and multifaceted our epistemic lives are. A certain smell can be evidence that the milk has gone bad, but so can a certain taste. Seeing for oneself that the outdoor thermometer reads 20 degrees Celsius is one kind of evidence for it being 20 degrees Celsius; another kind is the weather reporter's testimony that it is. Generally speaking, a belief can be evidenced by different kinds of evidence: there is perceptual evidence (the evidence from seeing, hearing, touching, smelling, and tasting); there is rational evidence (roughly, "seeing" that something is true; e.g., seeing that De Morgan's laws are true); and there is also testimonial evidence (for example, the evidence consisting in a psychologist testifying before the court that the accused person does not suffer from a personality disorder).

A standard way among epistemologists in the broadly analytic tradition to discuss the varieties of evidence is in terms of *sources of knowledge* (see Chapter 2 for references). Perception, memory, reason, and testimony, so the view goes, are sources of knowledge. It is therefore surprising that analytic epistemologists have paid virtually no attention to reading as a source of knowledge. The reason for this cannot be that many of the things that we can come to know through reading we can also come to know in other ways. For as the examples in the previous paragraph indicate, there are many things we can come to know through one source (e.g., visual perception) that we can also come to know through another source (touch, for example), without that being a reason for thinking that only one of them should count as a source of knowledge (both visual perception and touch are widely considered to be sources of knowledge). Generally speaking, that a source *X* delivers knowledge that can also be obtained through the operation of source *Y* is not a good reason for not paying attention to source *X*. Nor can the reason be that reading is just a way of attending to testimony and that testimony – which by now appears on almost every analytic-epistemologist's list of sources of knowledge – is the real source worthy of study. This cannot be the reason because there are many things we can come to know through reading that just don't qualify as instances of acquiring knowledge by attending to testimony. For instance, I came to know that the newspaper report on the bee count contains ninety words and four numerals, but that knowledge is not based on testimony. I may come to know through reading that a particular book is funny, yet it is not testified in the book that it is funny. You may come to know through reading it that a certain anonymous letter was written by Emily (you have evidence based on style and content), yet your belief that it was Emily who wrote the letter is not the result of attending to testimony. And there are many other such examples (I discuss a number of them in Chapter 4). This is not to deny, of course, that knowledge through reading often *is* knowledge on the basis of attending to testimony. But equally often, it is *not*. Nor can the reason that analytic epistemologists have paid no attention to reading be that reading just is an instance of seeing. For although seeing – in the case of braille, touching – is involved in reading, there is much seeing, even seeing of texts, that just isn't reading. For example, people who don't know Hebrew can still see Hebraic texts, and some can even see *that* the text is in Hebrew, although they can't read it. How seeing (touching) and reading relate is a delicate matter – again, one that analytic epistemologists have paid no attention to. These matters will be extensively discussed in Chapter 4.

What analytic epistemologists have virtually neglected is a topic of protracted attention on the continental end of the philosophical spectrum, especially among hermeneutical philosophers like Gadamer, Ricoeur, and Derrida. Although continental philosophers don't, for the most part, discuss reading (or, as I had better say, the *nature* of reading) explicitly either, in their discussions of textual engagement they *do* explicitly discuss what they feel is intricately or even necessarily connected with reading, viz., interpretation. Hermeneutical philosophy is about interpretation. It is, however, surprisingly difficult to find explicit statements of what interpretation is. More generally, it is surprisingly difficult to find explicit discussion of questions in which the notion of interpretation stands center stage, such as the following: What are we doing when we interpret? What is the aim of interpretation? When is one statement an interpretation of another? And when is an interpretation epistemically justified or rational, and when is it not? The surprises don't stop here, for although these questions are seldom explicitly discussed, a surprising consensus seems to exist about a number of claims that involve the notion of interpretation; for instance, all reading is interpreting; there is not one right or correct interpretation of a text; there is no such thing as one person interpreting a text *better* than another person, but only one person understanding a text *differently* from another person; all seeing involves interpretation; and Nietzsche's claim that there are no facts, only interpretations.

There is a further surprise. Hermeneutical philosophers wield the notion of interpretation in a way that makes virtually no connection with questions that have exercised analytic epistemologists for decades: What is the relation between knowledge and belief? What must be added to true belief to get knowledge? If we know, do we then know that we know?[2] In addition, a central concern in analytic epistemology has been what property or quality a belief should have if it is to be epistemically justified. Should the believing subject have done their level best to get things right, as friends of the deontological conception of justification have it? Or should the belief be, or be based on, what is self-evident or immediately evident, as foundationalists affirm? Or should the belief be based on evidence – or, rather, on *adequate* evidence, as evidentialists aver? Or should the belief be part of a coherent set of other beliefs that the subject has, or that a *rational* subject *should* have, or that the community to which the subject belongs has or should have, as coherentists think? Or should

[2] This question sparked the internalism–externalism debate. Some of the key papers are anthologized in Kornblith (2001).

the belief result from a faculty or belief-forming mechanism that is *in fact* reliable, as reliabilists maintain? Or is something else required? Even if no clear consensus has emerged on what is required for justification, these discussions have made it clear that beliefs can have a variety of epistemically valuable properties and display distinct epistemic merits, and, hence, that beliefs can be valued from different "dimensions of epistemic evaluation."[3] Philosophers on the continental end of the philosophical spectrum have for the most part paid no attention to the relevance of these distinctions when thinking about interpretation.

So, to put it starkly, what we seem to have is, on the one hand, analytic epistemologists paying no attention to reading and interpretation (even though, intuitively, both are sources of knowledge) and, on the other hand, continental philosophers dealing with interpretation in a way that is largely disconnected from the concerns addressed in analytic epistemology.

The purpose of this book is to argue that reading and interpretation are sources of knowledge. In order to accomplish this, a number of questions will be addressed, for instance: What precisely is required for something to qualify as a source of knowledge? What exactly *is* reading? How does it relate to perception and to testimony? What is it to interpret a text (or an author)? How do reading and interpretation relate to each other? What is required for an interpretation to be justified?

Before getting down to business, I make some remarks in the interest of clarifying the kind of project that I undertake in this book and highlight some general commitments that I shall adopt.

One. The project is to discuss reading and interpretation *generically*. What I will be saying about reading concerns *all* reading, irrespective of the genre of the text that is read or interpreted. So, it concerns the reading of newspaper articles as well as fables, scientific papers as well as poetry, reviews as well as novels, political pamphlets as well as holy books, email messages as well as medication prescriptions, and manuals as well as cookbooks. This makes the subject matter of the book a capacious one and sets it apart from much about reading that has been written in continental-philosophical works. Gadamer's *Truth and Method*, to mention just one classic, is written mainly with highbrow texts in mind – the great books of the philosophical tradition and the towering works of European literature. The notion of a fusion of horizons, a core notion of Gadamer's hermeneutical theory, just has no application – or is not

[3] For an overview and discussion of some twenty of such desiderata, see Alston (2005).

supposed to have one – when one is reading today's newspaper or the manual to one's new cell phone or a cookbook that has just come out.[4] There is merit, I believe, to aiming at an account of reading and interpretation that isn't focused on the reading of only a selection of textual genres, just as there is merit to aiming at an account of perception that isn't focused on the perception of only a selection of objects (say, of birds only).

Two. Although this makes the scope of the book very wide, it is radically restricted in another sense: it is restricted to *textual* interpretation only. Virtually all continental-philosophical authors make a point of affirming that what they say about interpretation is not restricted to the interpretation of texts but applies equally to the interpretation of all, or some, of the following items: what we see, hear, smell, touch, and taste; paintings; musical scores; human actions and behaviors; and situations (e.g., a man lying on the ground with a bloodstained face). Sometimes, the notion of interpretation is taken so widely – Gadamer is again an example – that the application of a rule of law to a particular case also qualifies as an interpretation of that law (Gadamer 1975, 291ff.). Along with others (Hemeren 1983; Dennett 1990), I have grave doubts about whether the interpretation of a poem and the interpretation of a musical score, for example, are two species of the same genus *interpretation* and, similarly, about whether the interpretation of Donald's behavior and the interpretation (application) of a rule of law are two other species of the same genus. It cannot just be assumed that the word *interpretation* in all these instances is used in the same sense. In other words, it cannot just be assumed that all things called *interpretation* are tokens of the same type. The case should be argued. But I have never come across such arguments. The simple fact that the same word (*interpretation*) is used is, of course, not a good argument. As Gilbert Ryle (1949, 23) once said, from the fact that we use the same word (*rising*) in the sentences "The tide is rising," "Hopes are rising," and "The average age of death is rising," it cannot be concluded that there is one and the same thing that the tide, hopes, and the average age of death are doing. Something similar, I aver, holds true for *interpretation*. The interpretation that this book is about is exclusively text oriented, or text based.[5]

[4] In Gadamer, *interpretation* and *understanding* are, in a way, burdensome enterprises because of the historical distance between interpreter and the objects of interpretation (see Gadamer 1975, part 2). I have chosen the examples in the body of the text because of the lack of historical distance in them.

[5] I use this admittedly somewhat vague phraseology, because I want *interpretation* to cover activities related to understanding texts, to understanding authors, and to understanding subject matters of texts (which I also call Matters; see Chapter 2).

Three. I work from the commonsense idea that writing is an action: it is something human agents do, and nonhumans do not and even cannot do.[6] As far as we know, only human agents perform actions of writing. Writing, moreover, is an action that humans normally engage in intentionally, deliberately, and knowingly. When they write, they have the *intention to write*, and not the intention to whistle, for example, or the intention to take a shower. In addition, when they write, they write *deliberately*; in other words, they write for a reason, such as to communicate that *p* or to convince others of the truth of *p*. Finally, when humans write, they write *knowingly*: they know both *that* they are writing and *what* they are writing. Normally, when we ask people what they're doing, they aren't puzzled by the question and will virtually always be able to answer it intelligibly. It rarely if ever happens that a person doesn't know what they are doing. That writing is an action, just as speaking is, is key in speech act theory as it was developed by J. L. Austin in his *How to Do Things with Words* (1962) and in some of his earlier essays (Austin 1970, especially essays 6 and 10), and further developed by John Searle (1969), Paul Grice (1989), and William Alston (2000). When humans write, they perform at least locutionary actions, and often also illocutionary actions and perlocutionary actions. I work from the commonsense idea that humans, by writing, perform such actions and normally also have the *intention* to perform them. Because of their intentionality, human actions are of another ontological category than such events as the rising of the tide or the blowing of the wind.

Four. Through reading and interpretation, we can obtain propositional knowledge. I work with the idea that knowledge requires at least true and justified or warranted belief, as well as with the idea that truth and justification can come apart: a true belief need not be a justified belief, and a justified belief need not be a true belief. Still, there is a connection between the two. Laurence BonJour describes it as follows (BonJour 1985, 7–8):

> We cannot, in most cases at least, bring it about directly that our beliefs are true, but we can presumably bring it about directly (though perhaps only in the long run) that they are epistemically justified. And, *if our standards of epistemic justification are appropriately chosen*, bringing it about that our beliefs are epistemically justified will also tend to bring it about, in the perhaps even longer run and with the usual slippage and uncertainty which our finitude mandates, that they are true. If epistemic justification were not

[6] I argue for this in the first section of Chapter 6, where I discuss commonalities between speaking and writing.

> conducive to truth in this way, if finding epistemically justified beliefs did not substantially increase the likelihood of finding true ones, then epistemic justification would be irrelevant to our main cognitive goal.

I should say that there is an element of hope here: we *hope* that things are such that justification is truth conducive, that more and better justification increases the likelihood of finding truth. We *hope* this to be the case, and we in fact *expect* it to be the case. I assume this also holds for forming beliefs through reading and interpretation: we hope, and in fact expect, that the better evidenced the beliefs are that we form through reading and interpretation, the more likely it is that they are true – if not the beliefs about the subject matter of the text, then surely about what it is that the author intended to convey by writing.

I should like to stress that nothing of what I have said so far entails that we do not read for other than epistemic purposes. We also read for purposes of delight, beauty, and aesthetic experience – especially, but not exclusively, when we read works of literature. We may also read for diversion and distraction. Be that as it may, one purpose of reading is to come to know and understand things. It is reading with epistemic purposes that this book is about.

Five. This brings me to a point about truth as a goal of reading and interpretation. In describing the tenets of hermeneutical philosophers, Jens Zimmermann (2015, 13) says:

> Hermeneutic thinkers hold that we arrive at truth because we already participate in something greater that conveys truth to us, such as the language and cultural tradition we inhabit. It is therefore misleading to pretend such influence does not exist or to repress it for the sake of supposed objectivity . . . . Instead, hermeneutic thinkers insist that we need to redefine objective truth as something we take part in rather than something we merely observe from a distance. We don't make truth happen; rather truth is something that happens to us. Truth is an event.

It is a truism that people participate in cultural traditions. However, why should we think that the truism pressures us to give up on objective truth as it is traditionally understood (so, as truth that is independent of the subject knowing it, believing it, or even entertaining it)? As I have argued elsewhere (Van Woudenberg 2014), the adjective *objective* in the expression *objective truth* affirms rather than adds to what is already present in the substantive *truth* itself. It functions as what the Polish logician Kazimierz Twardowski (1999) called an affirming adjective, another example of which is *actual* in the expression *in actual fact*. An affirming adjective affirms or highlights something that is already present in the noun it modifies: *objective* affirms or highlights what is already present in *truth*, just as *actual* affirms what is already present in *fact*. Affirming adjectives contrast with both determining and eliminating adjectives. The former add something to the substantives they modify: *red* in *the red coat* adds something to *coat* that is not already inherent in it. The latter take away something that is inherent in the substantives they modify: in *false friend* and *counterfeit money*, *false* takes away something that is inherent in *friend* and *counterfeit* something that is inherent in *money*.[7] To say that proposition *p* is objectively true is just to say that *p* is true, whilst the adjective is added for purposes of emphasis only (i.e., to stress that *p* is not merely believed to be true). What is it for a proposition to be true? I adopt a realist, nonepistemic conception of truth according to which proposition *p* is true if and only if what *p* says to be the case actually is the case; nothing more is needed (it is not needed that *p* has been proved or is known, believed, or even entertained by anybody), and nothing less will suffice.[8] The proposition that lemons are sour is true if and only if lemons are sour; nothing more is needed, nothing less suffices.

I can see no merit in talking about objective truth as "something that happens to us." That is a category mistake. The truth of a proposition just isn't the kind of thing that can happen. Of course, there are true propositions about events (e.g., "The ice caps are melting") but this fact doesn't turn the truth into an event. And of course, truths can be handed down by traditions that we grew up in and are part of, but that doesn't turn truth into an event either. And yes, it can happen that a truth strikes us emotionally or intellectually, but that still doesn't mean that truth is an event. When we read with epistemic interests, what we aim at is truth. When we read the bee-count article with epistemic interests, this means we want to know two things. First, what is the article (or its author) saying? Second, is what the article says true?[9] The two can come apart, as it is possible that through reading and interpretation we come to know what the article (or its author) says is *p*, yet *p* be false.

Still, there is an important point discernable in Zimmermann's statement of the tenets of hermeneutic thinkers. It is a truism, I said, that people participate in cultural traditions. Although it should not pressure us

[7] Note that *affirming*, *determining*, and *eliminating* are functional qualifications. One and the same adjective can be determining in one expression and eliminating in another. For example, in *false friend*, *false* is eliminating, but in *false statement*, it is determining.

[8] An extensive statement and defense of this is Alston (1996).

[9] This distinction gets elaborate treatment in Chapters 6 and 8, where I discuss two kinds of reading knowledge (RK_A and RK_B) and two kinds of interpretation knowledge (IK_A and IK_B).

to give up on the traditional concept of objective truth, this fact *should* pressure us to endorse the following claim: *which* beliefs we have is at least in part dependent on the traditions in which we participate. Geocentric belief is simply unavailable to us who are steeped in the tradition of modern science, whereas heliocentric belief was unavailable to the Scholastics who were steeped in the Aristotelian tradition. Beliefs about representative voting systems were simply unavailable to twelfth-century peasants, whereas belief in serfhood is unavailable to us who are reared in the tradition of liberal democracy. The fact should also pressure us to endorse the following claim: *which* evidence (or which kinds of evidence) is available to people is at least in part dependent on the traditions that people belong to and in which relevant pieces of evidence have or haven't been handed down. That is to say, which beliefs are *considered* to be justified will to a certain extent be influenced by the traditions we belong to. Adopting these claims, however, is entirely compatible with truth being objective.

Six. My next point is a comment on the claim that interpretation is always motivated by personal interests and concerns. As one commentator explains Heidegger's position: "Whether I read the Bible, an employment contract, or try to understand why my friend has not visited me in weeks, I want to know my 'fate,' that is, what these texts and actions mean to me. Interpretation ... is intrinsically guided by my present concerns, by the desire to hear an announcement that pertains to my own situation" (Zimmermann 2015, 5). Taken one way, the point is both trivial and overstated. The point is trivial, for of course we read and interpret while motivated by our personal interests and concerns: of course I want to know what the contract says before signing it – what it says means a lot to me. Our interests and concerns give us a focus. At the same time, the point is overstated because we sometimes read out of sheer curiosity, without practical and pressing matters motivating us. Sometimes, perhaps even often, we read just to get to know, say, the views of an author or how long the construction of the Cathedral of Notre-Dame in Paris took, without pressing interests and concerns motivating us here. Taken in another way, the point is even misleading insofar as it suggests that when we read and interpret text *T*, the beliefs we form are, content-wise, fully determined by personal interests and concerns. In other words, had we had other interests and concerns while reading *T*, the content of our beliefs would have been radically different. This suggestion is misleading, because the content of a newspaper article is independent of what readers pick up of it, just as the content of a scientific paper or a novel is independent of whether people read it and, if they read it, independent of what they make of it. There is a kind of fixedness to the objects of reading and interpretation that is independent of readers' interests and concerns.[10] And this means that readers cannot form just any belief in response to what they read – not, at least, when they read with epistemic interests.

Finally. Much of the discussion among hermeneutical philosophers about interpretation is motivated by the concern to safeguard the humanities against unwanted intrusions of the natural sciences and the related concern to carve out a kind of inquiry or scholarly investigation that differs from laboratory research. The way to accomplish this, many think, is to adopt, as intimated earlier, alternative notions of truth. I reject the remedy but share the concern. I share the concern because scientific research just isn't the exclusive way toward knowledge that friends of scientism claim it to be.[11] For in addition to what we know and can know through scientific investigation, there is much that we can know and do know independently of it – and knowledge entails truth. I know, for example, what schools I went to; I know the names of my siblings and of the streets I lived on; I know that there is only one even prime number; and I know that honesty is a virtue, and that when I make a promise, I thereby incur the obligation to keep it. All these things, and many others, I know independently of anything that merits the title *scientific research*. More pertinent to the topic of this book, I also know that the newspaper article says that the bee count has been extended, and this knowledge isn't based on scientific research but on reading. Similarly, my knowledge that Aesop's fable carries the message that flattery is the food of fools has been acquired through reading and interpretation, not through science. Very generally, through reading I can come to know truths about what a text (or its author) says – and reading is not a kind of doing natural-scientific or social-scientific research (although it can be part of it). Hence, scientism is false. Thus, the remedy for scientism is not to reject the notion of objective truth outside of science. Nor is the cause in favor of the humanities served by the rejection of the notion of objective truth. Rather, it is served by carefully showing

[10] In Chapter 1, I use Fred Dretske's information-theoretic account of knowledge and suggest that texts are carriers of information, and that the information they carry is independent of what readers pick up of it.

[11] A bold statement of scientism is Rosenberg (2011). Scientism – which Rosenberg endorses – is "the conviction that the methods of science are the only reliable ways to secure knowledge of anything" (2011, 6). He also says that "being scientistic means treating science as our exclusive guide to reality – both to our own nature and everything else's" (2011, 8). In Van Woudenberg (2018a), I offer an epistemological critique of Rosenberg's views.

that the sorts of objects studied in the humanities are different from the objects studied in the sciences and that (therefore) the humanities have their own aims, their own methods, and their own results that cannot be obtained through scientific (as opposed to humanistic) inquiry. As I have tried to show elsewhere (Van Woudenberg 2018b), the objects of the humanities differ from those of the natural sciences in that they have the following property: *meaning that derives from human conventions, human intentions, and/or human purposive behavior.* My proposal is thus not to pitch the humanities against the sciences but to engage in a division of labor. All the while we should keep in mind what is *common* between the sciences and the humanities, which, as I see it, is the aim of truth.[12]

Having introduced the main aim of the book and explicated a number of my commitments, I now offer a preview of the upcoming chapters.

In Chapter 1, I make it plausible that through reading we can acquire knowledge of three varieties: propositional knowledge, knowledge by acquaintance, and know-how. In Chapter 2, I explore the relations between reading and understanding. I distinguish various kinds of understanding and analyze how, by reading, we can come to understand texts, authors, and subject matters that authors write about. I also suggest that understanding requires knowledge (but I leave open the question of whether understanding is a kind of knowing).

Having thus argued that reading can give us epistemic benefits, I consider the question that has puzzled me for a long time: Why have philosophers, epistemologists in particular, never even considered the idea that reading is a source of knowledge alongside perception, memory, and reason? To address this matter I analyze, in Chapter 3, what it is for something to be a source of knowledge and also by what kinds of principles alleged sources of knowledge can be individuated. In addition, I study the principles by which the most widely discussed sources have been individuated. The conclusion is that there are no good reasons to *not* consider reading as a source of knowledge. However, one may feel that reading is not a source of knowledge in its own right in the sense that it reduces either to (attending to) testimony or to visual perception (in the case of braille, to tactile perception). In Chapter 4, I argue against the possibility of such reductions.

Having thus argued that reading should be considered as a source of knowledge in its own right, I look into it more closely. In Chapter 5, which is in a way the heart of the book, I distinguish between factive and nonfactive reading and provide unprecedented analyses of "*S* is

[12] Another proposal for a division of labor is Foley (2018).

reading" as well as of three kinds of (what I call) reading knowledge: RK_A, RK_B, and RK_C.

One may wonder whether there is something special about reading compared to listening. In Chapter 6, I argue that although the objects of reading and listening share important properties (notably, a fourfold intentionality), there is something special about at least *some* objects of reading, because they are the products of a special kind of writing, viz., what I call creative-investigative writing.

So far, nothing has been said about interpretation. But how do reading and interpretation relate? After distinguishing seven distinct notions of meaning, I offer a general account of interpretation according to which, roughly, an interpretation of text *T* is a statement of the meaning(s) of *T*. I also argue that meanings are not the sorts of things that can be known though scientific research.

In Chapter 8, I discuss three accounts of interpretation that fit the general account: first, the classical allegoresis interpretation, which digs for hidden and deeper meanings; next, the traditional difficulty account, according to which readers interpret texts only when they encounter difficulties in understanding what the text (or its author) says. Although the class of interpretative acts on the difficulty account is more capacious than on the allegoresis account, many feel it is not capacious enough. What I call the modernist view urges that *all* reading involves interpretation, even if texts have no deeper meaning and readers face no difficulties. I state this view in a way that I think is both entirely plausible and entirely devoid of the subjectivism and relativistic implications that the view is often thought to have.

The final chapter discusses four more notions of interpretation. First, I delineate what I call holistic textual act interpretation, which aims to specify what an author intended to communicate by the text as a whole. Second, I briefly identify a kind of interpretation that is a response to textual opacity, viz., interpretation as reconstruction. Third, I discuss what I call externalist interpretations; that is, interpretations that approach texts from a particular philosophical or intellectual perspective such as Marxism, feminism, or Freudianism. And finally, I critically discuss reader-response accounts of interpretation.

The discussion of interpretation in Chapters 8 and 9 has a threefold aim: first, to simply distinguish different kinds of interpretation; second, to explore the epistemic aspects of each of these kinds; and third, to argue that interpretation can be considered a source of knowledge. The final section of the book takes up this latter matter and also states the relations between reading and interpretation.

CHAPTER 1

Knowing and Reading

Readers can, and often do, reap epistemic benefits from reading, no matter the genre of the text. Reading can provide them with knowledge, understanding, insight, and other epistemic goods. In this chapter and Chapter 2, I unpack this remark that, at this high level of generality, must look like a boring truism. In this chapter, I explore the kinds of knowledge reading may yield; in Chapter 2, I explore the relations between reading and understanding, and I hint at some other epistemic benefits.

Reading can yield knowledge, I said, irrespective of the text's genre: we may acquire knowledge through reading newspaper articles, scientific papers, and historical narratives, as well as through reading poems, novels, and plays. The last part of this statement is controversial, but I will make this claim plausible as we go along. It is fairly standard among epistemologists to distinguish three forms, or kinds, of knowledge (see, e.g., Feldman 2003, 8–23): (1) knowledge of facts, also called knowledge of truths, or propositional knowledge; (2) knowledge by acquaintance, sometimes also called objectual knowledge; and (3) ability knowledge, or know-how. In this chapter I shall argue that reading can afford readers knowledge in each of these categories.

Before starting off, I should like to comment on certain locutions that are sometimes used when the relation between reading and knowledge is at issue, viz., that books *contain* knowledge and that works of literature *embody* knowledge.[1] These locutions suggest that just as there are bottles in which there is wine, there are items "in which" there is knowledge, and these items are books, articles – in one word, *texts*.[2] But how shall we understand this? For the proper subjects of knowledge are persons, not nonpersonal inanimate things such as sticks and stones and, indeed, texts.

[1] The latter locution is used in Gibson (2009).

[2] I use the word *text* as the most general word for what is written.

I suggest that the locution "This book contains knowledge" can be understood in one of two ways:

1. *In* or *through* or *by means of* a book, the author communicates things they *know* – not just things they *think* they know, but things they *actually* know.
2. If people read that book, they can – and, if all goes well, they will – acquire the knowledge the writer intended to communicate.

Let us call the former *writer's knowledge*, the latter *reader's knowledge*.[3] Writer's knowledge is not the totality of what an author must know in order to produce her text – it is exclusively the knowledge that she intends to communicate to her readership. It should be clear that what a writer must know in order to be able to produce her text exceeds the knowledge that she intends to communicate. Knowledge of a language, for example, is needed if one is to produce a text, but the writer may have no wish to communicate that knowledge to her readers. Also, knowledge of literary conventions is needed if one is to produce a literary text, but writers mostly don't intend to communicate their knowledge of those conventions. Writer's knowledge, then, is knowledge that the writer aims to communicate.

Writer's knowledge and reader's knowledge are different things. They can, as I will say, "come together," but they can also come apart. They come together when a writer wants to communicate some bit of knowledge to her readers, and upon reading what she wrote, readers pick up the knowledge. In such a case, what is known by the writer is in a sense identical to what is known to the reader.[4] We expect or hope this to be the case when students read textbooks or when we attentively read newspaper articles. And if poems and novels contain writer's knowledge, their – properly educated – reader can acquire the writer's knowledge, in which case writer's knowledge and reader's knowledge come together.

However, writer's knowledge and reader's knowledge need not come together; they can, and often will, come apart, at least to some extent. A book may contain knowledge that its reader just doesn't pick up. Such a person, upon reading, may either form false beliefs or no beliefs at all. If they form false beliefs, we think that they have misunderstood the text

[3] In Chapter 5, reader's knowledge is called reading knowledge *B* (or RK_B), and I offer an analysis of "*S* knows through reading that what text *T* (or its author) says (viz., *p*) is true."

[4] This leaves the conceptual distinction between writer's knowledge and reader's knowledge intact, of course.

(or the writer); if they form no beliefs at all, we think that they either misunderstood the text (or the writer) or paid insufficient attention to the text. The misunderstanding can be due to a variety of causes: inadequate grasp of the language, insufficient knowledge of literary conventions (the reader mistook the scientific paper for science fiction), fatigue, or sheer absentmindedness.

There is a further point here I should like to make, one that in the course of this book will play an important role. Readers may come to know, through reading, things that are *not* part of the writer's knowledge as I have defined it – these things are not part of what the author wanted to communicate through their text, yet they are things that readers may come to know by reading that very text. For instance, by reading the newspaper article quoted in the Introduction, I may come to know that it contains ninety words and four numerals. Or consider the following example. I read a book on musicians who have played on Bob Dylan's albums. All albums are discussed, *Slow Train* included. The author, however, doesn't mention Mark Knopfler, who played a prominent role in giving the album its unique musical texture. I thereby come to know that the author made a mistake, a mistake of omission. That the author made this mistake, however, isn't part of the writer's knowledge (as defined), for obviously the author didn't want to communicate that he made a mistake of omission by not mentioning Mark Knopfler. Yet I came to know this through reading. But now note that although the knowledge I've thus acquired can plausibly be called reader's knowledge, it is not reader's knowledge of the sort I have defined, for reader's knowledge as defined consists in picking up, through reading, what the author knew and intended to communicate. What we have here is another sort of reader's knowledge, which will be discussed in Chapter 5.

I now move on to a discussion of the various kinds of knowledge that reading can give rise to, starting with knowledge of facts, or propositional knowledge.

Propositional Knowledge through Reading

I shall discuss two accounts of propositional knowledge – the justified true belief account and Fred Dretske's information-theoretic account – and specify how knowledge acquisition through reading works on both accounts.

Propositional knowledge is knowledge of facts. If you know that the earth has a moon, you know a fact. In general, to know that *p* is to know the fact that *p*. We linguistically represent knowledge of facts with that-clauses, and they, in turn, express propositions about facts. The paradigmatic form of an ascription of that kind of knowledge is "*S* knows that *p*," where *S* is a variable for persons and *p* for propositions.

Propositions as I shall be thinking of them are nonlinguistic items that can be expressed by linguistic devices, have truth-value, are the objects of propositional attitudes, and stand in logical relations to each other.[5] By way of explanation, the English sentence "The queen is dead," the Latin sentence "Regina mortua est," and the Dutch sentence "De koningin is dood" express the same proposition.[6] This proposition, depending on who the queen is, is either true or false, and it can be believed, feared, hoped, or expected – that is, it can be the object of different propositional attitudes. You may believe that the queen is dead, other people may fear that she's dead, and yet others may hope that she's dead. Finally, this proposition stands in logical relations to other propositions, such as relations of entailment. It entails, for instance, the proposition that the queen no longer speaks, and it is entailed by the proposition that all royalty is dead.

True propositions are made true by facts. The proposition that the earth has a moon is made true by the fact that the earth has a moon. Propositions and facts are different sorts of items. Propositions have truth-value whereas facts do not. Facts can't be true or false; rather, facts obtain.

There are somewhat disguised forms of propositional knowledge, viz., various forms of knowing-wh: knowing *when* the match will start, knowing *where* the keys are, knowing *who* pushed the button, and knowing *why* she came. They are cases of propositional knowledge because when you know *when* the match starts, the following situation obtains: there is a true proposition that states the starting time of the match, and you know that proposition. This works similarly for the other examples (see Feldman 2003, 9–12).

One widely discussed account of propositional knowledge is that knowledge is justified true belief: to know that *p* is to have a justified true belief that *p*.[7] The motivation for the thought that knowledge requires belief is

[5] A defense of this view, sometimes called the mainstream view, is Cappelen and Hawthorne (2009); their defense is pitted against relativists.

[6] As I shall be thinking of it, the sentence "The queen is dead," used in a particular situation (one in which the queen referred to is Queen Elizabeth), expresses the proposition that Queen Elizabeth is dead, but used in another situation (one in which the queen referred to is Queen Juliana), expresses the proposition that Queen Juliana is dead.

[7] Because of Gettier problems, this analysis is problematic. Still, the wide consensus is that knowledge requires true belief *plus* something; the discussion about what that something is is more or less undecided. See Plantinga (1993b) and Shope (2002). The consensus breaker is Timothy Williamson

that, in order for you to know that *p*, the fact that *p* must in some way be represented to you, and believing that *p* fulfills that representational role. Also, knowledge seems to involve the subject's commitment to *p*. This is what G. E. Moore's paradox[8] helps to draw our attention to. When I say "I know that it is raining," I register my commitment to the belief that it's actually raining. That is why the addition "but I don't believe it" seems like a retraction of that commitment, which suggests that the commitment was part of the belief all along. It is a paradox to say "I know that it is raining, but I don't believe it" – hence, knowledge requires belief.

But merely believing that *p*, so merely being committed to the truth of *p*, is not enough to *know* that *p*. If believing *p* would be enough for knowing *p*, this would have highly objectionable consequences – e.g., by merely *believing* there is extraterrestrial life, you would *know* there is extraterrestrial life, and by merely *believing* you will get safely down the mountain, you would *know* that you will. However, this sounds wrong. You *don't* know these things simply because you believe them. So knowledge requires not mere belief but *true* belief. That is the reason why no one knows – and why no one *can* know – that Santa Fe is the capital of Chile: that proposition is false. It is another Moorean paradox to say "I believe that *p*, but *p* is false," because when you believe that *p*, you represent that *p* is true – you are committed to *p*'s being true.

Yet, as the account under discussion has it, true belief is still insufficient for knowledge. More is needed, as the following example bears out. If you form, prior to the draw, the true belief that the lottery ticket you bought is a winning ticket, you still don't *know* that your ticket is a winner, for you

(2001), who argues that knowledge is unanalyzable and that belief is *not* conceptually prior to knowledge. One argument he offers against the claim that belief is conceptually prior to knowledge is this: from the fact that some condition *C* (say, the presence of a belief) is necessary but insufficient for something to be an *X* (say, an instance of knowledge), it cannot be concluded that *X* must be analyzed as *C* + other conditions. His counterexample is that being colored is a necessary but insufficient condition for being red. And from this it cannot be concluded that being red can be analyzed as being colored + other conditions (Williamson 2001, 3). This argument, however, is unconvincing because the relation between being colored and being red differs importantly from the relation between believing and knowing. This can be brought out by reference to W. E. Johnson's distinction between determinables and determinates: "I propose," Johnson (1964, 174) wrote, "to call such terms as color and shape determinables in relation to such terms as red and circular which will be called determinates." *Colored* is a determinable in relation to *red*, or, conversely, *red* is a determinate in relation to *colored*. But the relation between knowledge and belief is not a determinable–determinate relation. This fact undermines the ground on which Williamson's objection against the conceptual priority of belief over knowledge is based. This, of course, is by no means a refutation of Williamson's knowledge-first epistemology (as it is usually called), but it does suggest that this analogy that he avails himself of is problematic. An illuminating evaluation and critique of Williamson's claim that knowledge is unanalyzable is Cassam (2009, 104–110).

[8] On Moorean paradoxes, see Moore (1993).

have no *reason*, or *ground*, for your belief. Although your belief is true (your ticket *is* a winner), it is true by sheer good luck. You are not *justified* in believing as you do.

There have been many different proposals as to what is required for a belief to be justified.[9] Does it require that the belief is based on evidence? On *sufficient* evidence? Or does it require that the subject has done their epistemic best in gathering and weighing the relevant evidence? Or does it require that the belief is coherent with the rest of the subject's beliefs, or with an appropriate subset thereof, or with the best scientific knowledge that we have? Or does it require that it is formed by a de facto reliable belief-forming mechanism – that is, one whose output beliefs are highly likely to be true? Or does knowledge require true belief that is warranted in the technical sense that Plantinga has elaborated, so formed by a reliable mechanism that is functioning properly in an appropriate environment and whose belief outputs have a high likelihood of being true?

I don't propose to enter these discussions here, nor will I enter the debate about so-called Gettier problems.[10] Rather, I will proceed from two assumptions. First, I will assume that knowledge is *almost* justified true belief, for an extra condition is needed. But I won't try my hand at determining exactly what that extra condition is. In the discussions of knowledge that follow, I will often reason as if having a true and justified belief is sufficient for knowledge, and not worry about the extra condition; it should be tacitly understood that the extra but unstated condition is also satisfied. Second, in these discussions I shall assume that what is required for a belief to be justified (in cases in which the belief is yielded by reading or by interpretation) is evidence.

What I suggest is this: even if we are not agreed upon the proper analysis of propositional knowledge, this should not deter us from supposing that we can and do acquire propositional knowledge through perception or

[9] See Alston (2005) for an informed discussion of these proposals.

[10] Many epistemologists have offered proposals about what would be sufficient for knowledge ever since Edmund Gettier argued that even justified true belief is insufficient. Here is a well-known case (a so-called Gettier case), due to Russell, that is often used to show that justified true belief is insufficient for knowledge. The restaurant of the company where Sam has been working for quite some time now has a clock. Sam looks at the clock and sees that it reads twelve o'clock; he forms the belief that it is twelve o'clock, and it is, as a matter of fact, twelve o'clock. So Sam forms a true belief. Sam is, moreover, justified in holding the belief – after all, it is based on his seeing the clock that he knows from experience to be an accurate timekeeper. He thus has a justified true belief. But (let us assume) the clock in fact stopped working twelve hours ago: therefore, Sam cannot be said to *know* that it is twelve o'clock. Sam has a justified true belief, but he doesn't have knowledge. This sort of case suggests that more is needed. For an overview of early discussions of the Gettier problem, see Shope (1983).

reason or memory – or reading. And it doesn't matter to which genre the text belongs: through reading the newspaper, we may come to know that the bee count has been extended; through reading a scientific paper, we may come to know that the emission of CO_2 is higher than ever; through reading Robert Browning's "My Last Duchess," we may come to know that the narrator is a heartless and cruel man; through reading the manual of the lawn mower, we may come to know how to lower the blades; through reading the business contract, we may come to know what is required of us; and so on and so forth. No one in their right mind should deny that we can and do acquire propositional knowledge through reading.

Some, as indicated, have qualms about the suggestion that we can acquire propositional knowledge through reading poetry, fictional stories, novels, and dramas. Noncognitivism, as the position is usually called, has its able defenders.[11] Yet it would appear, at least prima facie, that through reading a literary work we can come to know, for example,

- what its opening sentence is – e.g., through reading Graham Greene's *This Gun for Hire* (1936) we may come to know that its opening sentences read, "Murder didn't mean much to Raven. It was just a new job";
- what the story line is – e.g., through reading William Golding's *Lord of the Flies* (1954) we may come to know that a group of stranded schoolboys under Ralph's leadership developed extraordinarily aggressive behavior toward a red-headed boy named Piggy, whose life, in the end, is saved by a marine officer;
- what the topics or themes in the work are – e.g., a topic in Thomas Gray's "Elegy Written in a Country Churchyard" (1751) is the value of the lives of people of lowly origins; a theme in George Eliot's *Middlemarch* (1871–1872) is the position of women in society;
- the views of its author – e.g., through reading *Tess of the D'Urbervilles* (1891) we may come to know that Thomas Hardy despised the Victorian double standard concerning sexual morality; through reading *Animal Farm* (1949) we may come to know that George Orwell was extremely critical of Soviet Marxism;

[11] Lamarque and Olsen (1994), and Stolnitz (1992). Cognitivism, for a long time the minority position, is gaining traction again. See Graham (2005, 52–75) and Peels (2020), and especially Richard Gaskin's defense of literary humanism, which involves the theses that works of literature make or imply true or false statements about the world and that "some works of literature have cognitive value in the sense that, of the true statements that these works make or imply, some can be known to be true" (Gaskin 2013, 63). My approach in this book puts me in the cognitivist camp.

- general truths – e.g., through reading Aesop's fable of the fox and the crow (sixth century BCE) we may come to know the very general truth that we should guard ourselves against flattery; and
- facts – e.g., through reading Multatuli's *Max Havelaar* (1860) we may come to know how, in colonial times, the administrative system in Java worked.

Not everyone will agree with me on these examples. John Gibson's response to the first three examples is that they can be considered only as cases of *trivial* knowledge (Gibson 2009, 470). Even if that is right (which may be doubted, for what are the standards for triviality here? These standards seem, moreover, heavily context dependent), this is irrelevant to the point I am making, which is that through reading, including works of literature, we can acquire knowledge. We know many things, even if many of the things we know are, in some sense, and in some contexts, trivial. Concerning the other examples on the list, Gibson's response will conform to his general view that "literary works ... lacking declarative power ... are not in the business of articulating truths ... and thus they cannot be (or do not wish to be) vehicles of the sort of propositional-conceptual knowledge tied to it" (Gibson 2009, 477).[12] This response, however, begs the question, for it seems that the latter three examples *are* cases of knowledge acquisition. Moreover, it just doesn't seem right to say that literary works lack declarative power. First, it isn't *works* that make declarations – it is *persons* who do so. Second, persons who are literary authors often do make declarations, and they do so by writing their works: Charles Dickens, Thomas Hardy, Fyodor Dostoyevsky, George Elliott, and Multatuli do make – and intend to make – declarations on many different topics, albeit in indirect ways. But if they do, readers can come to know these declarations.

Of course, not everything that is written is true, and, hence, not everything we may come to believe through reading qualifies as knowledge. And of course, even if we come to believe something true through reading, the belief may be ill-founded and have no ground in the evidence that the text provides – it may thus be unjustified and hence not qualify as knowledge. Certain readings, certain interpretations, are unjustified, even

[12] Gibson argues that literature's goal is not the provision of propositional knowledge about the world but "the expansion and refinement of our understanding of social and cultural reality" (2007, 142). But if – as I shall suggest in Chapter 2 – understanding is propositional, then literature can, after all, give us propositional knowledge of reality. For a very informative critical discussion of noncognitivism, see Gaskin (2013, 118–153).

if they lead to true belief. As said, there is much more to reading literature than mere knowledge acquisition. But none of this should make us doubt the possibility and reality of acquiring propositional knowledge through reading.

To conclude, as a first approximation, on the justified true belief account of knowledge, person *S* comes to know that *p* through reading provided the following conditions are satisfied: (i) *S* forms the belief that *p* as a result of reading; (ii) *p* is true; (iii) *S*'s belief that *p* is justified on the basis of what *S* has read (plus background knowledge). In order for this account to work, conditions (i) and (iii) should be clarified. First, what exactly is it to form a belief as a result of reading? If you're reading and feel that reading makes you sleepy, then you form the belief that you're sleepy as a result of reading – but in this case, the belief doesn't result from reading in the right way. So how should a belief be related to reading in order for it to result from reading in the right way? This question will be explored in detail in Chapter 5. Second, when is *S*'s belief that *p* justified on the basis of what *S* has read? This matter will be explored in detail in Chapters 5, 8, and 9.

Let me now consider how the chips fall when we think about knowledge acquired through reading on Dretske's information account of knowledge. One formulation of this theory is that *S* knows that *p* iff *S*'s belief that *p* is caused (or causally sustained) by the information that *p* (Dretske 1981, 86). This is offered as a characterization of perceptual knowledge. Since reading involves visual perception (for blind people who have mastered braille, reading involves tactile perception), it looks promising to think about reading along Dretske's lines. Now, what is information supposed to be, and how exactly does Dretske construe the relation between information and knowledge?

As to the first question, on Dretske's account, information, or semantic content, is something that can be "carried" by signals. Consider one of Dretske's examples (1981, 21–22):

> There are eight mischievous boys and a missing cookie. Who took it? An inspection reveals crumbs on Junior's lips .... Any one of the eight boys could have taken the cookie, and any one was as likely to take it as any other one. Hence, Junior's eating the cookie represents a reduction of eight possibilities to one .... With some routine assumptions we may suppose that the crumbs on Junior's lips carry information about who ate the cookie.

The crumbs on Junior's lips are a signal that carries the information that Junior took the cookie. A further example is the red spots that Agnes developed on her cheeks: the red spots are signals carrying the information that she suffers from measles. And, finally, in certain conditions a double knock on the door is a signal, and the information it carries is that the coast is clear (Dretske 1981, 40).

As to the second question, concerning the relation between information and knowledge, Dretske says that "what information a signal carries is what it is capable of 'telling' us, telling us truly, about another state of affairs. Roughly speaking, information is that commodity capable of yielding knowledge, and what information a signal carries is what we can learn from it" (1981, 44). He also says that information "is a commodity that, given the right recipient, is capable of yielding knowledge" (1981, 47). These quotations contain various ideas about the relation between information and knowledge. One idea is that information is *capable* of yielding knowledge – i.e., it may or may not yield knowledge in some agent. Thus, when the information does not yield knowledge in anybody (i.e., when no one actually learns something from the information contained in a signal), this doesn't mean that there is no information. For information to be information, it does not have to yield knowledge in some agent. So, there may be information without knowledge; and although Dretske doesn't say so explicitly, he is assuming that if there is to be knowledge, there has to be information.

A second idea is that if information is to yield knowledge, there needs to be a "right recipient." Information isn't capable of yielding knowledge in just anything or anybody: the recipient must, so to speak, be sensitive to the signal and to the information it contains. A being that lacks the faculty of visual perception cannot pick up the visual signals that carry the information that Agnes has measles.

For what follows it is useful to add that one signal may carry a number of different informational contents – hence, that from one signal, the right recipient may learn several different things. Dretske illustrates the point as follows (1981, 72):

> The acoustic signal that tells us someone is at our door carries not only the information that someone is at the door, but also the information that the button is depressed, that electricity is flowing through the doorbell circuit, that the clapper on the doorbell is vibrating, and much else besides. Indeed, all the information that is nested (analytically or nomically) in these states of affairs is also part of the acoustic signal's informational content.

So Dretske says that signals are the carriers of information and that, given the right recipient, they are capable of yielding knowledge.[13]

[13] As I shall say, the world *contains* or *embodies* information; signals only *carry* information.

Suppose we apply this to reading. Then we may say that texts are signals, or perhaps bundles of signals; they are the carriers of information. Texts carry information even when they are not read (not, at least, by people other than the writer), even if no one actually learns anything from them. But given the right recipients, they *are* capable of yielding knowledge in readers. Right recipients for text signals are properly educated and adequately informed persons – roughly, persons who can read; that is, persons who know the language in which the text is written and who, perhaps, know about style and genre conventions. *Not*-right recipients are sticks and stones, cats and hawks, and humans who, for some reason or other, can't read. Even when people are actually seeing texts and are thus the recipients of signals, they may not learn anything from them if they're unable to decode or interpret the signs. This happens when the text is a Hebrew text and the reader doesn't know Hebrew. This example illustrates that in order to be able to pick up the information that is carried by a text, one needs to have specific knowledge in addition to the knowledge that comes from the text one is reading (in this case, one needs to know Hebrew).

One signal, Dretske says, may carry a number of different informational contents. This clearly also holds when the signals are texts. Texts carry a plethora of informational contents. A text may carry informational content about the text itself (what language it is in, how many words it counts, how its first sentence reads, etc.), about the author (what language they know [if the text is not a translation], what views they hold, which moods they are capable of describing, what they intend to convey to the reader, what their intentions are, etc.), and about the world (for example, that the ice caps are melting, that the moon always shows the same face to the earth, and who won the New York marathon).

Reading, then, can produce knowledge in people. It doesn't matter to what genre the text belongs. And it doesn't matter whether we think about knowledge as a form of true belief or along the lines of Dretske's information-theoretic account.

Knowledge by Acquaintance through Reading

As Bertrand Russell famously suggested, not all knowledge is propositional, not all knowledge is knowledge of truths.[14] Someone who knows many truths about Burgundy wine doesn't, just in virtue of knowing those

[14] See Russell (1948), chapter 5, which bears the title "Knowledge by Acquaintance and Knowledge by Description."

truths, know the taste of a Burgundy. In order to know the taste of a Burgundy, one has to taste it – drinking the wine is the way to get acquainted with its taste. We can have knowledge by acquaintance, then, of tastes; and of colors, too. You may know many truths about colors, but these truths don't give you knowledge by acquaintance of colors. The only way to obtain such knowledge of a particular shade of blue is by visually seeing that shade. This is one of the points Frank Jackson made in his famous paper about what Mary didn't know (Jackson 1986). Mary, so the story goes, is confined to a black-and-white room, and she's educated through black-and-white books and through lectures relayed on a black-and-white television. In this way, she learns everything there is to know about the physical world. Well, not *everything*. For when she is let out of the room, she learns something new – she learns what it is like to see, say, something blue. She gains knowledge by acquaintance of the color blue.[15]

Thought of in this way, knowledge by acquaintance is, as Mark Johnston (2006) has it, "knowledge of what something is like." To know *X* in this sense is "to know what *X* is like." To revert to the examples given above: to know the taste of a Burgundy is to know what a Burgundy tastes like (it is to know how it tastes because one has tasted it oneself), and to know the color blue is to know what blue, or a blue thing, looks like (it is to know how blue looks because one has seen blue things oneself). Similarly, to know stomach pain is to know what a pain in the stomach feels like (it is to know how a pain in the stomach feels because one has experienced it oneself); to know happiness is to know what happiness feels like (it is to know how happiness feels because one has been happy oneself).

Thinking about knowledge by acquaintance in this way entails of course that someone who's never drunk a Burgundy doesn't know (in this sense of knowing) the taste of a Burgundy, that a color-blind person doesn't know (in this sense) the color blue, that a man doesn't know (in this sense) what it is like to give birth to a child, and so forth. Knowledge by acquaintance, then, has two features: it is first personal, and it is experiential. This is why I cannot have pain in your head, nor you in mine.[16]

[15] Jackson's knowledge argument (as it is usually called) is standardly taken to show that Mary comes to (propositionally) know new facts – viz., nonphysical facts; and more generalized, the argument is taken to show that, in addition to physical facts, there are nonphysical facts. In the context of the present chapter, my take on the argument is akin to Conee (1994), where it is defended that the argument shows that upon her release, Mary obtains nonpropositional acquaintance knowledge of colors.

[16] We can have knowledge by acquaintance, then, of tastes and colors. It has also been suggested (e.g., by Feldman 2003, 11) that we can have knowledge by acquaintance of persons. We have such

Many acquaintance theorists hold that a what-it-is-like experience is nonconceptual – i.e., that one can have the experience without the involvement of concepts, that the experience doesn't consist in the application of concepts.[17] One can experience the taste of a Burgundy without applying any concept. Also, one can visually experience the color blue without applying the concept *blue* or any other concept. Since acquaintance involves no concepts, it doesn't involve judgments or beliefs either. Knowledge by acquaintance is compatible with forming no beliefs at all.

This is not to deny that there might be a relation between a person's experience of what *X* is like and certain beliefs of that person about *X*. It may very well be, as foundationalists have argued, that one's experience of what *X* is like *justifies* some of one's beliefs about *X* (see, for instance, Fumerton 2001). For example, your experience of blue may justify your belief that what you are seeing is blue as well as your belief that Hester's shoes are blue – at least, if what you are seeing are Hester's shoes. But in order for you to be acquainted with the blueness of Hester's shoes, you don't have to have concepts, nor form beliefs about the shoes' color (even if you typically will have such beliefs).

Knowledge by acquaintance, then, is knowledge that can exist without belief. Thus, the question can be raised whether knowledge by acquaintance really is *knowledge*. It has been argued that it is not, and hence that we should not confuse acquaintance with foundational knowledge of truths acquired (and justified) by acquaintance.[18] I agree that we should not confuse these, but I don't agree that we therefore should refrain from speaking about knowledge by acquaintance. I disagree because long-standing linguistic practice suggests that acquaintance, whether or not it gives rise to propositional knowledge or justified belief, is itself a form of knowledge – albeit of a different nature than propositional knowledge. In the end, however, nothing much hangs on whether we call it knowledge: what is most important is that we recognize the phenomenon.

knowledge of others when we've met them, shook hands with them, talked with them, dined with them, and so on. You may know many truths about Angela Merkel – e.g., that she originates from former East Germany, that her father was a parson, that she has a degree in physics, and that she's become a very influential politician. But unless you have met with her, talked with her, and so on, it would be seriously misleading for you to say "I know Dr. Merkel," even if you know all the truths about her that I mentioned. So there is a sense of *know* in which you don't know a person unless you've met them, viz., the knowledge-by-acquaintance sense. Russell denied that we can have knowledge by acquaintance of persons, but he affirmed that we can have knowledge by acquaintance of universals (Russell 1948, 52).

[17] Nonconceptualism is defended by Dretske (1981), Evans (1982), and Peacocke (1983).

[18] For more on this, see Hasan and Fumerton (2017).

By my counting there are at least four different relations between reading and knowledge by acquaintance conceived of as being first personal, what-it-is-like experiential, and nonconceptual. First, when we read, we have – and *must* have – knowledge by acquaintance of the words and sentences that we're reading. Just as you cannot smell a rose without being acquainted with its fragrance, so you cannot read a text without being acquainted with its words and sentences. This acquaintance is obviously a first-person experience. Moreover, the experience has a distinctive what-it-is-like quality. What it is like to see words and sentences when reading is very different from what it is like to see a giraffe or a house, and it is even more different from what it is like to hear a drum beat or what it is like to taste a Burgundy. Finally, the first-person experience of seeing words and sentences is nonconceptual: you don't have to have the concept *word* or the concept *sentence* in order to have knowledge by acquaintance of words and sentences. You can have knowledge by acquaintance of Cyrillic letter forms even when you don't know the Russian language.

But how exactly should we think about this relation between reading and knowledge by acquaintance of words and sentences? It isn't that reading *gives rise to* knowledge by acquaintance (in the way reading can and often does give rise to propositional knowledge). Rather, it is, as suggested, that reading a text *requires* that the reader has knowledge by acquaintance of words and sentences. The relation is one of a *precondition*: it is a precondition for reading that the reader has knowledge by acquaintance of words and sentences.

A second type of knowledge by acquaintance that comes with reading, we might say, "builds on" the knowledge by acquaintance just discussed. Acquaintance with words and sentences of the sort just mentioned can go hand in hand with acquaintance with the *meaning* of the words and sentences. You see, for example, the word *woods* in the sentence "Whose woods these are I think I know" and immediately grasp its meaning. This grasping of the meaning of the word *woods*, I suggest, is a second type of knowledge by acquaintance. Your grasping the meaning of the word is a first-person experience: it is you who grasps the meaning, and the grasping, moreover, is experiential in the sense that it has a distinctive qualitative feel to it. What it is like to grasp the meaning of the word *woods* is different from what it is like to grasp the meaning of the word *odd* or the meaning of *perpendicular*.

The what-it-is-like character of grasping word meanings, moreover, is nonconceptual. This may initially seem strange, but I don't think it is. To say that knowledge by acquaintance of a patch of blue is nonconceptual is to say that one doesn't need a concept – not the concept *blue* nor the concept *patch* – to be acquainted with that color. Likewise, to say that knowledge by acquaintance of the meaning of the word *woods* is non-conceptual is to say that in order to be acquainted with its meaning one doesn't need (other) concepts. One can be acquainted with the word's meaning without, for example, being able to provide a synonym or a definition for it. Thus, we don't necessarily need concepts in order to have knowledge by acquaintance of word meanings.

I take it that Russell adopted a somewhat similar view when he wrote: "We also have acquaintance with what we shall call *universals*, that is to say, general ideas, such as *whiteness*, *diversity*, *brotherhood*, and so on .... Awareness of universals is called *conceiving*, and a universal of which we are aware is called a *concept*" (Russell 1948, 51–52). So having a concept, say, the concept *brotherhood*, is identical to being aware of a universal (the universal *brotherhood*), and universals are objects of acquaintance, as are colors, smells, and tastes. There is a difference, though, between Russell's view and the view that I've tried to articulate. On my view we have, or can have, knowledge by acquaintance of word meanings. Now, *some* word meanings are universals: the meaning of the word *brotherhood*, for example, is the universal *brotherhood*. But we're also acquainted with word meanings that are *not* universals – for example, syncategorematic words like *and* and *this* and indexicals like *here* and *now*. On my view, we can have knowledge by acquaintance of the meaning of these words, too.

It bears pointing out that we can also have *propositional* knowledge of word meanings – e.g., knowing that the meaning of *to procrastinate* is "to put things off." But the present point is that we have *acquaintance* knowledge of word meanings.

As to the exact relationship between reading and knowledge by acquaintance of word meanings, we must say that reading doesn't normally[19] *give rise to* knowledge by acquaintance of word meanings but, rather, that reading *requires* it. One isn't reading unless one is acquainted with the meanings of the words one is reading. (This is compatible, of course, with incidental ignorance of the meaning of some of the words one is reading.)

There is a third type of knowledge by acquaintance associated with reading. It builds on the previous two types. Via acquaintance with the words and sentences, and via acquaintance with the word and sentence meanings, when things go well, we can come to know the thoughts of an

[19] "Normally," because it is possible to get acquainted with the meaning of a word by consulting a dictionary.

author; that is, we can come to know what they intended to convey or "get across," what they wanted to endorse, suggest, criticize, ask, and so on. Through reading a newspaper article, one may come to know the author's thought that something is terribly wrong in Angola, or that Bob Dylan's voice sounded surprisingly good at last night's concert. Knowing that the newspaper article says any of these things isn't knowledge by acquaintance – it is knowledge of facts. Knowing, on the basis of reading the newspaper, that there is something terribly wrong in Angola or that Dylan's voice sounded good last night aren't cases of knowledge by acquaintance either: these cases lack the first-personal and experiential character that marks out knowledge by acquaintance. Yet, as I shall now suggest, even here knowledge by acquaintance is involved. Suppose you read the newspaper and come to think the author's thought expressed in the article, viz., that there is something terribly wrong in Angola; or suppose you come to think the thought that the reviewer expressed when he wrote that Dylan's voice sounded surprisingly good. Now, thinking these thoughts is surely a first-personal affair: it is you who's having the thoughts. There is, moreover, a what-it-is-like aspect to thinking these thoughts: thinking that there is something terribly wrong in Angola has a qualitative aspect that is different from the qualitative aspect that comes with thinking that Dylan's voice sounded surprisingly good.

The point of saying this is that through reading, we come to think thoughts. Thinking thoughts involves almost always entertaining propositions: whether one, through reading, comes to believe that *p*, doubt that *p*, hope that *p*, fear that *p*, or whatever, it always involves having proposition *p* in mind. Propositions, if we think of them in a Platonist-realist vein, are abstract objects. And like universals, propositions can be objects of acquaintance: we can have knowledge by acquaintance, for example, of the proposition that there is something terribly wrong in Angola. In thinking that proposition, we have knowledge by acquaintance of it. But my acquaintance with that proposition doesn't by itself amount to my *knowing that* there is something terribly wrong in Angola. For if that proposition is false, then when I think that thought I lack the propositional knowledge that there is something terribly wrong in Angola – for knowledge is factive. Nevertheless, I have knowledge by acquaintance of that proposition: I know what it is like to think it. Finally, knowledge by acquaintance of propositions is a nonconceptual affair. When I merely entertain a proposition, I don't need (other) concepts in order to be able to entertain it. I don't need the concept *proposition*, for example, in order to be able to entertain the proposition that Dylan's voice sounded good.

So, propositions can be objects of propositional knowledge as well as of knowledge by acquaintance. And it would seem that we can only have propositional knowledge if we also have knowledge by acquaintance of the proposition involved. But knowledge by acquaintance of a proposition is insufficient – though necessary – for propositional knowledge of it.

What exactly is the relation between reading and knowledge by acquaintance of propositions? There's a difference between this type of knowledge by acquaintance and acquaintance with words and word meanings. For reading often does give rise to the kind of knowledge by acquaintance under discussion: it is *through reading* that a reader comes to entertain certain propositions and not others. This type of knowledge by acquaintance is not a precondition for reading – it results from it.

There is, finally, a fourth type of knowledge by acquaintance that comes – or can come – with reading, which I call secondhand knowledge by acquaintance, or proxy acquaintance, for reasons that will emerge in a moment. The reality of proxy acquaintance can perhaps best be illustrated by reference to what happens or may happen when one reads works of literature, especially novels. (But reading other genres – e.g., poems, biographies, autobiographies, and historical narratives – may work the same wonder.) Through reading works of literature one may, to use Dorothy Walsh's phrase, "vicariously live through" (Walsh 1969, 129) an experience or a way of living or a position in life that one has no acquaintance with by one's own experiences. For example, through reading Thomas Hardy's *Tess of the D'Urbervilles* (1891), one may have a proxy experience of what it is like for a woman to live in a culture in which what is allowed to men is denied to women. Through reading Iris Murdoch's *The Sea, the Sea* (1978), one may experience what it is like to project one's feelings on someone else while having no idea that one is doing so. Through reading John Steinbeck's *Of Mice and Men* (1937), one may come to feel what it is like to shoot someone for whom one has cared deeply. Through reading Marilynne Robinson's *Home* (2008), one may come to feel what it is like for a father to have a son whom he doesn't understand. Through reading Dostoyevsky's *The Brothers Karamazov* (1880), one may feel what it is like to belong to a family that falls apart, and what it is like to be attracted to a truly holy man (the starets Zosima). Through reading literature, then, one may have a what-it-is-like experience of something that one has no firsthand experience of.

To be sure, this isn't knowledge by acquaintance in the strict sense, for one doesn't have a first-person experience of the real thing. But it's close enough to qualify as proxy knowledge by acquaintance. There is *some sort of* first-person what-it-is-like experience that one is undergoing in these cases. The most important reason why proxy acquaintance isn't real acquaintance is that, whereas in the genuine article the experience is nonconceptual, in proxy cases, the experience in the reader is mediated and induced by concepts – you can't have a proxy experience unless you have concepts. And there is a variety of ways in which the feat can be accomplished. For instance, the extreme is when a certain what-it-is-like experience is induced in the reader through various concepts, *none* of which describe the experience. For instance, through reading Marilynne Robinson's first novel, *Housekeeping* (1980), a reader can get a (kind of) what-it-is-like experience of living in a dysfunctional household. But nowhere in the entire novel is the notion *dysfunctional household* explicitly used. As a matter of fact, it takes quite some time for the reader to realize that the household that is being described is dysfunctional. Another example of this extreme is Iris Murdoch's *The Sea, The Sea*, in which readers can get a what-it-is-like experience of being deluded by one's own wishful thinking, without the notions *delusion* and *wishful thinking* ever being used in the novel. Many other books, the reading of which can give the reader a proxy acquaintance with something, are at some remove from this extreme in that they do use concepts that more or less directly describe the experience.

What is, precisely, the relation between reading and secondhand knowledge by acquaintance? It is not that proxy acquaintance is a requirement for reading – rather, reading can induce and generate proxy acquaintance.

To sum up, reading requires knowledge by acquaintance of words and sentences; it also requires knowledge by acquaintance of word meanings. Reading can yield, or generate, or give rise to, knowledge by acquaintance of propositions. And reading can induce and generate proxy knowledge by acquaintance of, for example, experiences. Beings incapable of the first three types of knowledge by acquaintance cannot read. (Hence acquaintance is included in the analysis of reading that I offer in Chapter 5.) Beings incapable of proxy acquaintance miss out on important cognitive gains involving empathy (for this, see Keen 2007).

Knowing-How through Reading

Epistemologists often distinguish a third form of knowledge, viz., knowing-how, knowing how to *do* something – for instance, knowing how to play the guitar, how to play "Stairway to Heaven," how to speak Dutch, how to pronounce the sentence "Een schelle schicht schoot schichtig uit den hogen," or how to cook a gourmet dish. Gilbert Ryle argued that knowledge-how cannot be reduced to knowledge-that – i.e., propositional knowledge – and that those who think such a reduction *is* possible are in the grips of "the intellectualist legend," according to which intelligent actions must be preceded by the intellectual acknowledgment of rules or criteria (Ryle 1949, 27ff.). He concedes that sometimes this is the case; for instance, when a chess player takes some time to plan their moves before they make them. He points out, however, that there are many things we know how to do without prior acknowledgment of criteria or rules: for example, someone may know how to make good jokes and how to detect bad ones without having a recipe available to themselves, and people can reason correctly even if they don't make an internal reference to the rules of reasoning.

Adam Carter and Ted Poston (2018) have recently advanced a new argument for the irreducibility of knowing-how to knowing-that. The argument is that, whereas knowing-that can easily be transmitted by testimony, knowing-how cannot. The argument proceeds from considering inferences about knowledge transmission like the following:

(A) (1) Rutger knows that Robert Schumann wrote *Kinderszenen*; (2) Rutger tells Sophie that Schumann wrote *Kinderszenen*; (3) so, Sophie knows that Schumann wrote *Kinderszenen*.

(B) (1) Rutger knows how to play Schumann's *Kinderszenen*; (2) Rutger tells Sophie how to play Schumann's *Kinderszenen*; (3) so, Sophie knows how to play Schumann's *Kinderszenen*.

It seems obvious that (A) looks good and (B) bad. From inferences like these, Carter and Poston draw the general conclusion that knowing-how cannot be easily transmitted by testimony, whereas propositional knowledge can. This evidences that knowing-how cannot be reduced to knowing-that.

If this line of reasoning is correct, this rather obviously suggests that knowing-how cannot easily be transmitted by reading either. Consider the following inferences:

(B*) (1) Rutger knows how to play Schumann's *Kinderszenen*; (2) Sophie has read what Rutger wrote about how to play *Kinderszenen*; (3) so, Sophie knows how to play *Kinderszenen*.

(C) (1) Ludmila Pagliero wrote about how to do a pirouette; (2) I have read Pagliero on how to do a pirouette; (3) so, I know how to do a pirouette.

These are bad inferences.

However, the claim that knowing-how cannot easily be transmitted through telling – or, more relevant in the current context, through reading – is unconvincing, because it faces many counterexamples. We read cookbooks so as to acquire knowledge about how to prepare certain dishes. We read books about gardening to come to know how to tend roses or how to prune an elm tree. We read self-help books to overcome anxieties. We read travel guidebooks to find out how to walk from Barcelona's Jewish Quarter to the Sagrada Familia. We read instructions in order to learn how to calculate sales taxes. And by reading the relevant manuals, we come to know how to use our new computer, sewing machine, central heating system, Spotify, and so on.

The claim, then, that know-how cannot easily be transmitted through testimony or reading is false: in fact, know-how transmission is often quite easy. The problem with the discussion on know-how, as Stephen Grimm (2020) has pointed out, is that it has suffered from a one-sided diet of examples. If we expand the diet, the picture becomes more complex, but also more interesting, for whether or not know-how can be transmitted through reading depends then on two factors, viz., the complexity of the know-how and the abilities of the reader, as I will now explain. If the know-how is involved and complex (as in knowing how to play Schumann's *Kinderszenen*, or how to make a pirouette, or how to operate an aircraft, or how to calculate a nation's gross national product), then transmission through reading is much more difficult than if the know-how is simple and easy (as in knowing how to flip the light switch, or how to inflate the tires of your bicycle). It also depends on the abilities of the reader – not only their reading abilities but their other abilities as well. If you're a well-trained pilot, picking up through reading the know-how of operating a new type of equipment will be much easier than if you're a novice in the world of aviation. So, how easy or difficult the uptake of know-how through reading is depends on both the complexity of the information and the reader's abilities.

As Grimm has rightly noted, contrary to what Carter and Poster aver, there is no serious difference in this respect with the transmission of propositional knowledge. It just isn't the case that the transmission of knowing-that through reading, for instance, is always easy. If you barely know French, then even reading an easy French sentence expressing a simple truth will not transmit that truth. And even if you have mastery of the language, the transmission of truths through reading in the areas of, for instance, quantum mechanics, the EU system of taxes and subsidies, or

McTaggart's arguments for the unreality of time and space may be very difficult. Again, whether the uptake of knowledge-that is easy or difficult depends on two factors, viz., the complexity of the proposition(s) involved and the reader's abilities, linguistic and other. These abilities have at least in some part to do with how much the reader already knows about a particular subject matter. If you're a well-educated physicist, the transmission of truths in the area of quantum mechanics will be easier than if you're a biologist or a historian or someone with elementary education only.

The discussion so far leaves it unresolved whether know-how can be reduced to propositional knowledge. For present purposes, there is no need to take a stand on this. The upshot of the discussion in this section is that *it is possible* to acquire know-how through reading, and that the reality of knowledge transmission depends on both the complexity of the know-how and the reader's receptiveness – receptiveness that is due to education, training, and experience. This conclusion stands, regardless of whether knowing-how can be reduced to knowing-that.

The conclusion of this chapter, then, is that reading can give a rich cognitive yield. It can give readers propositional knowledge, knowledge by acquaintance, and know-how. But reading not only yields knowledge – it also requires knowledge, especially knowledge by acquaintance of words, sentences, meanings, and propositions.

In the next chapter, I argue that the cognitive yield of reading is even more capacious.

CHAPTER 2

Reading and Understanding

To *know* something is one thing; to *understand* something seems quite another, as the saying "The more we know, the less we understand" suggests. In this chapter, I distinguish various forms of understanding, specify the kinds of understanding that reading can yield, and explain why we can think of understanding as being built on knowledge. Finally, I mention some additional epistemic benefits of reading.

Three Types of Understanding

Knowing and understanding, I said, are different things. But I should be more precise because they sometimes amount to virtually the same thing. When you say (referring to the upcoming meeting of local shopkeepers and entrepreneurs) "I understand that Starbucks will be represented by Claire," this is virtually the same as saying "I know that Starbucks will be represented by Claire." Often, however, understanding is not the same as knowing – it goes, in a way that I will try to explain, beyond knowing. They can come apart in that one may have knowledge but lack understanding. Let me offer some examples. One may know that the United Kingdom has such an institution as the House of Lords and yet have no understanding of its role in the political system, how it relates to the House of Commons, what its voting rules are, or what the role of the Speaker of the House is. One may know that Lincoln gave a speech in Gettysburg and yet not understand its content, its significance, or its influence. One may know that water freezes below zero degrees Celsius and normal atmospheric pressure and yet not understand the physics of freezing. One may know that Jack the Ripper killed the so-called canonical five and yet not understand why he did that. One may know that Robert Browning wrote "Two in the Campagna" (1855), one may even know all its words by heart, and yet one may not, or not really, understand what the poem is about.

Can the difference between knowing and (this kind of) understanding be pinpointed? Linda Zagzebski (2001, 241) has suggested that "the object of understanding is not a discrete proposition," implying that the objects of knowledge *are* discrete propositions. This suggestion looks good if we assume that it is propositional knowledge she has in mind. For consider such propositions as that the earth has a moon, that every even number smaller than 100,000 is the sum of two prime numbers, and that Copenhagen is the capital of Denmark. These propositions can be, and in fact are, the objects of knowledge, but it seems they can't be the objects of understanding; at least, such sentences as "I understand that the earth has a moon" and "He understands that every even number smaller than 100,000 is the sum of two prime numbers" and "She understands that Copenhagen is the capital of Denmark" sound peculiar. *Why* do these sayings sound strange?

Such sayings (can) sound strange because understanding requires that the object of understanding is *either* something complex, something with "parts" that "interact," and to understand it is to "see" how the parts interact, *or* something that itself is part of a larger whole (or structure, or system), and to understand it is to see how it interacts with other parts of the system. Thus, to understand the House of Lords is either to understand its "inner workings," its aims, rules and regulations, and so on, or to see how it fits in the British political system and how it interacts with other parts of that system. To understand the Gettysburg Address is either to understand its content, so how its parts hang together so as to make one formidable, although short, speech, or to see why it had the effects that it had, how it fitted in the bigger reality of American politics and society of the 1860s, and so on. To understand the freezing of water is either to see what happens inside the "water parts," or to see how those parts interact. The objects of (this kind of) understanding are complexes with interacting parts: you understand things insofar as you see how its parts interact. This entails that objects without parts and that are not part of anything bigger cannot be understood. This doesn't constitute much of a limitation on the scope of understanding, however, as almost *everything* either has parts (either literally or in a metaphorical sense) or is part of something bigger. Zagzebski, then, is right: "Understanding is the state of comprehension of nonpropositional structures of reality" (Zagzebski 2001, 242).

Stephen Grimm has added a modal twist to the analysis of (this kind of) understanding, which he thinks of as an analysis of *understanding the natural world*. (I shall suggest in a moment that his analysis has a broader scope, though.) Grimm introduces the modal twist in a discussion of an eight-year-old child who sees, for the first time, someone fill a balloon with helium and release it so that it rises into the air. The child tries to figure out why the balloon rose and wonders whether it is the color that made a difference to the rising, or the time of day when it was released, or where it was released, or by whom. Through a series of observations, the child comes to believe it was none of these things and concludes it was the presence of a mysterious gas, the helium, that made the difference. In this way, the child has obtained some understanding of why the balloon rose. And the understanding consists in the child's having grasped a real relation of dependence that obtains in the world. The child has got, as Grimm (2018) says, "command over the 'modal space' around the focal event" – i.e., it will appreciate how changing the value of certain variables will lead to changes in the focal event, while changing the value of other variables will not.

I think that Grimm's analysis of (this type of) understanding is not confined to the natural world: we can have this kind of understanding also of the House of Lords, of the significance of the Gettysburg Address, of university administrations, and of many other social realities.

Zagzebski's and Grimm's accounts both enable us to make sense of the intuitively plausible idea that understanding admits of degrees, so that one person may have a better understanding of something than another person. To have a better understanding of phenomenon *X* is to better see how *X*'s parts interact, or to see more of the relations that *X* stands in – it is to see deeper into the "modal space" surrounding *X*.

Both Zagzebski and Grimm suggest that there is a practical dimension to understanding that is absent from mere propositional knowledge. Zagzebski (2001, 240) says that understanding is a cognitive state arising from *techne*, which includes practical activities that are not wholly cognitive. And Grimm speaks of understanding as having "command over the modal space" surrounding the phenomenon – and the command, as suggested by the example of the child, has a practical side to it.

We should note that there are types of understanding that are not captured by the above accounts. For there is a type of understanding that we aim for when we try to understand *people*.[1] Suppose you have a neighbor *A* who always leaves his house on Monday evening at 7:00 p. m., and another neighbor *B* who, when the moon is full, opens all the windows and doors of her house. Both of your neighbors' behaviors

[1] Grimm (2016) has pointed out a number of differences between understanding people and understanding the natural world.

display structure in such a way that you can predict with reasonable certainty what *A* will do on Monday evenings at 7:00 p.m. and what *B* will do when the moon is full. So you have a modicum of "command over the modal space" of *A*'s Monday evening movements and over *B*'s full moon movements – that is, you understand their actions at those evenings and nights. So far, this is still the sort of understanding presented in Grimm's child-with-balloon example.

However, there is another sense (or type) of understanding in which you *don't* understand *A*'s and *B*'s behaviors: you don't understand *why* they behave in these ways. Suppose now that *A* tells you that on Monday evenings, he sings in a choir. This provides you with another kind of understanding of *A*'s Monday evening behavior. You now understand *A* (or *A*'s behavior) because you see that it serves a purpose; it has a point. Now suppose also that *B* tells you that she opens doors and windows at full moon so that the bats can fly in. Then you understand *B* (or *B*'s behavior) in the same way that you understand *A* (and *A*'s behavior): you see that *B*'s behavior also serves a purpose; it too has a point. Of course, understanding what purposes a person's particular pattern of behavior serves is different from understanding *that* a person's behavior fits a pattern. They constitute two different types of understanding.

But we should not stop here; for there is yet another type of understanding. That further type is such that you presumably understand *A* in a way in which you presumably *don't* understand *B*. You understand *A* in this further sense that you see that the purpose of *A*'s Monday evening behavior – i.e., singing – is not only in fact desired but also desir*able* (or, at least, it can be considered desirable). The goal that *A* pursues by his behavior is not only chosen – it is choice*worthy*, and you can see that it is. But you presumably *don't* understand *B*'s behavior in this further sense, since the goal of *B*'s behavior (i.e., hosting bats), although in fact desired by *B*, does not look desir*able*. And although in fact chosen by *B*, it doesn't look choice*worthy*.[2] Understanding *A* in this further sense is a way of endorsing *A*'s behavior; that is, agreeing that *A*'s aim is indeed desirable and choiceworthy. Not understanding *B* in this further sense is *not* endorsing *B*'s behavior but rather *denying* that *B*'s aim is desirable and choiceworthy.

What this discussion brings to light is that we should distinguish the following three types of understanding:

[2] This discussion owes much to Grimm (2016).

- Type I: understanding *X* consists in seeing how *X*'s parts hang together (or what *X*'s place is in the broader scheme of things) or grasping how *X* fits a pattern; to understand *X* is to grasp the modal space surrounding *X*. Here, *X* can be a part of the natural world, but it can also be a social constellation or token behavior.
- Type II: understanding *X* consists in grasping the desired goals that *X* aims to attain. Here, *X* is a person (or a person's behavior) or a collective of persons, such as a choir, a board, a sports team, or a company (or a collective's behavior).
- Type III: understanding *X* consists in grasping (and so endorsing) the desirability of the goals that *X* aims to attain. Here, too, *X* is a person or a collective of persons (or a person's or a collective's behavior).

Reading can yield understanding. In fact, the relations between reading and understanding are manifold. One way to organize them is this: when we read, our aim can be (i) to understand a text, (ii) to understand the author(s) of the text, or (iii) to understand the subject matter (or, the Matter) of the text.

Reading and Understanding Texts

An important aim when reading a text is to come to grips with how its parts hang together. Our default attitude toward the texts that we read is – and perhaps ought to be – the expectation that its parts hang together. Or, which comes to the same thing, when reading a text, we proceed – and perhaps should proceed – from the presumption that the text's parts form a meaningful whole, a coherent unity. And *one understands a text to the extent that one sees or grasps that or how its parts hang together so as to form a meaningful whole*. The type of understanding involved here is Type I understanding. This section explains and explores these thoughts.

First, the italicized statement entails that texts can be understood by readers to various extents: they can be fully understood, but also only partially, and the latter to various degrees. The more one has grasped the relations between its parts, the better one has understood the text. This holds generally. But we shouldn't assume that between the parts of different texts the same number of relations or even the same kinds of relations exist. Old-fashioned telephone books, for example, have only very few relations between their parts – each part being an entry consisting of a name, telephone number, and home address. Between its parts, only alphabetical and local relations obtain (i.e., the names are of persons who live in the same town or village). Between the parts of Dostoyevsky's *The Brothers Karamazov*, many other relations obtain, which is why it is so much harder to understand this literary masterpiece than it is to understand a telephone book.

Second, when we read texts, our presumption is that the text's parts hang together so as to form a meaningful whole, a coherent unity. This expectation however may sometimes be frustrated: some text's parts may *not* form a meaningful whole. Or to be more precise, texts may be meaningful wholes only to a certain degree. *Being a meaningful whole* is a gradable notion. Lesser degrees of textual unity can be due to such factors as hastiness of composition, incompetence, or mental fatigue on the part of the author during the writing process. But a low degree of textual coherence could also, in principle, be a conscious choice – a choice made so as to make a particular point. All of this is possible, and it indicates that reaching a Type I understanding of a text can be a daunting task – if it is possible at all. Be that as it may, this should not make us drop our default attitude.

Third, we may ask: What is it about texts that gives them some degree of unity, or meaning-coherence? Intuitively the idea may seem clear enough, but it is somewhat difficult to make it fully precise. The degree of unity and coherence seems to depend upon such factors as

- whether the text has a more or less clearly discernable main point that emerges from the text as a whole and not from only some of its parts – a point that any summary of the text should contain, lest it be inadequate;
- whether the text contains parts that are disconnected from the rest of the text and that could be omitted without loss;
- whether the text has a clearly discernable structure or recognizable organizing principles. Examples of such structures/principles in non-fictional texts include (i) a presentation of premises leading up to a conclusion based on them, (ii) the presentation of a theory plus supporting pieces of evidence, (iii) the discussion of a number of different objections to a claim, (iv) the historical order of narrated events, and (v) a thematic structure – e.g., "We start with impressionism, next comes expressionism, which is followed by cubism." Examples of such structures in fiction include (vi) the recurrence of a particular theme or topic in a novel (estrangement, miscommunication, causes of true happiness, mother-daughter relations, etc.), (vii) stylistic features (association, hyperbole, rhyme and rhythm, etc.), and (viii) a discernable time line and order of described events; and

- whether the contents of the parts of the text are consistent with each other – that is, whether what is said or implied in one part isn't taken back in another (at least, not without there being a seeming intention behind the inconsistency). In order to secure consistency in tragedies, the Aristotelian tradition required unity of place (a tragedy should take place in one physical location), unity of time (the sequence of tragic events should take place over no more than 24 hours), and unity of action (a tragedy should have one principal action).

Factors like these, then, contribute to a text's unity. But what is it supposed to *be* for a text to have unity? Do Aesop's fable of the fox and the crow and the newspaper article about the bees have the same property, viz., the unity property? Or should we say that the fable has more of that property than the article, in a way that is analogous to saying that an aircraft has more mass than a bike? Peter Unger's distinction between absolute and relative terms may be of help here. An absolute term, he says, "purports to denote a limiting state or situation to which things may approximate more or less closely" (Unger 2000, 46). Examples he offers of such terms are *flat* and *useless* (and, more controversially, *certain*). Absolute terms denote absolute states, that is, states that have no degrees. A thing is either flat or it isn't – there is no third possibility. This is not to deny that we do sometimes say, for instance, "That is the flattest thing I have ever seen," thus seemingly implying that flatness *does* come in degrees and hence is no absolute state after all. However, as Unger points out, this way of speaking can be paraphrased so that the suggestion of degrees disappears: "That's the only absolutely flat thing that I have ever seen" or "That's closer to being absolutely flat than anything else I have ever seen." Absolute terms contrast with relative terms. Relative terms do *not* denote limiting states or situations to which things may approximate more or less closely. Examples are *tall* and, if Robert Adams (1972) is right, *good*. There is nothing that is *absolutely* tall, because for every tall thing there is another thing that is even taller; and, according to Adams, there is no best of all possible worlds because for every good possible world, there is an even better one. Relative terms really denote matters of degree.

It seems to me that *unity* is not an absolute term, at least not when we are talking about textual unity. We can see that some texts have more unity than others, but there just doesn't seem to be a limit of unity which texts can approach more or less closely. Or at least, I have no idea what that limit could be. *Unity*, I therefore suggest, is a relative term – which is not to deny that in practice it will often be difficult to say just which of two texts has more unity. But the list of factors offered above does give us some clues as to what to look for.

Fourth, so far I have talked about "parts" of texts without specifying what those parts are supposed to be. Here we have a whole nomenclature to avail ourselves of. All of the following terms denote parts of texts: books (as in "the book of Leviticus," which is a part of the Hebrew Bible, and "book 4 of John Locke's *An Essay concerning Human Understanding*"), chapters, sections, subsections, acts and scenes (as in "*Hamlet*, act 2, scene 2"), verses (as in "The opening verse of the book of John reads 'In the beginning was the Word'"), couplets and stanzas (as in "The final stanza of George Herbert's 'The Elixir' speaks of the philosopher's stone"), paragraphs, sentences, and words. Between the parts of texts, mereological relations exist that are not wholly unlike the relations between the parts of houses: walls, roofs, rooms, ceilings, staircases, corridors, windows, doors, and so on. Books are usually composed of chapters. Chapters in turn are often composed of sections, and if not, they are composed of paragraphs. If they are composed of sections, then the sections are composed of subsections, and if not, they are composed of sentences. If sections have subsections, then the subsections are composed of sentences. And the sentences, finally, are composed of words. This holds for scientific books as well as for philosophical ones, and also for works of literary art. Poems usually have no chapters or sections or paragraphs, but they do have parts, as indicated: stanzas, couplets, and, of course, sentences and words. Texts can also have other kinds of parts; for example, story lines, arguments, and motifs.

To conclude, reading can yield an understanding of texts that can be thought of as involving Type I understanding: it is understanding how their parts hang together so as to form a meaningful whole and unity. No doubt, there is more to reading than understanding how the parts of the text one is reading hang together. Reading often also involves understanding the writer. But understanding a text in the sense explained in this section is an important part of the reading experience.

Reading and Understanding Authors

My discussion of another relation between reading and understanding takes its point of departure in the commonsensical idea that when people write things up – or, to put it abstractly, when they produce texts – they normally have reasons for doing so. Those reasons are often connected with the goals they aim to attain through the production of the text. One epistemic aim we have when reading is to come to understand authors – i.e., to understand the aims they had and tried to attain through the production of the text. To the extent that one has grasped the authorial aim or aims for the text, one has understood the author. The following comments flesh out the notion of *reading aimed at understanding authors*.

First, by the phrase *authorial aims* I mean what could also be called *authorial intentions*. The phrase doesn't refer to just any old aim that an author might have in the production of a text (getting rich or famous, for example, falls outside its reference). It refers to what speech-act theorists have called illocutionary act intentions and perlocutionary act intentions. Examples of illocutionary act intentions are the intention to *assert* that *p*, the intention to *proclaim* that *p*, the intention to *request* that *p* be done, the intention to *question* whether *p*, the intention to *command* that *p*, the intention to *promise* that *p*, and the intention to *warn* that *p*.[3] Examples of perlocutionary act intentions are intentions to secure a certain effect in one's readers, such as to *persuade* them of *p*, to *baffle* them by saying *p*, to *encourage* them by saying *p*, and to *scare* them by saying *p*. It seems clear that when we write emails, old-fashioned letters, op-eds, academic papers, and books, we have illocutionary as well as perlocutionary act intentions. It barely (if ever) happens that people write things and *not* have intentions of these sorts.[4] Accordingly, our default attitude toward a text, *any* text, is and should be that it embodies authorial intentions of both the illocutionary and the perlocutionary variety.

Second, and related, when we read texts and want to understand the authorial intentions, we want to understand not only the *illocutionary force* of what the writer wrote but also *its propositional content*. Reading an email from a student, I come to understand that he apologizes for not attending my class. Reading an email from one of the editors of *Synthese*, I come to understand that I'm invited to compose a review report for them. Reading the announcement poster, I come to understand that van Inwagen's talk will be on the problem of evil, will be held in the auditorium, and will start at 4:00 p.m. tomorrow. When we read, we are almost always interested in *what it is* that authors intend to communicate (the illocutionary force of their words and their propositional content) as well as what effects they intended to secure. To be sure, readers may sometimes want other things

[3] Alston (2000), Chapters 4 and 5, distinguishes five main categories of illocutionary act intentions and perlocutionary act intentions, which he baptizes assertives, expressives, directives, commissives, and exercitives.

[4] For more argument on this, I refer to the first section of Chapter 6.

from reading than grasping what the authors intended to convey. They may, for instance, just be curious about whether Bach or Napoleon or Bohr are mentioned in the text, whether it contains a quotation from Kant or Shakespeare, or whether the text's style is solemn or playful or analytic or angry. But we do often read in order to grasp authorial intentions. And insofar as we grasp these, we understand the author.

Finally, understanding an author is different from understanding a text. Understanding a text, as I indicated above, is grasping how the text's parts hang together so as to form a meaningful whole; it instances Type I understanding. But understanding an author has nothing to do with grasping the interaction of textual parts. Understanding an author (in the sense expounded so far) has to do with grasping the goals the author aimed to attain through the production of the text – i.e., grasping the author's illocutionary and perlocutionary act intentions as well as their propositional contents. Understanding an author in the sense intended here, then, instances Type II understanding.

Readers can have a Type II understanding of an author whose work they're reading and *not* understand the author in another sense. What I have in mind are cases analogous to the case of your neighbor who opens her house's doors and windows when the moon is full: although you grasp the goal she aims to attain by doing this (viz., to host bats), you don't understand why that goal should be deemed desirable, why acting that way should be choiceworthy. You have a Type II understanding of your neighbor's actions at full moon, but you lack a Type III understanding of them (and of her).

Having a Type III understanding of an author means, in a way, that you *agree* with the author, whereas having merely a Type II understanding does not mean that you do. For to have a Type III understanding of an author is to grasp the value of what the author intended to convey. And to grasp the value of someone's intentions is to agree with the intender. You cannot see the value, the desirability, the choiceworthiness of what an author intended to convey and yet disagree with her. I do not Type III understand what a philosopher, a politician, a cultural critic, a literary author, or a journalist wrote unless I can agree that what the author intended to communicate is worthy of communication and, hence, is something desirable.

The point about the difference between Type II and Type III understanding can be put in terms of Max Weber's two well-known notions of rationality: *means rationality* and *value* (or *ends*) *rationality*.[5] Given a certain end (goal, aim), the selection of one instrument to attain it can

[5] For a discussion of the intellectual background of this distinction, see Apel (1984, 15–19).

be more rational (efficient, likely to help attain the goal) than the selection of another. For example, given that your only goal is to make as firm an ecological footprint as possible when traveling to Amsterdam, and you can choose between a car and a bicycle, the selection of the car is the more rational choice – it is *means rational*. But it isn't *value rational*, for why would you want to set yourself a goal like that? Setting yourself this goal violates what have been called the principles of substantive rationality. When we try to understand what an author intended to say, the first thing to do is to ascertain what it is that she intended to convey by the text – which cannot be done unless we pay detailed attention to the textual means offered. We normally conclude to what it is that an author intended to convey by scrutinizing the means used (i.e., the text), and we form ideas about whether those means are rational, given what we have identified as the author's goal. But doing this doesn't imply anything about the substantive rationality of the end that the author selected. Capturing authorial intentions – i.e., the ends that the author aimed to secure – by reading the author's production – i.e., the means through which she aimed to secure her ends – is what constitutes Type II understanding. It involves gauging the means rationality of the author. Type III understanding of the author, by contrast, involves gauging the end rationality of the author and seeing that the intended end is valuable and choiceworthy. In other words, a Type II understanding of a text is understanding *why* its author says what she says – that is, *why* she endorsed the content. And one has a Type III understanding of a text when one agrees with the author that the endorsed content is worthy of endorsement.

Distinguishing various types of understanding can be helpful in the interest of avoiding misunderstanding and for diagnosing what is going on in certain discourses. Let me offer a real case example. Peter van Inwagen, a truly brilliant philosopher, is famous for saying about certain theses or claims that he doesn't understand them – and, by extension, that he doesn't understand the proponents of those claims.[6] For example, one claim he says he doesn't understand is what he calls anti-Realism, and hence one group of philosophers he doesn't understand are anti-Realists. Anti-Realists deny the existence of objective truth; proponents of anti-Realism include, by van Inwagen's admission, Richard Rorty (especially Rorty 1981) and Hilary Putnam (e.g., Putnam 1987, lecture 1). At one

[6] One of his papers bears the title "Why I Don't Understand Substitutional Quantification" (van Inwagen 1981).

place, van Inwagen engages these philosophers and prefaces his discussion with the following words (van Inwagen 2009, 96):

> Let the reader be warned. It must be evident that I am unable to enter into the smallest degree of imaginative sympathy with those who deny that there is such a thing as objective truth. I am therefore probably not a reliable guide to their views. Perhaps, indeed, I do not understand these views. I should like to think so. I should prefer to think that no one actually believes what, on the surface at least, it very much looks as if some people believe.

A few paragraphs further down he asks, "What, then, *is* the thesis of anti-Realism?," and he continues in the same vein: "I confess I have had a very hard time finding a statement of anti-Realism I can understand" (van Inwagen 2009, 97). Van Inwagen, then, suggests that perhaps he doesn't understand the views of anti-Realists. Yet he has given an – admittedly crisp – description of the view, viz., objective truth doesn't exist. And he goes to great lengths to explain how these words should be understood, making the plausible suggestion that they should be understood, roughly, as follows: whatever we think is true, is true thanks, somehow, to humans that apply concepts. He goes on to argue that the arguments for anti-Realism are unconvincing, and even that there is a killing objection against it. I take it that what is going on in the quoted passages and in van Inwagen's discussion of the merits of anti-Realism is something like this:

1. Initially at least, van Inwagen doesn't know or grasp the thesis that anti-Realists are so enthusiastic about; he doesn't understand what thesis the words "Objective truth doesn't exist" are meant to express.
2. Next, he suggests that those words should be taken to express the claim that whatever we think is true, is true thanks, somehow, to humans that apply concepts. He has thus come to an understanding of the words "Objective truth doesn't exist." This, in my terminology, is a Type II kind of understanding: it is an understanding of what it is that anti-Realists intended to endorse.
3. Finally, he argues that the arguments adduced by anti-Realists are unconvincing, and even that there is a killing argument against anti-Realism. Having reached this stage, van Inwagen now lacks a Type III kind of understanding of the anti-Realists. Adopting anti-Realism (given his Type II understanding of it) just isn't rational, has no value, and is not a valuable thing to do.

This short case study enables me to highlight two important points.

First, van Inwagen's nonunderstanding of anti-Realism referred to in (1) above is neither a Type I nor a Type II nor a Type III kind of nonunderstanding. It is the lack of yet another type of understanding. To bring that out, I first single out for contrasting purposes a type of understanding that van Inwagen does *not* lack in the example – a type that I call *linguistic understanding.*[7] To have linguistic understanding is to know what the words that compose a sentence jointly mean. Van Inwagen surely has a linguistic understanding of the words "Objective truth doesn't exist" – as many people *lack* linguistic understanding of the words "Pa natten och jag sovar inget" and "No llores, mi querida, Dios nos vigila" (and as no doubt most non-English speakers lack linguistic understanding of the words "Objective truth doesn't exist"). The understanding van Inwagen says he lacks can be dubbed *propositional understanding* – i.e., an understanding of what proposition is meant to be expressed by a particular sentence. When someone produces an ambiguous sentence and there are no contextual clues to disambiguate it, then one lacks propositional understanding of the sentence. I suggest that what van Inwagen claims in my (1) is that he lacks propositional understanding of the words "Objective truth doesn't exist." We may often have the feeling that we lack propositional understanding of sentence-composing words. This may be due to readers' inabilities and deficiencies, but it may of course also be due to the incompetence of an author. So, the first important point is that the three-item list of types of understanding above is incomplete and should be augmented with linguistic as well as propositional understanding.

Second, my account of Type III understanding entails that you cannot have and do not have a Type III understanding of something if you believe it to be incorrect, inadequate, or untrue. This came out in my (3) above: van Inwagen doesn't have a Type III understanding of anti-Realists because, as he holds is the case, there is a killing objection against their view. So, because he believes he *knows* that their view is false, it is not possible for van Inwagen to Type III understand anti-Realists.

These distinctions are also relevant more generally. One can have a Type II understanding of Berkeley's *Treatise* or Hegel's *Phenomenology of the Spirit* and yet not have a Type III understanding of them, that is, not appreciate these works, not see why one would think the things they say, and disagree that such things are worthy of endorsement.

[7] For a discussion of this type of understanding, see Fricker (2003).

Reading and Understanding the Text's Subject Matter

Through reading, we can come to understand not only texts and authors but also what might be called *the subject matter* of the author's text.[8] For although we often read in order to find out what an author intended to convey, it is also true that we hope that, by figuring out what the author intended to convey, we gain knowledge and understanding of the subject matter that the author is writing about. Through reading, say, Richard Westfall's *The Life of Isaac Newton* (1993), we expect to gain an understanding not only of Westfall's intentions but also of the person Isaac Newton himself, of his scientific and intellectual achievements, and of his time and cultural setting. Readers of Westfall's biography may come to have a Type I understanding of Newton as a person in that they get a sense of how the various parts of his life hang together, how his scientific projects hang together, how the work he became famous for relates to his biblical studies, and so on. Readers of Westfall's biography can also gain a Type I understanding of Newton's character and how his character traits hang together with the projects he took up. The understanding of Newton we can get through Westfall's book is of the modal kind, as Grimm calls it, in that we can gain insight into the modal space around Newton: insight in what, given his character, his interests, and the social realities at the time, were genuine possibilities and what were not. We get some sense of the likelihood of counterfactuals of the sort "Had Newton been in situation *X*, he would have done *Y*."

Reading biographies and other historical works, but also reading philosophical texts, will often lead to an understanding of the text, of the author, and of some Matter at the same time. Reading Thomas Reid's *An Inquiry into the Human Mind on the Principles of Common Sense* ([1764] 1997), for example, a reader may obtain an understanding of the text – i.e., of how its parts hang together so as to constitute a meaningful unity, which is a Type I understanding. The modal-space element here is that the reader comes to understand that Reid could not possibly have included a chapter on evolutionary explanations of our intellectual and active powers, but that he *could* have included a chapter on moral belief, as it fits the general topic of the *Inquiry* (viz., how the human mind obtains knowledge, or justified belief). In addition, a reader may come to Type I understand its author; for instance, his deep commitment to Newtonianism and his antiskepticism, and how they hang together. A reader may also obtain a

[8] Here I am using Gadamer's concept of "die Sache."

Type I understanding of a number of the Matters that Reid writes about. One may come to understand, for example, the complexity of the relations between seeing and touching, and come to understand the role of what Reid called commonsense beliefs in our cognitive lives – understanding that consists again in seeing how things hang together and grasping the modal space around them.

Not all reading of texts will lead to such a rich menu of understanding. Think of cookbooks. We read them first and foremost with an eye to understanding how to prepare certain dishes, which is a Type I understanding in that we come to see which ingredients jointly make a good dish (if well prepared). Through reading such books, we may also gain an understanding of authorial intentions: some cookbook authors make claims about healthy eating, fair products, the morality of vegetarianism or veganism, and so on. In this way we may come to a Type II understanding and, if we endorse the tenets of the writer, even a Type III understanding of the cookbook's author. But we read such books mainly because they can give us an understanding of the book's subject matter (i.e., dishes) – a Type I understanding.

Many books are like this. When we read them, we don't obtain (and aren't looking for) an understanding of their authors in any significant sense. If we read a relatively simple cookbook, we come to an understanding of dishes, what goes into them, and how to prepare them. Or think of vacuum cleaner manuals, train schedules, medication prescriptions, etc. By reading them, we can get an understanding of how this vacuum cleaner works, which train options we have, and when the medication should and should not be taken. Reading texts of this nature (can) give us an understanding almost exclusively of a Matter. I say *almost* exclusively – for we may also come to understand the authorial intentions in these texts. But since they are entirely obvious, we usually don't single them out for special attention. Still, being of a humble but most helpful kind, these intentions exist – viz., the intention to explain how the vacuum cleaner works, to indicate train options, to prescribe when to take the medication, etc. Thus, these intentions are real, and they can be the objects of understanding. And so reading may lead to a Type II (and even a Type III) understanding of a writer.

Most scientific textbooks are like this. I. C. S. Staff's *Plane Trigonometry* (1941), for instance, is a long series of instructions about how to calculate distances. The authorial intention is obviously to instruct. Reading the volume doesn't enable you to Type II understand its author. And that, of course, is as it should be, for that is not the function of the book. The function of the book is solely to enable the reader to come to understand the subject matter of plane trigonometry. And this understanding is of the Type I kind: an alert reader comes to see how the various parts of plane trigonometry hang together. Similar examples are Henk Tijms's *Understanding Probability* (2012) and Ethan D. Bloch's *Proofs and Fundamentals: A First Course in Abstract Mathematics* (2011). Reading these works can give readers a serious understanding of their subject matters – probability theory and mathematical proof, respectively. The authorial intentions can be quickly grasped: they are informing and instructing. Through reading these books, we don't come to understand Henk Tijms and Ethan Bloch as persons; our focus is not on understanding the authors, but on Type I understanding the books' subject matters.

As many readers testify, literary or fictional texts can give us as good an understanding of Matters as manuals and prescriptions can, although their Matters will normally be more complex and interesting than how to put a vacuum cleaner to work or when to take a pill. For example, through reading Susan Howatch's six *Starbridge* novels (1987–1994), readers can gain a Type I understanding of the inner workings of the Church of England. Through reading Marilynne Robinson's *Gilead* (2004), one can come to Type I understand the interior life of a person of Calvinist faith. The books that I mentioned in the discussion of how reading can yield knowledge by acquaintance can do double duty here. For there is a close relationship between acquiring proxy knowledge by acquaintance through reading fiction and acquiring a Type I understanding of a literary text's Matter. Reading *The Brothers Karamazov*, we may acquire proxy knowledge by acquaintance of how family relations can work, while we also get a Type I understanding of some of those relations. It may not be the primary purpose of these works to give readers such understandings, but that is currently beside the point.

In an autobiography, the Matter and the author are identical in the sense that understanding the autobiography's Matter coincides, at least to some degree, with understanding its author. Reading St. Augustine's *Confessions* (c. 379) or Teresa of Avila's *The Book of My Life* (c. 1565) or Mark Twain's *Autobiography* (1906) can impart to readers an understanding of those books' Matters, which is at the same time an understanding of those books' authors. These are Type I understandings since they consist in seeing the modal space surrounding these authors. But they are also Type II understandings because we can appreciate *why* they did what they did (which includes appreciating why they wrote what they wrote); we can appreciate their aims. And this may even lead to a Type III understanding if we can see that what these people did (wrote) can be deemed desirable and choiceworthy.

A related phenomenon may occur with poems. It is possible that understanding the poem's Matter is at least in part (the same as) understanding the poet – that is, when the poem has an autobiographical element. A rather beautiful example of this is A. E. Housman's "Because I Liked You Better" – the poet himself being the Matter of the poem. Readers of the poem can get some understanding of Housman's interior life, at least, if they know something of Housman's biography. Of course, we should keep in mind that in poetry, the first-person pronoun doesn't necessarily refer to the poem's author. But sometimes there are good reasons to believe it does, as in the case of Housman's poem. Understanding an author and understanding a text's Matter are the same in such cases. In all its crispness, the understanding can be of all three types at the same time.

Reading, then, can give us understanding of many things: of texts, of authors, and of Matters. There is no need to set literary texts apart from more businesslike nonfictional texts: reading literary texts can yield the epistemic benefits of understanding texts, authors, and Matters to the same extent that reading journalistic reports or works of history or cookbooks can. The claim is not that every text, irrespective of its genre, gives readers equal measures of understanding of texts, authors, or Matters. This is false. The more modest and more realistic claim is that in each genre there are texts the reading of which can yield the benefit of understanding it, its author, or its Matter.

Is Understanding a Kind of Knowing?

Reading, then, can yield knowledge as well as understanding. But how do the two relate? In the philosophy of science literature it has been argued – for instance, by Peter Lipton (2004, 30) – that understanding just *is* knowledge: it is knowledge of causes. Among epistemologists, the tendency has been to argue that they are different. Unlike knowledge, it has been argued, understanding does not require truth (Elgin 1996), it is transparent (Zagzebski 2001, 246), and it cannot be Gettierized (Kvanvig 2003, 198–199). This tendency has not been without its detractors, however. Stephen Grimm (2006), for example, has argued against these alleged differences, in favor of the conclusion that understanding is a species of knowledge.

I don't propose to discuss the relation between knowing and understanding in its generality, but only how they relate when we reap epistemic benefits through reading. I have indicated at the beginning of this chapter that knowing and understanding can come apart; this claim that can now be made more precise. I draw attention to the fact that the examples I offered were cases in which a person knows something but lacks understanding. This leaves open the possibility that understanding *builds on* knowledge, that it *requires* knowledge. So the two can come apart in the sense that it is possible to have knowledge without understanding, even if it is not possible to have understanding without knowledge. It is this claim, in the context of reading, that I mean to defend. The way to do this is to consider cases of the various types of understanding through reading that I have distinguished and then show that understanding requires knowledge.

Understanding texts, I suggested, consists in seeing that or grasping how a text's parts hang together so as to make a meaningful whole. This is a Type I understanding. Now in order to arrive at such an understanding, a reader must know what the parts are (this knowledge is propositional). Understanding a text thus builds on knowing the text's parts.

Understanding authors, I suggested, consists in grasping the aims they tried to attain through the production of the text. This in turn consists in knowing the illocutionary and the perlocutionary act intentions of the author, as well as knowing the propositional content of the speech acts. This is a Type II understanding. Type II understanding of an author just *is* an instance of propositional knowledge.

I suggested furthermore that we can also have a Type III understanding of authors, namely, when we can see that the aims they had in producing their text can be deemed desirable and choiceworthy. This type of understanding obviously builds on the reader's knowledge of what is, or can be deemed, desirable and choiceworthy. But equally obviously, it is not identical to it.

Finally, I suggested that understanding a text's subject matter is a Type I understanding: it consists in seeing how the parts of the text's subject matter hang together. And so, in order to be able to see this, one must know what the parts are. Again, understanding builds on knowing.

Type I understanding of *X* is seeing how *X*'s parts hang together, and this can be unpacked, as Grimm does, as grasping the modal space around *X*. In the previous section, I suggested that insight into the modal space around *X* amounts to knowing counterfactuals that involve *X*. Referring to

Westfall's biography of Newton, I said that by reading it we can come to understand the person of Newton, his character, and his time, and that we can get a sense of the likelihood of such counterfactuals as "Had Newton been in situation so-and-so, he would have done that." Now, counterfactuals are propositions; they have a truth-value. From this it seems to follow that an adequate grasp of the modal space surrounding *X* consists in knowing a fair number of true counterfactuals that involve *X*. And so it seems that this type of understanding consists in, or at least involves, knowledge of true counterfactuals.

If *X* is a text, then what a Type I understanding of it amounts to is this: it is to know the truth-value of such counterfactuals as "If this part of the text had been left out, what is said in other parts of the text would have been unmotivated"; "If this paragraph had been added to the text, then the general message would have been much clearer"; and "If the order of the text's parts had been changed in this or that way, the reader would have felt seriously confused." If *X* is an author, then what a Type I understanding of the author amounts to is this: it is to know the truth-value of such counterfactuals as "If the author had aimed to secure aim *A* by the production of this text, then that would have been an infelicitous choice" and "If the author had not written what he wrote in this particular fashion, he would not have reached his goal." If *X* is a text's subject matter, then what a Type I understanding of it amounts to is this: it is to know the truth-value of such counterfactuals as "If this hadn't been the case, then that would not have happened" and "If this had happened earlier, then the effect would have been much greater."

All of this suggests that understanding, if it isn't knowledge, is built on it. I therefore think that we should improve on Zagzebski's earlier-quoted suggestion that the "the object of understanding is not a discrete proposition." The improvement is this: one's understanding of *X* is not so much knowledge of a single proposition about *X* as knowledge of a set of counterfactual propositions about *X*. And the greater that set, the deeper one's understanding of *X*; the smaller, the shallower.

In the subsequent chapters of this book I will mainly deal with knowledge through reading and interpretation. If the argument in this section is correct (so, if understanding either is knowledge or builds on it), this means that at some remove I am also dealing with understanding through reading and interpretation.

A final remark. Modal knowledge is knowledge of what is possible or necessary (more precisely, it is knowing that *p* is possible or knowing that *p* is necessary) – it is the knowledge that we have when we understand the modal space surrounding some focal fact or event. Modal knowledge is traditionally conceived to be the yield of the faculty of reason. It is through perception that we know, say, that the car is blue, but it is through reason that we know that it is possible to paint it black. It is through perception that we know (see) that the wheel is round, but it is through reason that we see that the wheel could not possibly lack a middle point. If this is correct, this means that, whenever we have a Type I understanding of something, reason is involved. Thus, acquiring, through reading, a Type I understanding of a text or an author or a Matter involves or requires reason. (This is a topic I will return to in Chapter 5.)

Other Epistemic Benefits through Reading

Readers may reap other epistemic benefits through reading than knowledge and understanding. In this final section I will draw attention to some of them, but I won't discuss them in any detail.

First, reading may kindle a reader's imagination. This surely isn't exclusively true of reading literary works: philosophical works or popular science books like Martin Rees's *On the Future* (2018) and Bill Bryson's *A Short History of Nearly Everything* (2003) can also fire one's imagination. But it is especially true of the great works of literature. Although *imagining* something is surely different from *knowing* it, it can be argued that there is a road that leads from imagination to knowledge (see Van Woudenberg 2006). Without the faculty of imagination, scientists would be unable to devise radical new concepts, hypotheses, and theories. It takes imagination to devise the concept of curved space, or to hypothesize that all organisms are genetically related to each other, or to come up with the idea that some physical laws are statistical. The epistemic value of imagination-generated concepts, hypotheses, and theories will, of course, have to be evaluated by other and independent means. But this should not lead us into thinking that imagination has no epistemic benefits. It does have such benefits, even when the route from imagination to corroboration is long and winding.

Second, and related, reading works of literature can suggest certain explanatory hypotheses that can be tested independently. From his study of some mainly nineteenth-century French novels, literary scholar René Girard developed the hypothesis that desire has what he calls a "mimetic" structure (Girard 1976). The hypothesis is that when a person *S* desires a particular, nonshareable state of affairs *SOA* (such as being married to Jane), that person does not desire *SOA* because it is desirable *in se*, but because there is some other person *S** whom *S* knows to desire *SOA* and whose desire for *SOA S* is mimicking. Next, Girard uses this mimetic structure of desire to explain violent interactions between people. Thus, reading works of literature can enable people to devise explanatory hypotheses. Even if the hypothesis cannot be independently confirmed, it remains the case that distilling explanatory hypotheses by reading fiction is a significant cognitive feat. If we assume that many literary authors have great insight into human psychology, we can expect their works to suggest explanations of, for example, suicidal tendencies in persons, the occurrence of feelings of depression, and what causes happiness.

Reading is an important way in which we may come to know and understand the views that others have or have had. Reading sometimes is a channel of testimony – it is one way in which testimony reaches us. And testimony is widely regarded as a source of knowledge. Although I agree with this consensus, I disagree with the view that all there is to reading, from an epistemological perspective, is attending to testimony. In the next two chapters I explain why I disagree with that view, and I expound my alternative. The notion *source of knowledge* plays a crucial role in my disagreement; therefore, Chapter 3 is devoted to this notion. I discuss a number of alleged sources of knowledge and suggest it is surprising that reading is never viewed as a source of knowledge, even though for all the world, it looks like one. In Chapter 4, I inquire whether reading can be reduced to one of two widely acknowledged sources of knowledge – viz., testimony and perception. I argue that it cannot. In Chapter 5, I argue that reading is a source of knowledge in its own right, offering a detailed analysis of both reading and the source that reading is.

CHAPTER 3

Sources of Knowledge and Their Individuation

As I argued in the previous chapters, through reading we can come to know and understand many things. Philosophers have talked much about sources of knowledge.[1] The question arises whether reading should be considered as a source of knowledge. This chapter and Chapter 4 address this question. But before I start, some preliminaries are in order.

First, although epistemologists distinguish, as noted in Chapter 1, between propositional knowledge, knowledge by acquaintance, and know-how, the notion *source of knowledge* is almost exclusively used in discussions of propositional knowledge.[2] I will not follow this practice, because very often what seems to be the same source yields both propositional knowledge and knowledge by acquaintance, and sometimes also know-how (although this is more controversial).

Second, as I show in the next section, epistemologists talk a great deal about sources of knowledge, but never about sources of understanding. This may reflect a tacit assumption that understanding really is a form of knowledge, but it may also reflect the fact that the concept of knowledge has received much more sustained attention than the concept of understanding. Since I argued that the understanding that reading may yield is based on knowledge that reading may yield, in my discussion of whether reading is a source of knowledge, *source of knowledge* should be understood as "source of knowledge and understanding."

[1] Chisholm (1977, 122); Audi (1998, part 1). Philosophers also talk about the following notions as synonyms or near-synonyms for *sources of knowledge*: belief-forming processes (Goldman 1979), belief-formation methods (Nozick 1981), modules of our epistemic establishment, epistemic powers, faculties, belief-producing mechanisms (Plantinga 1993a), doxastic mechanisms, ways, modes, or procedures of forming beliefs, habits, doxastic practices (where a doxastic practice "is not a single belief-forming disposition, but some family, grouping, or system of individual dispositions, bound together in some important way," as Alston [1993, 8] has it), virtues, and competences (Sosa 2007). Dancy (1985, part 3), apparently dealing with the same topic, writes about forms of knowledge.

[2] Witness the works referred to in the previous note; also witness Zagzebski's, Kvanvig's, and Grimm's work on understanding (see the list of references).

The present chapter addresses two questions, in the interest of a third. First: What is it for something to be a source of knowledge, as opposed to not being one at all? Alternatively, what are the individuation conditions of something being a source of knowledge? Second: What distinguishes one particular source of knowledge from another? Alternatively, what are the individuation conditions of a specific alleged source of knowledge?[3] I study these questions in the interest of a third: Should we think of reading as a source of knowledge? It is a remarkable fact that although analytic epistemologists have distinguished a great number of sources of knowledge, reading has never been one of them, even though, as I argued in the previous chapters, we seem to know much through reading. Is there a principled reason for this state of affairs, or is this just an oversight? If the latter, shouldn't reading be added to the list of sources of knowledge?

This chapter is organized as follows. First, I show that the notion of source of knowledge plays a key role both in a number of epistemological theories and in the formulation of a number of well-known philosophical problems; hence, we cannot do without it even if it is (as is the case) in some respects a puzzling notion. The second section addresses my first question, viz., what it is for something to be a source of knowledge, and the third section offers a list of alleged sources. I then move on to suggest that there are five kinds of individuation principles for sources of knowledge. The section entitled "Sources Individuated" studies how some widely acknowledged sources are individuated by these principles, thus addressing my second question. In the concluding section, I suggest that reading meets all the conditions for being a source of knowledge, and I indicate how it is individuated.

Epistemic Work Done by the Notion *Source of Knowledge*

Whether or not something is a source of knowledge is by no means a minor matter. The notion plays a central role in a number of ways and does important, nonnegligible, theoretical work.[4] I provide four illustrations.

The notion has taken center stage, first, in broadly externalist theories of knowledge and justification. On Alvin Goldman's account of justification,

[3] Generally speaking, a specification of the individuation conditions of *X*s enables us, first, to determine whether or not something is an *X* and, second, to count the number of *X*s.

[4] Hamlyn held that "the question of the sources of knowledge is unimportant and irrelevant" (Hamlyn 1970, 284; echoing Popper 1960). Later epistemologists proved how deeply he was mistaken.

one's believing that *p* is justified iff one's so believing "results from a reliable cognitive belief-forming process (or set of processes)" (Goldman 1979, 10). And on Plantinga's account, one knows that *p* iff one has a warranted true belief that *p*, and one's belief that *p* is warranted if it is produced by a belief-forming apparatus (or faculty, or power) that is "functioning properly" (Plantinga 1993a, 4). What these approaches have in common is that they analyze important epistemological notions, viz., justification and warrant, in a way that involves the notion *source of knowledge* or a near-synonym.[5]

The notion also plays a key role in Chisholm's celebrated formulation of the problem of the criterion. Chisholm depicts certain moral skeptics as holding that experience (i.e., perception, memory, and consciousness) and reason are the only sources of knowledge, and as reasoning as follows: "There is no source of knowledge other than experience and reason. Experience and reason do not yield any knowledge of ethical facts. Therefore we do not have knowledge of any ethical facts" (Chisholm 1977, 124). The problem of the criterion cannot be formulated without using the notion of source of knowledge.

The notion has furthermore center stage in William Alston's discussion of the problem of epistemic circularity. This is the problem of whether we can show in a noncircular way that our basic sources of belief are reliable – i.e., yield mostly true beliefs. Alston argues that sense perception, which he holds to be a basic source, cannot be shown to be reliable in a noncircular way: any argument for the conclusion that sense perception is reliable will have to proceed from premises that you can only accept if you've already committed yourself to the truth of the conclusion (Alston 1993, chapters 1–11). He calls such arguments epistemically circular, as opposed to logically circular. And what holds for sense perception, he argues, also holds for other basic sources of belief, such as induction, deduction, memory, introspection, and rational intuition (Alston 1993, 115–119). Clearly, the very issue that Alston discusses cannot be discussed without the notion of source of knowledge.[6]

Finally, this notion also functions centrally in many skeptical arguments. One basis for skeptical arguments is the possibility that our beliefs

[5] Nozick's (1981) sensitivity account of knowledge, albeit less ostensibly, also relies on the notion of source of knowledge. For in-depth explanations, see Alfano (2009) and Baker-Hytch (2018).

[6] To this I add that empirical studies about the reliability of introspection (for example, Wilson 2002; Schwitzgebel 2008), reasoning (for example, Gilovich 1991), and memory (for example, Kahneman 2011) intend to assess entire sources.

are yielded by sources that, unbeknownst to us, are unreliable (see Machuca and Reed 2018).

Source of knowledge, then, is a central notion in epistemology, and many discussions assume such sources to be real. And if we are to make progress in these discussions, as well as in the discussion of whether reading should be seen as a source of knowledge, it will be helpful to have a proper understanding of the notion. But such understanding is not readily obtained. For although the notion is widely *used*, it has hardly been *analyzed*.

What Is It for Something to Be a Source of Knowledge?

Axel Gelfert has rightly noted that "systematic investigations of the question of what constitutes a source of knowledge are surprisingly rare" (Gelfert 2014, 55). There is, really, no general account of *source of knowledge* that we can turn to when we seek to answer the question whether reading should be considered such a source – no account, that is, that tells us which conditions *X* must satisfy in order to be a source of knowledge.

Many epistemologists have provided lists of what they think are sources of knowledge – in other words, lists of *X*s that they think satisfy the (unstated!) conditions of being a source of knowledge. Strangely enough, reading does not occur on any of these lists.[7] This is puzzling, for it has been said that a source of knowledge or warranted belief is that "from which" knowledge or warranted belief "comes" (Moser, Mulder, and Trout 1998, 101; Audi 2002, 82). It has also been suggested that a source of knowledge is "roughly, something in the life of a knower . . . that yields belief constituting knowledge" (Audi 2002, 72). Given these suggestions, one would expect reading to qualify as a source. After all, as the previous chapters have made abundantly clear, there is much that we can and do know that comes from reading; reading *is* something in the life of a knower that yields belief constituting knowledge.

An initial worry one might have here is that if we take the phrases "that 'from which' knowledge or warranted belief 'comes'" and "something in the life of a knower that yields belief constituting knowledge" at face value,

[7] None of the following textbooks and nontextbooks mention reading or interpretation as even possible candidate sources of knowledge: Chisholm (1957); Dretske (1969); Dancy (1985); Moser (1989); Alston (1993); Plantinga (1993a); BonJour (2002); Gendler and Hawthorne (2006); Pritchard (2006); Audi (2010).

it is not only reading that will qualify as a source but also such unlikely items as the following:

1. *Walking.* Your knowing that the soil is marshy in the Okavango Delta in Botswana *comes from* your walking; walking is something in your life that yields the belief that the soil is marshy, and this belief constitutes knowledge.
2. *An open door.* Your knowledge that Sissy's room is a mess *comes from* the door that is usually closed but is now open; alternatively, the opened door is something in your life that yields the belief that Sissy's room is a mess, and this belief constitutes knowledge.
3. *Raising your arm.* Your knowledge that your shoulder is hurting *comes from* raising your arm; so, raising your arm is something in your life that yields the belief that your shoulder is hurting, and this belief constitutes knowledge.

Intuitively, these aren't sources of knowledge. Why not? A likely response to (1) is that your knowing that the soil is marshy doesn't *really* come from walking but from the operation of your visual and somatic senses – *these* are the true sources of your knowledge. Walking through the Okavango Delta *enabled* your visual and somatic senses to pick up the information that the soil is marshy. Walking brought your perceptual apparatus to the right place, but walking isn't therefore (part of) the source of your knowledge: what *enables* a source to deliver its cognitive goods shouldn't itself be conceptualized as (part of) that source. As to (2), it isn't the open door as such that is the source of your coming to know that Sissy's room is a mess. The open door merely *enabled* you to see the mess – *seeing* is the source, and the open door is what enabled you to see the messy room. Concerning (3), it seems more adequate to say that the raising of your arm *causes* the pain in your shoulder, and that your knowledge that your shoulder is hurting comes from nociception, which is the real source. Raising your arm was a triggering condition – i.e., it *enabled* you (brought you in a position) *to feel* the pain. But, again, what enables the source to deliver its cognitive goods shouldn't itself be conceptualized as (part of) the source.

The distinction between sources of knowledge and enabling circumstances is an intuitive one and has been noticed by others. Plantinga, for example, has it that a belief constitutes knowledge only if it is generated by a faculty or mechanism that works *in an appropriate environment* (see Plantinga 1993a, chapter 1). Your visual faculty does not generate knowledge in an environment with bad lighting conditions. Good lighting conditions thus enable you to acquire knowledge. The distinction is akin to the distinction familiar in the philosophy of science between causes and enabling conditions. The match that was lit, to use a standard example, caused the explosion. But without oxygen the explosion would not have happened, which is why the presence of oxygen is called an enabler. It has often been remarked that it is difficult to draw a clear line between the two, and that whether or not something should be looked at as the cause of an event or merely as an enabling condition is interest and context relative.[8] But there is no analogous difficulty for the distinction between source of knowledge and enabling condition. Walking, the open door, and raising your arm are not the kinds of things that, given certain interests, or in certain contexts, could meaningfully be referred to as sources of knowledge or belief-forming mechanisms.

These considerations do not yet tell us what a source *is*, or in other words, how a source is distinct from what is *not* a source. My proposal is this:

> *X* is a source of knowledge iff *X* is a process or mechanism that
>
> (i) occurs only "in" subjects
> (ii) is triggered or set to work in certain conditions
> (iii) due to being so triggered yields
>   a. acquaintance, and/or
>   b. practical insight in how to do something, and/or
>   c. beliefs that can, and in the preponderance of cases do, constitute knowledge

By way of explication, I offer four comments. *First.* The base clause of the account is that a source of knowledge is a *process* or *mechanism.* I won't try to specify in any detail what a process or mechanism is but merely note that it is *not* an individual thing; it is not a substance. This means that stones aren't sources of knowledge, and neither are trees, cats, chairs, spoons, books, libraries, computers, and other people, as none of these are processes or mechanisms. The choice of this base clause, as can be easily seen, prevents walking, an open door, and raising your arm from qualifying as sources of knowledge. Sometimes, faculties such as perception, reason, and memory are called sources of knowledge. On my account, however, it isn't, strictly speaking, these faculties that are sources of knowledge but rather the processes or mechanisms they sustain.

[8] For discussion of this, see Ewing (1962, chapter 8). An interesting discussion of the notion *enabling condition* is Dancy (2004, 44–49), where he seems to suggest that the cause–enabler distinction is not, or not always, context and interest relative.

Second. Sources of knowledge are processes or mechanisms *of a specific sort* – they are processes and mechanisms that as (i) has it, occur "in subjects" and that as (iii) has it, yield acquaintance and/or practical insight in how to do something and/or belief. I won't try to specify in any detail what a subject is, but instead I'll give a nonexhaustive list of examples of subjects: human beings, higher primates, aliens from other planets, angels, and demons (if these last three exist). Nothing is a source of knowledge, on this analysis, unless it is a process or mechanism that takes place "in" subjects like these. The sun's rising this morning and the president's giving a speech are therefore not sources of knowledge – they don't take place in subjects. And many processes that in the relevant sense do occur in subjects are *not* sources of knowledge: your heart pumping blood through your veins and your headache making you unfocussed are processes that don't yield knowledge. Positively, and intuitively, a process that is a source of knowledge is in a subject provided the process takes place in the *mind* of the subject. In the case of human subjects, this means that the process also takes place within the bounds of skin and skull. I won't analyze the notion *in subjects* any further here.[9] But I do want to say this: the sense of *in subjects* as I wish it to be understood is fully compatible with the following two facts. First, a source of knowledge can be triggered by items that are fully external to the subject – i.e., that are not located in the mind, nor within the skin and skull of a subject – as I presume is the case with seeing a tree or reading a book: trees and books are not in subjects, yet in subjects they trigger processes that may yield knowledge. Second, informative theories can be developed of more holistic situations that have subjects, what is in subjects, and the subjects' environments as their parts.

Third. As condition (ii) states, the processes or mechanisms yield acquaintance, know-how, or belief only in certain circumstances. These circumstances include triggering conditions; i.e., conditions that set a mechanism at work ("the input," as I shall call it) as well as enabling circumstances. If those conditions don't obtain, the yields won't obtain either.

Fourth. If a source occasionally yields a false belief, this doesn't necessarily disqualify it from being a source of knowledge. Perception is widely viewed as a source of knowledge, even though it occasionally yields false beliefs. The qualification "in the preponderance of cases" in condition (iii. c) is an acknowledgement of this fact. What this condition rules out is that *X* qualifies as a source of knowledge when *X cannot* yield knowledge or when in the preponderance of cases it yields false beliefs. As explained in

[9] The discussion on extended cognition addresses this very topic in great detail.

Chapter 1, propositional knowledge requires more than mere true belief: it requires *warranted* true belief (where warrant is that property or quality that bridges the gap between knowledge and mere true belief). These conditions prevent wishful thinking, cognitive biases, fantasy, and self-deception, as well as extrasensory perception, telepathy, and clairvoyance (assuming these words refer to realities) from qualifying as sources of knowledge. These mechanisms don't yield in the preponderance of cases of true belief; this is either because they are not aimed at truth or because they are unsuccessfully truth aimed. And in those cases in which the beliefs they yield are true, these beliefs lack warrant because their truth is due to luck.[10] Hence, these mechanisms don't yield knowledge and don't qualify as sources of knowledge on the proffered analysis.

This account does not bar, at the very least, the *possibility* that reading is a source of knowledge. For reading can sensibly be viewed as a process or mechanism that (i) takes place in subjects and (ii) is triggered in certain conditions and is sensitive to enabling conditions. Moreover, condition (iii) is satisfied: as I argued in Chapter 1, reading can yield acquaintance, know-how, and propositional knowledge.[11]

Having thus offered a general account of what it is for something to be a source of knowledge, I make in the next section a rather quick and dirty tour of a number of sources of knowledge that epistemologists have identified. The point of doing this is twofold. First, it will enable us to see how widely acknowledged sources are individuated by radically different *kinds* of principles, and how some are individuated by more than one principle. And this, second, is a setup for the discussion of the question whether reading should be thought of as a source of knowledge – and if so, how it is individuated.

An Inventory of Sources of Knowledge

Each of the following has been deemed by at least some philosophers and cognitive scientists to be a source of knowledge:

a. perception (visual, auditory, gustative, olfactory, somatic)[12]
b. memory[13]

[10] The luck at hand is what Pritchard (2005, 146) has identified as veritistic epistemic luck, it being a matter of luck that the subject's belief happens to be true.

[11] In Chapter 9 I discuss a number of conditions that may trigger interpretative processes; all of them have to do with difficulties that readers may encounter due to their ignorance.

[12] E.g., Chisholm (1977); Goldman (1986); Alston (1993); Plantinga (1993a); Audi (2010).

[13] E.g., Chisholm (1977); Goldman (1986); Alston (1993); Plantinga (1993a); Audi (2010).

c. consciousness (or self-awareness, or reflection)[14]
d. reason, or rational intuition[15]
e. induction and probability[16]
f. testimony[17]
g. moral intuition, or moral sense[18]
h. *sensus divinitatis*[19]

In the broad area of human perception, cognitive scientists have distinguished, in addition to the five traditionally recognized perceptual senses, a number of other senses (the list lays no claim to completeness):

i. a sense by which we sense temperatures: thermoception
j. a sense by which we sense "from the inside" the location of our limbs: proprioception
k. a sense by which we sense pain: nociception
l. a sense by which we sense our balance: equilibrioception
m. a sense by which we sense vibrations: mechanoreception
n. a sense by which we sense hunger and thirst

These senses, like the five traditional ones, are associated with specific sensory systems – i.e., with specific groups of "receptors." For instance, vision is associated with photoreceptors in the retina, hearing with mechanoreceptors, and thermoception with cold and heat receptors. Cognitive scientists also point to senses that are *not* associated with specialized receptors:

o. a sense of time: chronoception
p. a sense of direction
q. a sense of agency

Even if epistemologists don't talk much about these nontraditional senses as sources of knowledge, there would seem to be no principled reason why, if the traditional senses are called sources of knowledge (or belief), these nontraditional sources should not also be deserving of the name.

The above list is not only not exhaustive, it is also controversial. While most philosophers take perception, memory, consciousness, and reason to be sources of knowledge, there is serious discussion about the reality of

[14] E.g., Chisholm (1977); Alston (1993); Plantinga (1993a); Audi (2010).
[15] E.g., Chisholm (1977); Goldman (1986); Alston (1993); Plantinga (1993a); BonJour (1998); Sosa (2007); Audi (2010). Reason is often taken to be the faculty that sustains deductive reasoning.
[16] Alston (1993); Plantinga (1993a); Audi (2010).
[17] Lackey (2008); Audi (2010).
[18] Chisholm (1977); Audi (2013).
[19] Plantinga (2000).

moral intuition and of the *sensus divinitatis*. Still, the latter have able defenders. Other alleged sources, not mentioned on the list, are even more controversial, and these seem to be without able defenders: extrasensory perception, telepathy, and clairvoyance.[20] Whether or not (a)–(q) really are sources of knowledge is presently not the issue. What is at issue is how defenders of the reality of these sources have individuated them. In the next section, I present five different kinds of individuation principles.

Five Kinds of Principles of Source Individuation

An individuation principle of a source of knowledge is a principle by which that source is distinct from other sources and that enables us to tell – at least, when we *know* the principle – whether or not something is *that* source of knowledge. (And I am thinking here of source types, not of source tokens.) Philosophers have availed themselves mainly of five kinds of principles.

A first kind of principle is the presence of externally observable "organs" that are supposed to be responsible for the knowledge acquisition, such as eyes and ears.[21] This criterion has sometimes been used to argue against the existence of moral intuition, since we cannot identify organs by which we come to know that, say, stealing is morally wrong. However, *externally observable* could also be taken more broadly so as to encompass brain processes that are externally visible by means of brain scanners.

We can ease our way into further kinds of principles by taking note of Goldman's remark about the notion of a belief-forming process: "Let us mean by a 'process' a *functional operation* or procedure, i.e., something that generates a *mapping* from certain states – 'inputs' – into other states – 'outputs.' The outputs . . . are states of believing this or that proposition at a given moment" (Goldman 1979, 11; similarly Alston 1993, 5).

Goldman, then, thinks of belief-forming mechanisms as having inputs and outputs. This means that belief-forming mechanisms can, in principle, be individuated by reference to their inputs, by reference to their outputs, by reference to mechanisms that work on the input so as to generate the belief output, and by a combination of these.

[20] I note that philosophers such as Henry Sidgwick and C. D. Broad have offered rather interesting epistemological reflections on clairvoyance and telepathy. See Broad (1969, 7–115).

[21] Maimonides is an example here. He held that God cannot see or hear, because God, who is immaterial, has no eyes and ears. See Wolterstorff (1995, 10).

Finally, there are principles that refer to (the nature of) the objects about which the beliefs are formed. This means there are at least[22] five kinds of individuation principles by which sources of knowledge can be individuated; namely, principles that refer to

A. the externally visible organ that is active in the knowledge acquisition;
B. the kind(s) of inputs that the source takes – i.e., whatever it is that triggers the source, whatever it is that puts it into operation;
C. the kind(s) of outputs of the source: this could be knowledge by acquaintance and/or know-how and/or the belief attitude vis-à-vis propositions with a specific kind of content;
D. the "mode of operation" of the source – i.e., the nature of the process that is responsible for the way the inputs are processed so as to yield the output; and
E. the (nature of the) objects about which the beliefs are formed.

In the next section I discuss, in an admittedly very sketchy way, the individuation principles of a selection of sources. The selection is based on whether or not the alleged source plays a role in in this book.

Sources Individuated

Visual Perception

Each of the five senses has been individuated[23] by reference to the externally visible sense organs that are active in knowledge acquisition, so by what I shall call *A*-principles. Seeing has been individuated by reference to the eyes. Seeing has also been individuated by reference to the unique kind of input it takes, which is, very roughly, light that strikes the retina and that causes us to have visual experiences. Hence, it has a *B*-individuation as well.[24]

[22] *At least* – for Alston (1991, 165–168) makes the case for yet another kind of principle, one that refers to what he calls the overrider system of a doxastic practice. I will put this to one side, since it seems to have a role only in Alston's specialized discussion of differences between mystical practices.

[23] I speak both of sources being individuated by principles and of us being able to individuate sources by wielding individuation principles. I take the former locution to refer to the basic phenomenon. When the latter locution is used correctly, we must suppose that we have been able to correctly identify and formulate the principle. I use these locutions interchangeably but don't think this creates problems for the understanding.

[24] An instructive textbook that offers much scientific detail about the working of our perceptual faculties is Wolfe et al. (2019). More detailed *B*-individuations are offered by Chisholm (1957, 43–52), Alston (1991, chapter 1), and Plantinga (1993a, 91–93).

As to a *C*-individuation (one that refers to outputs), we must consider three categories of cognitive output: acquaintance, know-how, and propositional knowledge. Seeing acquaints us with an immense variety of visual shapes and colors. No other source yields that particular array of acquaintance – hence, this *C*-individuates vision. As to know-how: suppose you see a spruce tree. Does this give you any know-how? It doesn't seem so. Does seeing yield any know-how *at all*? Not much has been written about this. It seems that we don't get new know-how by seeing objects but that we *can* obtain new know-how by seeing how someone else does something. I can acquire knowledge about how to use an unfamiliar corkscrew by seeing you successfully manipulating one. However, the know-how that seeing can yield has no principled limits – it is not restricted to a particular kind of know-how. Hence, there is no *C*-individuation to be found here. Nor can seeing be *C*-individuated by reference to *belief content*. Such an individuation would exist if vision exclusively yielded beliefs like "I see that the flowers are wilting" and "I see that the dog is running." Then vision would be uniquely marked by the fact that it yields beliefs that have as part of their propositional content *that one sees* thus and so. However, vision also yields beliefs like "The flowers are wilting" and "The dog is running," which do *not* include a reference to one's seeing. More importantly, such beliefs can also be the yield of other sources, for I can also *smell* that the flowers are wilting and *hear* that the dog is running.[25] So yielding the belief that the flowers are wilting doesn't ground a distinction between seeing and smelling, and yielding the belief that the dog is running doesn't ground a distinction between seeing and hearing.[26] The conclusion is that there is a *C*-principle for seeing and it refers to knowledge by acquaintance, but not to know-how nor to propositional knowledge.

A *D*-principle, so a principle that individuates by reference to the nature of the belief-yielding process, *must* exist for vision. For even if we can come to know that the vase is cubical through vision as well as through touch, the same belief is formed through radically different processes. It may not

[25] Many more examples are given in Dretske (1969). That the five senses are distinct from each other should not obscure the fact that in normal environments the five senses are stimulated simultaneously, which creates opportunity for improved performance. This fact is foundational to the psychology and philosophy of multimodal perception. See Bertelson and de Gelder (2004) and O'Callaghan (2012).

[26] To add to the complexity, we must note that some beliefs can be the yield of only one sense. The belief that the dress is red, for example, can only be the yield of vision – we cannot hear, smell, taste, or sense that the dress is red.

be easy to formulate these principles, but psychologists and cognitive scientists can be expected to pave the way here (see Wolfe et al. 2019).

There is, finally, no *E*-individuation of vision, no principle that refers to specific objects. For, as indicated, spruce trees, corkscrews, wilting flowers, and running dogs are not exclusively objects of vision – they are also the potential objects of touch and of smell. The objects about which beliefs are formed by sight constitute no theoretically unified group.

Vision, then, is individuated by *A*-, *B*-, *C*-, and *D*-principles.[27]

Memory

Turning to memory, we can note straightaway that it has no *A*-individuation because there is no externally observable organ associated with remembering. Brain scientists using fMRI scanners or other technical devices, however, are finding out that certain parts of the brain are associated with memory. Potentially this makes for an *A*-individuation of memory. Whether potentiality will ever become actuality is uncertain for reasons having to do with the brain's plasticity. Moreover, the entire enterprise of associating brain parts with memory depends on the availability of an independent kind of individuation. Memory must be identified in a way that is independent of brain states in order for brain scientists and psychologists to be able to correlate it with brain states.

To assess whether memory has a *B*-individuation, we must make a distinction. Memory has inputs in the sense that whereas some things are stored in one's memory (for example, the experience of seeing the Old Man of Hoy), others are not (the things we did or experienced but have forgotten). Those that have been stored qualify as inputs. But memory has also another kind of input; for once something is stored in one's memory, a variety of things may *trigger* memories so that what is stored is retrieved. Let us call the former "storing inputs," the latter "triggering inputs."

There seems to be no unity among the storing inputs of memory. For what can be stored is of a huge variety. First, a variety of knowledge by acquaintance can be stored: we can remember the smell in the pig stable, the taste of the kumquat, the look on the child's face. Second, know-how can be stored: we can remember how to use the corkscrew and how to hoist the sails. Third, different kinds of propositional knowledge can be stored: knowledge based on first-person experiences, but also things we have learned from our teachers, from conversations, from books. There is

[27] I note for the record, but won't argue, that the same is true for the other four traditional senses.

no theoretical unity among the things that can be stored in memory. But neither is there a theoretical unity among memory's triggering inputs. A smell may trigger a memory, or a song, a particular word, a photograph, a face – anything. Hence there is no *B*-principle for memory.

Nor is there an individuation that refers to output. There is a tendency to think we can only remember things that lie in the past and that this grounds a *C*-individuation of memory.[28] But this won't do in the case of remembered acquaintance. We (say we) remember the taste of kumquats, or the color of the Taj Mahal; but what is remembered in these cases is nothing particularly to do with the past. When you (say you) remember the taste of kumquats, what you remember is not how they tasted in the past, nor the moment at which you first got acquainted with that taste, but *the taste of kumquats*.

Somewhat similar things are true of remembering how to do things. When you (say you) remember how to strum a diminished seventh chord on the guitar, or how to prove that the square root of two is not a rational number, your remembering is nothing particularly to do with the past. When you remember these things, what you remember is not how you did them in the past, nor the moment when you learned how to do them, but *how to do them*.

Perhaps surprisingly, similar things hold for propositional knowledge. We (say we) remember that Orkney lies north of the Scottish mainland, that the keys are on the table, that table salt is NaCl, and so on. Of course, if we remember these things, we must have learned them in the past. But what is remembered when we (say we) remember them is not necessarily something *about* the past, or about something *in* the past. When we (say we) remember these things, this isn't shorthand for saying that we remember when or how we learned them. We may even (be said to) remember these facts when we have no memory at all about when or how we learned them. So, *being about the past* is not what unifies the belief outputs of memory, and there is nothing else that does. Hence, memory has no *C*-individuation.

There does seem to be a unifying individuation of memory, one that refers to the mode of operation of the source. Ernest Sosa once observed that there are faculties of two broad sorts, viz., "those that lead to beliefs

[28] Reid, for example, said that "it is by memory that we have an immediate knowledge of things past" (Reid [1785] 2002, 253). Plantinga agrees with Aristotle who said that memory is of the past (Plantinga 1993a, 57). Audi (2010, 60–64) makes useful distinctions between memory, remembering, and recalling.

from beliefs already formed, and those that lead to beliefs but not from beliefs" (Sosa 1991, 225). The former he called transmission faculties and the latter generation faculties, and he suggested that memory is a transmission faculty: it takes beliefs as its input and leads to beliefs. I aver that this is only half right. The right half is that memory is not a "generation" source: it is not a productive faculty; it doesn't generate new knowledge. It is, as Sosa has it, a transmission faculty, although I prefer to say that it is a "retentive" faculty. The wrong half is his suggestion that memory leads from beliefs to beliefs. This is only right for propositional knowledge, not for knowledge by acquaintance and neither for know-how. If I now believe, on the basis of memory, that I once visited Orkney, that belief is indeed formed from an earlier belief – the earlier belief being the not-memory-based belief "I am now visiting Orkney" that I formed when I was actually visiting Orkney. But when I remember the smell of the stable, there is no belief formed from an earlier belief. And when I remember how to open the safe, there is no belief formed from an earlier belief either. Yet in these cases there is retention. This suggests that, if retention is the essence of memory,[29] the following *D*-delineation of memory is possible: memory is a source that has as its inputs *one's own* not-memory-based knowledge by acquaintance, know-how, and propositional belief, and it *retains* these. This individuation gives theoretical unity to memory and makes it distinct from testimony, where the input is *not* one's own not-memory-based acquaintance, know-how, and propositional belief.

Given the previous discussion, it is clear that there is no *E*-individuation of memory. The things remembered, the objects of memory, have no theoretical unity. So, whereas perception has four individuation principles, memory has only one – a *D*-principle.

Reason

Reason is traditionally supposed to have two "offices," or to be a combination of two related yet different sources, viz., rational intuition and deduction.[30] Rational intuition is considered to be the source or faculty

[29] This hasn't gone uncontested. Ginet (1975, 148–153) has argued that there might also be "generative" memory. If this is correct, the principle alluded to in the body of the text individuates at best only a part of what is usually called memory.

[30] See Locke ([1689] 1975), book 4, chapter 2; Reid ([1785] 2002), essay 4, chapter 4. Chisholm (1977) makes the distinction in terms of truths of reason and the indirectly evident. Plantinga (1993a, 107) says that tradition was inclined to distinguish "two parts or aspects to reason, two subfaculties": intuition and deduction.

through which we intuit certain truths. A truth is intuited when we can "see" it to be true directly – i.e., without argument or adducing evidence. As the tradition has it, self-evident propositions are intuited; and a proposition is self-evident provided understanding it suffices for seeing, or intuiting, that it is true. For example, consider the following propositions: "2 + 1 = 3"; "If *A* is taller than *B*, and *B* taller than *C*, then *A* is also taller than *C*"; "No prime number is a prime minister"; "Nothing can be wholly red and wholly green at the same time"; and "If you make a promise, you thereby incur an obligation." Understanding (the content of) these propositions, tradition has it, suffices for seeing that they are true. But something must be added; for it isn't only that through rational intuition we see that these propositions are true, but we also see that they *must* be true, that they *could not* be false, that they are *necessarily* true.[31] Whereas we can know through visual perception that *A* is taller than *B*, that *B* is taller than *C*, and that *A* is also taller than *C*, we don't know, and can't know, through visual perception that if *A* is taller than *B* and *B* taller than *C*, then *A must* be taller than *C* too. The latter requires rational intuition. But through rational intuition we can not only come to know what is *necessary* but also come to know what is *possible*; for example, that it is possible that a person with blond hair is a mathematician. The yield of rational intuition is thus modal knowledge – knowledge of what is necessary and of what is possible. If we think about reason this way, we must note that rational intuition is involved in Grimm's account of understanding as grasping the modal space surrounding a focal event.

Reason defies *A*-individuation, unless brain scanners will help us identify the brain correlates of reason. But this requires a prior, brain-independent individuation of reason.

Whereas it is rather clear what triggers visual perception (light striking one's retina), it is less clear what triggers reason. The objects of reason are often supposed to be abstract and hence incapable of exerting causal influence – hence also incapable of exerting causal influence on the faculty of reason.[32] If we accept that sources must have inputs, and also that the objects of reason are abstract, this means we must take seriously the idea that the triggers of reason work in a noncausal way. Plausible candidates for being the inputs of rational intuition are intuitions conceived of as

[31] The relevant notion of necessity here is what Plantinga (1974, 3) has called "broadly logical necessity." It is broader than logical necessity, but narrower than physical or causal necessity.

[32] This is why Goldman's causal theory of knowledge is not supposed to account for mathematical knowledge. This gave rise to Benacerraf's (1973) problem.

intellectual seemings (Bealer 1999, 246–248). For you to have an intuition that *p*, as Bealer thinks of it, is just for it to *seem* to you that *p*. *Seems* should not be understood as a cautionary term here but as a term that refers to a genuine conscious episode that is distinct from belief. Intellectual seemings are distinct from beliefs because they can come apart. For instance, I believe that the square root of two is not a rational number, but that theorem does not *seem* true to me, nor does it *seem* false to me; I believe it nonetheless because I know how to prove it. Also, it often *seems* to me that what is called the gambler's fallacy is not a fallacy; yet I believe it is a fallacy for all the usual reasons. Intellectual seemings, then, are not beliefs. Nonetheless, the seemings function as inputs for the source under discussion, reason, which yields belief. This suggests there is a *B*-individuation for reason, on the assumption that no other source takes intellectual seemings as its input.

While reason does not seem to yield know-how, it yields propositional belief in abundance. And those beliefs have very specific content – *modal* content. This binds the output beliefs of reason together. Although memory and testimony can also yield beliefs with modal content, there is this difference: reason yields modal belief in a productive way, whereas memory and testimony do so merely in a reproductive way. As to knowledge by acquaintance, I suggested in Chapter 1 that we know propositions by acquaintance. This can be thought of as the yield of reason. And so this suggests there is a *C*-individuation of reason.

As to the mechanisms that, given the input, yield belief in necessary truths, there is controversy. Rationalists tend to hold that the mechanism is "rational insight," or direct apprehension that "the claim in question cannot fail to be true" (BonJour 1998, 101). Empiricists tend to be skeptical about the very idea of necessary truth and for them, the question about mechanisms is otiose.[33] Since my project is not to decide whether a putative source of knowledge is genuine but only, if it *is* genuine, what kind of individuation principles hold for it, we may say that, if rationalism is correct, reason admits of *D*-individuation. For by means of Sosa's distinction between generation and transmission sources, we can say that reason is *D*-individuated by the fact that only reason *generates* belief in necessary truths through rational insight. This sets reason apart from testimony and memory, which can, at best, merely *transmit* belief in necessary truths.

[33] Quine (1961) is the influential case against necessary truths. It has met with very serious opposition by BonJour (1998, chapter 3) and Bealer (1999).

Unsurprisingly perhaps, reason admits of no *E*-individuation. For although the objects that it gives us knowledge of are theoretically unified in that they are necessarily true propositions, both memory and testimony can also yield belief in them.

The second "office" of reason, many have held, is inference. This names the source or faculty by which we can deduce conclusions from premises. These premises are not marked out by any specific content, nor are their conclusions: they can be about geography, history, mathematics, ethics, *anything*; and they may be necessary or contingent, true or false.

Since there is no externally visible organ that does the reasoning, there is no *A*-type individuation of deduction, although, perhaps, brain scanners can help identify the brain correlates of inference – which requires an individuation that stays clear of a reference to the brain.

The inputs of reasoning are propositions. But this is not unique to reasoning, since memory has propositional inputs too, and so has testimony. Nor is there, as indicated, content-wise, anything that binds the propositional inputs together. So there is no *B*-individuation of reasoning.

With respect to *C*-individuation, things are more complicated. For as I have indicated, the outputs of reasoning, the conclusions, content-wise can be about anything (and they can be necessary as well as contingent) and hence they lack theoretical unity. However, deductive reasoning can only be deemed a source of knowledge if it yields belief. Now one can validly deduce a conclusion from premises without believing the conclusion – for instance, because one has no idea whether the premises are true. However, we can think of deductive reasoning as nevertheless invariably yielding belief, albeit not belief in the conclusion per se. The belief yielded by deductive reasoning can be thought of as belief in a conditional, namely, the belief that if the premises $P_1 \ldots P_n$ are true, then conclusion *C* must be true too. Yielding belief in conditionals that are necessarily true is what individuates deduction and makes it different from both rational intuition (which involves no moving from premises to conclusions) and inductive reasoning (which cannot yield belief in necessary truths.) Hence, deductive reasoning is *C*-individuated. I note that deduction also yields knowledge by acquaintance of the propositions that are the conclusions of the deduction. Moreover, deduction may yield know-how. From "I know how to prune fruit trees" and "A pear tree is a fruit tree," you can deduce "I know how to prune pear trees."

Deductive reasoning as a source is also individuated by its mode of operation: it operates in such a way that if the premises are true, then so must be the conclusion(s). This sets it apart from induction and uniquely characterizes deductive reasoning, which is, hence, individuated by a *D*-principle. Since, as indicated, reasoning can be about anything, there is no specific kind of object to which it is directed; hence, no *E*-individuation of reasoning is possible.

I conclude that rational intuition admits of *B*-, *C*-, *D*-, and *E*-individuation, while deductive reasoning admits of *C*- and *D*-individuation. If we accept all this, it means that rational intuition and deductive reasoning are really different sources. Finally, rational intuition and deduction may one day admit of *A*-individuation.

Testimony

Thomas Reid wrote that an "original principle implanted in us by the Supreme Being, is a disposition to confide in the veracity of others, and to believe what they tell us" (Reid [1764] 1997, 194). The disposition is to accept the testimony of others. Ever since the groundbreaking work of C. A. J. Coady, epistemologists unanimously regard testimony as a source of knowledge. The basic idea is clear enough: we form beliefs on the basis of others telling us things, and often simply *because* others tell us things. The beliefs we so acquire often constitute knowledge. For present purposes we need not worry about what exactly constitutes testimony, as a substantial part of the next chapter is devoted to that. For now we need only the basic idea.

Hearing and seeing are involved in attending to testimony, and so are the externally visible organs for seeing and hearing. But since there is a lot of hearing and seeing that isn't attending to the thought expressions of others, this doesn't distinguish testimony from hearing and seeing – if there *is* such a distinction. For it might be thought that attending to testimony is just one way of using ears and eyes, and that believing on the basis of testimony reduces to perception plus some other sources. In fact, whether this is so or not is the central issue between reductionists and nonreductionists about testimony.[34] Nonreductionists like Reid and Plantinga (1993a, 79–80) hold that testimony (which is shorthand for, roughly, "forming beliefs on the basis of the word of others") is a sui generis source – i.e., a "fundamental" source, so a source that cannot be decomposed into more elementary sources – like perception or memory or reason. Reductionists, by contrast, think that testimony does reduce to more basic sources, notably, to perception and some form of reasoning.

[34] For an overview of the issues, see Gelfert (2014, 95–123).

On the reductionist approach, if one is to acquire knowledge through testimony, one should not only perceive the testimony but by some form of reasoning also convince oneself of the reliability of the testifier. Usually, however, the difference between reductionists and nonreductionists about testimony is framed in terms of justification. The nonreductionist holds that a testimony-based belief can be justified simply in virtue of the fact that the testimony has been issued, and that it *is* justified provided the subject has no reason to think the testifier is unreliable (insincere, mistaken, mislead). The reductionist, by contrast, holds that a testimony-based belief can be justified only if the subject has evidence of the testifier's reliability – and such evidence might include the testifier's past track record as a testifier, the present behavior and demeanor of the testifier (if still alive), and specific circumstances of the testimonial encounter. In order to obtain that sort of evidence, the subject will have to use perception, memory, and reason – so, more elementary sources of evidence.[35]

These considerations, I take it, lead to the conclusion that no *A*-individuation of testimony is possible. Nor is there a *B*-individuation. We may say that testimony as a source has propositional input. But testimony isn't unique in this respect, for we observed that memory and reasoning have such inputs as well. Moreover, there is nothing that content-wise binds the testified propositions together; they can be about anything and everything. The outputs of testimony include know-how[36] and propositional knowledge. But the know-how can be about anything, and belief outputs can have virtually any content.[37] Hence testimony defies *C*-individuation. There is no *E*-principle for testimony either: there is no specific class of objects that testimony is *about*.

What *is* characteristic of testimony as a source is its mode of operation, the particular process that, given the propositional input, generates the belief output. In cases of testimony, if proposition p is the input of the process, then the output is belief in the same proposition. This marks a distinction with deductive reasoning, for in cases in which deduction is the source, the output belief *differs* from the propositional input of reasoning. The point is a bit subtle, for of course we can deduce p from p. However,

[35] I note that at this point usually a lot of hand-waving is going on. Reductionists usually don't care to explain how exactly testimony decomposes into more basic sources, how exactly testimony involves perception or reasoning, or how it involves linguistic understanding – which it must!

[36] See for this the third section of Chapter 1, and Grimm (2020).

[37] *Virtually* – because it has been claimed that in certain areas testimonial knowledge is impossible; notably, mathematics, ethics, aesthetics, and philosophy. These are matters of debate. Ranalli (2019), for example, argued for the possibility of testimonial knowledge in philosophy.

the belief yielded by deduction is not the belief that *p*, but the belief that if *p*, then *p*, whereas the belief yielded by testimony, given that it is testified that *p*, is the belief that *p*. Hence, there is a *D*-principle that individuates testimony and that sets it apart from other sources.

Moral Intuition

A fair number of philosophers have held that there is a source that yields moral knowledge, both of the acquaintance and of the propositional variety.[38] It yields acquaintance with moral properties that are instantiated in persons and relations. For example, people can be acquainted with the compassion of Florence, and the wrongness of what Harvey did to them. It also yields propositional beliefs that fall in two broad subclasses: first, belief in general moral principles (such as that promises ought to be kept) and second, particular moral beliefs (such as that Jane should not have kept silent). Philosophers who take this line mostly hold that the yields of moral intuition are accompanied by moral feelings like moral anger, sympathy, indignation, and admiration. They hold that since neither perception nor memory nor consciousness nor reason yields moral knowledge, there must be a special source for it, which is variously named conscience, moral sense, or moral intuition.[39]

The view that there is a source of moral knowledge has, of course, come under very serious attack from a great number of twentieth-century philosophers, such as A. J. Ayer, John Mackie, and other noncognitivists (see McNaughton 1999, chapters 2, 4, and 11).The point of this section is, again, not to adjudicate between these positions but merely to get some grip on what individuates the source that yields moral knowledge – if there is one. Since moral noncognitivists hold there is no moral knowledge, for present purposes their views can be put to one side.

If the reasoning of moral cognitivists who accept a separate source of moral knowledge is sound, moral intuition clearly has a *C*-individuation: the yields of this alleged source have unique *moral* content. This source

[38] This position is usually called moral realism. A strong recent defense is Cuneo (2007); an older one is Ewing (1953, chapter 7). A reliable guide through this complex terrain is McNaughton (1999).

[39] For this argument, see Chisholm (1977, 123–126). Advocates of the argument include Thomas Reid ([1788] 1969), W. D. Ross, and A. C. Ewing. Allies include Jonathan Dancy (2004) and Robert Audi (2013). There are philosophers who acknowledge that moral knowledge exists but deny a special source for it. Some of these philosophers hold that moral knowledge is the yield of one of the other sources – reason, for instance.

generates moral knowledge, acquaintance with moral properties, accompanied by moral emotions.

Moreover, the objects of moral knowledge constitute a unified class: the objects are the moral properties with which we can get acquainted, and propositions with moral content. Since none of the other sources is directed to these, moral intuition is also *E*-individuated.

This source defies *A*-individuation as there is no externally visible organ connected to moral intuition; but with brain scanners we may find brain correlates of this source. This however requires (as I've remarked a couple of times now) a brain-independent individuation of moral intuition.

What is the input of moral knowledge supposed to be? It is often argued that moral properties supervene on natural properties and that if two things have identical natural properties, they also have identical moral properties. In order to notice the natural properties of things, we need perception. And perception is always of what is concrete. Now, visual perception is unfit for noticing moral properties. For, many moral realists maintain, moral properties are *nonnatural*.[40] But then, in order to notice moral, so nonnatural, properties, we need another source, namely, moral intuition. On this approach, then, moral intuition does have a special kind of input, viz., nonnatural input – input that rides piggyback on natural properties that we come to know via perception. This way we can account for knowledge by acquaintance of Florence's kindness as well as of the belief that Jan ought to have kept his word.

But this way we cannot account for belief in general moral truths, since these, by their very nature, cannot supervene on anything natural. So, what input triggers moral intuition in such a way that it yields belief in general moral truths? Robert Audi has argued that moral intuition is triggered by reflection, and the moral belief that is yielded by such reflection is a "conclusion of reflection" as opposed to a "conclusion of inference" (Audi 1999, 278–285). Coming to know the general moral truth that promises ought to be kept, he holds, requires reflection on the concept of a promise – and such reflection yields the belief that promises ought to be kept. Thought of in this way, the input of moral intuition includes reflection on concepts and their interrelations.

The inputs for moral intuition yielding moral knowledge of both varieties are unified and set them apart from other sources in that they are nonnatural. Hence, moral intuition has a *B*-individuation. If there is a

[40] Cuneo and Shafer-Landau (2014) argue for the nonnaturalness of moral properties, as did A. C. Ewing and W. D. Ross. Moral realists mostly maintain that moral properties are nonnatural.

D-individuation of moral intuition, it isn't one that we seem to know. We don't have a clue as to how to describe in informative terms the mechanism that has nonnatural input and yields moral knowledge. Moral intuition can thus be thought to be individuated by *B*-, *C*-, and *E*-principles.

Reading as a Source of Knowledge

After this very rough and sketchy study of individuation principles, I now make a brief foray into the third question that I posed in the beginning of this chapter: Should we think of reading as a source of knowledge? I first discuss whether reading satisfies the general conditions for being a source at all, and next the issue of its individuation principle(s).

The conditions for something being a source at all are satisfied, for reading *is* a process or mechanism, as the base clause of the account says it should be. This is not only intuitively clear, but in his fascinating book *Reading in the Brain*, Stanislas Dehaene (2009) has also described many aspects of this process in great scientific detail. Next, reading is a process that occurs in the relevant sense "in" subjects. Here too Dehaene's book offers ample details. Condition (i) is satisfied. And so is condition (ii): the process is triggered by the presence of texts; if there are no texts, there is no reading. Of course, all sorts of other conditions must be satisfied if one is to read, but the presence of texts is among the triggering conditions. More discussion of this is in Chapter 5, where I offer an analysis of "*S* is reading." Finally, condition (iii) is satisfied as well, since the reading process can yield knowledge in three varieties. As to (iii.c), beliefs yielded by reading can, but need not, constitute knowledge. That it *can* yield knowledge was amply illustrated, I trust, in Chapters 1 and 2. But it *need* not. In Chapter 5, I also offer an analysis – in fact, two analyses – of "*S* knows through reading that *p*." The initial suggestion, then, is that reading satisfies the conditions for being a source of knowledge.

Before taking up the issue of individuation conditions for reading, I must acknowledge a fact that I have so far almost entirely ignored. Some sources can operate only if other sources do. Deduction cannot yield knowledge unless memory works – memory being the source by which we retain knowledge of the premises. And if memory doesn't work, many instances of perceptual knowledge would be impossible, such as seeing that the birds are flying or seeing that that is a long-eared owl. In a similar vein, testimony cannot yield knowledge unless visual perception, the channel through which testimony comes to us, works. Also, we often have knowledge of particular moral facts (e.g., of the fact that Jane's treatment of Suzy is immoral), because another source works as well (e.g., perception by which we visually see how Jane treats Suzy).

Now, from the fact that in these examples one source cannot yield knowledge unless another source does too, no one, as far as I know, has concluded that *therefore* the one is not a source in its own right.

This is relevant for whether reading can be thought to be a source of knowledge. It is clear that reading can't yield knowledge unless other sources work as well. First and obviously, reading requires that visual perception (or, in the case of braille, tactile perception) works. But, on the basis of what emerged from the previous paragraph, it cannot be concluded that reading is therefore not a source in its own right. Second, reading requires that memory, the retentive faculty, works, because one cannot read unless one remembers what the words one is reading mean and unless one remembers the earlier parts of what one is reading.

The only way, it seems, in which it could be argued that reading is not a source in its own right is by showing that reading fully reduces to allegedly more basic sources in the way in which reductionists argue that testimony reduces to sense perception, memory, and induction. Reductionism with respect to reading would be the thesis that reading is either just an instance of one basic source or an instance of a conjunction of more basic sources. The two most likely candidates to which reading might seem reducible are perception (visual and tactile) and testimony. It is the burden of Chapter 4 to show that reading doesn't reduce to perception, nor to (attending to) testimony. If the argument in Chapter 4 is successful, this will clear the way for thinking of reading as a source in its own right. Now suppose my argument *is* successful, by what principle(s) is reading in that case individuated?

First, there is a *B*-type individuation for reading as its input is unique: it is written (or, in the case of braille, touched) words. There is of course similarity here with hearing, as well as some overlap with testimony. But it makes for a real difference, obviously, whether the words are received through the eyes (or through touch) or through the ears. There is overlap with testimony, since a lot of testimony comes to us by way of reading. But there is a lot of reading – as well as a lot of acquiring reading knowledge – that just isn't attending to testimony. (This is clear in the case of knowledge by acquaintance, but it is also true for large stretches of propositional knowledge, as I will argue in Chapter 4.)

There is no *C*-individuation of reading, because the knowledge that reading can yield (of all the three kinds we have distinguished: acquaintance, practical, and propositional), is not confined to particular contents. I again refer to Chapters 1 and 2 for examples and argument. Accordingly, there is no *E*-individuation of reading either: there just is not a theoretically unified set of objects that reading gives us knowledge of.

There is a *D*-principle for reading, however, so a principle that refers to a mode of operation. The process that has texts as its input so as to yield knowledge is very different from the process that has visible objects as its input and that yields knowledge about those objects. Coming to know, through reading, that the bee count was not successful is a very different process from seeing a bumblebee and, through seeing, coming to know that it is a bumblebee. Dehaene has argued that the reading process comprises two what he calls "reading routes"; that is, two routes to meaning. One is the phonological route, which goes from the seeing of words, via the inner articulation/pronunciation of the words, to their meaning. The other is the lexical route, which goes directly from the seeing of words to their meaning. In a well-known passage in his *Confessions* (book 6, chapter 3), St. Augustine writes that he saw Ambrose reading in silence, as if it were a remarkable and noteworthy feat. In Dehaene's terms, St. Augustine was struck by the lexical route that he noticed to be at work in Ambrose. Here is a key passage in Dehaene (2009, 26) on the two routes:

> Whether our mind ever goes straight from the written word to its meaning without accessing pronunciation or whether it unconsciously transforms letters into sound and then sound into meaning has been the topic of considerable discussion. The organization of the mental pathways for reading fueled a debate that divided the psychological community for over thirty years. Some thought that the transformation from print to sound was essential – written language, they argued, is just a by-product of spoken language, and we therefore have to sound the words out, through a *phonological route*, before we have any hope of recovering their meaning. For others, however, phonological recoding was just a beginner's trait characteristic of young readers. In more expert readers, reading efficiency was based on a direct *lexical route* straight from the letter string to its meaning.
>
> Nowadays, a consensus has emerged: in adults, both reading routes exist, and both are simultaneously active.

Later on he nuances the dual-route view of reading by stating that "two parallel paths . . . can be used simultaneously, *depending on what is to be read*" (Dehaene 2009, 104; my italics). The phonological route is used when we are confronted with infrequently used words and neologisms, while the lexical route is used when we are confronted with frequently used words and words whose spelling does not correspond to their pronunciation.

The dual-route view, I suggest, should at least be a *part* of the *D*-individuation principle of reading, since it describes at least a part of what is going on when textual inputs set the reading process at work.

Dehaene argues that it can be made plausible that the two reading routes correspond to two distinct networks of brain areas (Dehaene 2009, 107). The brain route from letters to sounds, for example, involve the superior regions of the left temporal lobe. The brain route from visible words to meanings is distinct from this and involves other regions of the brain, such as the left middle temporal region, the middle and ventral regions of the left temporal lobe, and the inferior frontal cortex. Dehaene also strikes an important cautionary note when he says that "overall, although researchers have managed to map several of the relevant brain areas, how meaning is actually coded in the cortex remains a frustrating issue. The process that allows our neuronal networks to snap together and 'make sense' remains utterly mysterious" (Dehaene 2009, 111).

These remarks indicate that to date we have at best some ingredients for an *A*-individuation principle of reading. Nonetheless, the ingredients are there, and we know what to look for when we aim at an *A*-principle. But we should not forget that we must know *what reading is* – so, have one or more individuation principles for reading to our avail – before we can research the *A*-principle for reading. This final section suggests that we do have such a principle, namely, of the *B*-type.

This is no more than a gesture toward the conclusion that reading is a source of knowledge in its own right. In Chapter 4 I discuss whether reading can be reduced either to attending to testimony or to perception. I argue it cannot.

CHAPTER 4

Why Reading Doesn't Reduce Either to Attending to Testimony or to Perception

In Chapter 3, I said it is a puzzling fact that epistemologists in the broadly analytic tradition never discuss or even mention reading, not even in passing, as a possible candidate source of knowledge. In this chapter I discuss two possible explanations of this fact and argue that both are wrong. I should say up front that I have never seen these explanations in print. But many colleagues with whom I discussed this matter offered these two explanations, mostly in a tentative mood, as throwaway suggestions. I didn't throw them away, however – rather, I tried to see whether they could be developed into convincing explanations. The first explanation is that reading is just a form of attending to testimony; the second, that it is just a special case of perception. Hence, according to these explanations, the epistemology of reading reduces to either the epistemology of testimony or the epistemology of perception. Reading thus merits no special attention and should not be thought of as a source in its own right with unique individuation conditions. As indicated, I argue that both explanations are wanting. Seeing *why* they are wanting puts us in a position to develop an informed account of what reading is – I say *informed* because up till now we have worked with an intuitive and unanalyzed notion of reading. The analysis of reading is offered in Chapter 5.

I first discuss whether reading reduces to attending to testimony; next, I inquire whether it reduces to simple seeing. The final section discusses whether reading reduces to what Thomas Reid called "acquired perception" or to what Dretske called "secondary epistemic seeing."

Reading Isn't Only or Merely Attending to Testimony

In order to be able to evaluate the first explanation – i.e., reading reduces to testimony – we need to get clearer about what testimony is, which requires moving beyond the highly general and intuitive notion of testimony that I worked with in Chapter 3. Various accounts of testimony have been offered. I discuss three of these and argue that on each of them knowledge acquired through reading is not identical with knowledge acquired through testimony. More specifically, I argue that much knowledge that we acquire through reading does not qualify as testimonial knowledge on the accounts of testimony offered by C. A. J. Coady, Elizabeth Fricker, Robert Audi, Ernest Sosa, and Jennifer Lackey.

C. A. J. Coady (1992) has offered the following account of "natural" testimony (as opposed to "formal" testimony of the sort that is offered in courtrooms):

> A speaker *S* testifies by making some statement *p* iff
>
> (i) *S*'s stating that *p* is evidence that *p* and is offered as evidence that *p*
> (ii) *S* has the relevant competence, authority, or credentials to state truly that *p*
> (iii) *S*'s statement that *p* is relevant to some disputed or unresolved question (which may, or may not be, *p*?) and is directed to those who are in need of evidence on the matter

There are two points I should like to make about this account. First, given this account, there are many cases of acquiring knowledge or warranted belief through reading that just aren't cases of acquiring knowledge or warranted belief through testimony. Suppose you open a copy of Graham Greene's *This Gun for Hire*, read the opening sentence "Murder didn't mean much to Raven," and thereby acquire the knowledge that Greene's novel opens with that sentence. Then you don't acquire this knowledge on the basis of Coadyan testimony, for condition (i) isn't satisfied: Greene doesn't offer his statement as evidence that murder didn't mean much to Raven.[1] Nor is condition (iii) satisfied: Greene's opening sentence isn't relevant to some disputed or unresolved question, and it isn't directed to people who are in need of evidence on the matter of Raven. And this isn't an isolated case. All of the following examples are things one may come to know through reading, in the contexts sketched in parentheses, while the knowledge is not acquired through Coadyan testimony (for ease of future reference I include the example just given):

[1] The example does not show, and is not supposed to show, that in the ordinary processes of reading one forms beliefs like this one. Upon reading the second sentence of Greene's novel ("It was just a new job"), one typically doesn't form the belief that that is the novel's (or, as Greene called it, entertainment's) second sentence. That would be an over-intellectualizing of reading. Nevertheless, one *may* come to know this fact through reading implicitly. The situation is not wholly unlike what happens in typical cases of visual perception: we typically form such beliefs as "The sun is up" and "The sky is blue" mostly implicitly.

a. That the first line of Graham Greene's novel *This Gun for Hire* reads "Murder didn't mean much to Raven" (you have opened the book that you know was written by Graham Greene, and you have read the opening sentence).
b. That the text contains a lot of metaphorical expressions, or that the text contains no typos (you have read the text and noticed these facts).
c. That the poem is a sonnet (you are familiar with the formal characteristics of a sonnet).
d. That the book is humorous (the writer doesn't say or imply this, but upon reading, you find yourself laughing).
e. That the article contains an invalid argument (you followed the argument and noticed that the conclusion doesn't follow from the argument).
f. That the review is based on a misunderstanding of the book (you know the book very well).
g. That the book is a warning call for people not to harbor grudges (this point is not explicitly stated, but from the development of the book's main character you conclude as much).
h. That the author of the novel assumes that *p* (he doesn't say this explicitly, but it is the inevitable though unobvious conclusion you must draw, given the points that the author does explicitly make).
i. That the author is intimately familiar with the Scottish Enlightenment (you are a historian who specializes in that period, and even though the book is not a history book, it contains so many adequate allusions to the Scottish Enlightenment that the conclusion forces itself upon you).
j. That what the Dutch did in the Caribbean was wrong (the reader is offered a "clean," neutral statement of facts and figures without the author making any moral or evaluative statement whatsoever).
k. That the square root of two is not a rational number (you have followed and comprehended the proof that was offered and you judged it, rightly, to be sound).

Before putting these examples to use in this chapter's argument, I make some general remarks. First, what these examples have in common is that one can come to know the indicated things through reading without reading them. Less enigmatically put, these examples have in common that they are cases in which one comes to know *through reading* some proposition *p* without *reading that p*. You come to know *through reading*, say, that the book is humorous, but you don't *read that* it is humorous.

You can come to know *through reading* that the opening line reads "Murder didn't mean much to Raven" without *reading that* that is the opening line. (Although for what follows nothing hangs on it, I note that this distinction seems to be unique to reading: you cannot come to know *through seeing* that the apple is greenish and not *see that* it is greenish; you cannot come to know *through tasting* that the milk has gone bad and not *taste that* the milk has gone bad; and you cannot come to know *through hearing* that the instrument is a trumpet and not *hear that* it is a trumpet.)

Second, the things on the list, I claimed, can be known through reading: in the cases as described, one would not have come to know the things that one did come to know unless one had engaged in reading. For the piece of knowledge to be acquired, reading was required. But this doesn't mean that such sources of knowledge as reason, inference, memory, or the moral sense did not also play a role in the process. Coming to know, through reading, that the article contains an invalid argument – as in (e) – also involves reason. Coming to know, through reading, that the review is based on a misunderstanding – as in (f) – involves memory: one must remember the contents of the book under review. Likewise, coming to know, through reading neutral statements, that something was morally wrong – as in (j) – involves the operation of the moral faculty. Sources join forces. We noted other instances of this at the end of the previous chapter: for example, if testimony is to work as a source of knowledge, perception is involved as well, since recipients of testimony should *hear* the testimony, or *see* it (in case it is written down), or *touch* it (in the case of braille).

Finally, the list is not exhaustive. In the Introduction, as well as in Chapter 1, I gave many other examples of knowledge through reading. Many of them were *also* cases of knowledge through testimony. Reading often *is* a matter of attending to testimony. But equally often, it is not. The list offered above is peculiar in that its cases show that not all knowledge from reading is testimonial knowledge – or so I shall argue.

Returning to Coady's account of testimony, I note that the point of this list is not that these things *cannot* be known through Coadyan testimony, for surely there are contexts in which one can and does come to know them on the basis of Coadyan testimony. Knowledge of all the propositions listed can be acquired when Coady's three conditions are satisfied. Rather, the point of the list is that one can come to know these things through reading in a way that *does not* qualify as believing on the basis of Coadyan testimony, viz., in the contexts in parentheses. For in none of these cases are Coady's three conditions jointly satisfied. Condition (i) is not satisfied in any of the cases on the list, since the propositions specified aren't offered as evidence. Neither is condition (ii) satisfied: the sketches of the contexts provide no indication of the authors' competence, credentials, and authority. Nor is condition (iii) satisfied: the propositions aren't relevant to some disputed or unresolved question, nor are they directed to people who are in need of evidence on the matters at hand. But even though Coady's conditions aren't jointly satisfied (and so, knowing the specified propositions in the contexts as sketched cannot be considered as knowledge based on Coadyan testimony), knowing the specified propositions (in the contexts specified) does qualify as knowledge acquired through reading. From this it follows that reading isn't coextensive with attending to Coadyan testimony.

My second point about Coady's account is that, as Jennifer Lackey has argued, it doesn't capture what we ordinarily take testimony to be, since there are clear cases of testimony that don't satisfy (i) and/or (ii) and/or (iii). Statements in posthumously published private journals and diaries that were never intended by their writers to be read by others fail Coadyan condition (i): they aren't offered as evidence, nor need they be relevant to some disputed question. But now suppose, to adapt an example from Lackey (2008, 18), you read Sylvia Plath's posthumously published diary, in which she says that she was regularly deeply depressed. Then you likely come to know that Plath was regularly deeply depressed. When asked what the source of your knowledge is, the intuitively correct answer, Lackey says, is that it is testimony. For you don't know this through visual perception (you haven't *seen* her depressed), nor through memory (you don't remember it), nor through reason (this is not a self-evident truth of reason, nor do you derive it as a conclusion from a number of facts that you are aware of), nor through introspection, nor through any combination of these sources. You acquired this knowledge from an expression of Plath's own thoughts – her thoughts are, for you, testimony. This example also shows that Coady's condition (iii) isn't necessary for someone's testifying: after reading her diary, you will know through Plath's own testimony that she was regularly depressed, but you had no evidential needs.

As Lackey (2008, 17) has also argued, for what we ordinarily take testimony to be, Coady's condition (ii) isn't necessary either. This condition entails that one doesn't testify unless one has the competence, authority, or credentials to state truly that p. Now, someone who lacks these properties may not be a very *reliable* testifier – but she is still capable of testifying. Her testimony may not be an epistemically good source of belief, but she can testify nonetheless. People who give false testimonies testify; they testify falsely. And false testimony is still testimony, the same way that a bad squash player is still a squash player.

All of this is obviously relevant for my argument that reading is not coextensive with attending to testimony. For if Coady's account of testimony is wrongheaded, then it does not bear much argumentative weight that there are things we may come to know through reading even though that isn't attending to Coadyan testimony.

Let us therefore turn to another account and see whether on that account acquiring knowledge of the things that are on the list (in the contexts sketched in parentheses) *does* qualify as the acquisition of knowledge through testimony. On this account, testimony is "people's telling us things" (Audi 1998, 131) or "tellings generally" with "no restrictions either on subject matter, or on the speaker's epistemic relation to it" (Fricker 1995, 396–397). Related is the view that testimony requires "only that it be a statement of someone's thoughts or beliefs, which they might direct to the world at large and to no one in particular" (Sosa 1991, 219). The essence of this broad view, as Lackey (2008, 20) has called it, can be put as follows:

> *S* testifies that *p* iff *S*'s statement that *p* is an expression of *S*'s thought that *p*.

It is clear that this view is not vulnerable to the objections just raised against Coady's account. On this view, Sylvia Plath's statements in her private diary qualify as testimony, as do expressions of thoughts that are false. That is to say, on this account one can testify that *p* even if one doesn't offer one's thought as evidence, even if one doesn't have the relevant competence, authority, or credentials to state truly that *p* (i.e., even if the testimony is false), and even if one doesn't express one's thought that *p* to people who are in need of evidence regarding *p*.

Regarding the broad view of testimony, I also make two remarks. First, on this view too, the knowledge acquired of the propositions on the list does not qualify as testimonial knowledge. Take (b), for example, "That the text contains a lot of metaphors": someone can know this through reading even if this proposition is not an expression of the author's thought. The same holds for (c), "That the poem is a sonnet": this can be known through reading even when this proposition isn't part of the thought that the poet wanted to express. The same holds for most, or perhaps even all, of the other items on the list.

Let me just cover case (a), which may seem an exception. It may seem an exception because the fact that Greene's *This Gun for Hire* opens with

"Murder didn't mean much to Raven" might be considered to express a thought that Green had about one of his fictional characters and therefore might be considered as testimony. However, we must tread carefully here. For the knowledge that a reader may acquire upon reading the opening page of the novel is *that the first line of the book reads "Murder didn't mean much to Raven.*" But this proposition is not a thought that is expressed in the opening page of Greene's fine novel. Hence that proposition is not broadly testified by Greene, which means, in turn, that the reader's knowing that proposition on the basis of reading is not an instance of knowing that proposition on the basis of broad testimony.

I am not going down the list any further here, but my point should be clear by now: there are cases of acquiring knowledge through reading that don't qualify as instances of acquiring knowledge on the basis of broad testimony. The point is well made even if some of the items on the list were to be instances of knowledge by broad testimony.

My second remark, however, is that the broad view is too broad. There are expressions of thought that, intuitively, do not qualify as testimony. What prevents these expressions of thought from qualifying as testimony is that they are noninformational. Here is an example. It is a beautiful day, you are hiking in the mountains with a friend, and you say, "Oh, what a beautiful day it is!" This is an expression of your thought, but it isn't testimony, for, as Lackey says, this expression of your thought "is neither offered nor taken as conveying information" (Lackey 2008, 21). Of course, in special circumstances, the very same expression of your thought *can* qualify as testimony; for instance, when the person you're with is blind and takes the expression of your thought as conveying the information that it is a beautiful day. What this suggests, Lackey says, is that when an expression functions merely as a conversational filler, as it does in the initial example, it doesn't qualify as testimony.

In addition to mere conversation fillers, there are other kinds of expressions of thought that do not qualify as testimony. Adapting a point from Lackey, we may think of exhortations. You say to your son who is training for the half marathon: "You can do it!" By saying this, you express a thought of yours, but it isn't testimony, as you don't offer what you say as conveying the information that your son can do it, nor does your son take what you say as conveying the information that he can do it.

This is relevant for my argument, for it means that if the broad account is unsatisfactory, my argument that we can come to know things through reading that don't qualify as cases of knowledge by broad testimony doesn't bear much weight. I therefore turn to Lackey's disjunctive account of testimony that I take to be the best account of testimony to date. It takes its cue from the distinction between testimony as an intentional act on the part of a speaker or writer and testimony as a source of belief or knowledge for the hearer or reader (Lackey 2008, 27). This distinction forms the basis for Lackey's distinction between speaker testimony (*s*-testimony) and hearer testimony (*h*-testimony). Before presenting the full account, I need to introduce some terminology. First, the notion of an act of communication:

> *A* is an act of communication iff by performing *A* a speaker or writer intends to express communicable content. (It does *not* require that the speaker or writer *also* intends to communicate that content to others.)

When Plath wrote in her diary for only private purposes, she was engaging in acts of communication: she had the intention to express communicable content, even if she had no intention to communicate that content to others. Of course, the two intentions might go together, but the point is that they need not.

Second, the notion of conveying information. Acts of communication – for instance, Plath's writing in her diary – convey information. What does it mean for an act of communication *A* to convey the information that *p*? Rather than defining this notion, Lackey provides paradigmatic cases. She says an act of communication *A* conveys the information that *p*, for example, (1) when *A* is the utterance of a declarative sentence that expresses proposition *p* or (2) when <*p*> is an obvious (uncancelled) pragmatic implication of *A* (Lackey 2008, 31).

With the notions *acts of communication* and *conveying information* thus clarified, Lackey (2008, 30, 32) defines speaker testimony and hearer testimony as follows:

> **Speaker testimony**: *S s*-testifies that *p* by performing *A* iff, in performing *A*, *S* reasonably intends to convey the information that *p* (in part) in virtue of *A*'s communicable content.

> **Hearer testimony**: *S h*-testifies that *p* by performing *A* iff *H*, *S*'s hearer, reasonably takes *A* as conveying the information that *p* (in part) in virtue of *A*'s communicable content.

The account of *s*-testimony requires that a speaker intends to convey information to their hearer and in that sense requires a speaker's *A* to *be offered as* conveying information. The phrase "(in part) in virtue of *A*'s communicable content" is included in order to exclude cases like the following: you sing in a soprano voice "I have a soprano voice," and you intend to convey the information that you have a soprano voice in virtue of the *perceptual* content of your sung assertion, *not* in virtue of the *communicable content* of your sung assertion. So, you intend to convey the information that you have a soprano voice by your singing in a soprano voice, and not by the content of the words that you sing. In this case, you are not *s*-testifying that you have a soprano voice. But if you just *said* "I have a soprano voice" or "I have one of the female voice types, but not the alto," you *would* be *s*-testifying that you have a soprano voice. Had you said the latter, you would still have conveyed the information that you have a soprano voice – there is a reasonably obvious connection between "I have a soprano voice" and "I have one of the female voice types, but not the alto."

Whereas *s*-testimony requires some intention on the part of the speaker to convey information, no such intention is required for *h*-testimony: *h*-testimony captures the sense in which testimony can serve as a source of belief or knowledge for others, regardless of the testifier's intention to be such an epistemic source. Crucial for *h*-testimony is that the hearer or reader *takes* the speaker's or writer's *A* to convey information.

It follows from these accounts that a speaker or writer can *s*-testify without *h*-testifying, and vice versa. But they can also go together. Lackey's official statement of the disjunctive view of the nature of testimony is as follows (Lackey 2008, 35–36):

> *S* testifies that *p* by making an act of communication *A* iff (in part) in virtue of *A*'s communicable content (1) *S* reasonably intends to convey the information that *p* and/or (2) *A* is reasonably taken as conveying the information that *p*.

Let me now return to the question for which the presentation of Lackey's account was propaedeutic: Is all knowledge we can acquire through reading based on Lackeyan testimony? Let me go down the list. Regarding (a): as indicated, the knowledge that a reader of the first line of *This Gun for Hire* acquires through reading is that the first line of that book reads "Murder didn't mean much to Raven." This knowledge is not based on Greene's *s*-testimony, as Greene did not intend to convey the information that the first line of *This Gun for Hire* reads "Murder didn't mean much to Raven." This is not to deny that it is possible to think up a scenario in which someone's knowledge of this *is* based on Greene's *s*-testimony.[2] But in the case as originally described, the reader does not

[2] For example: suppose Jane is Greene's neighbor, and she has asked him what the title of his new book will be and what its opening sentence will be. Greene's answer is that the title is *This Gun for Hire* and its opening line is "Murder didn't mean much to Raven." In this case, Jane's knowledge

acquire the indicated knowledge through *s*-testimony. Nor does the reader acquire it through *h*-testimony, for it is not the case that, upon reading "Murder didn't mean much to Raven," a reader takes this to convey the information that the first line of *This Gun for Hire* reads "Murder didn't mean much to Raven." So, the knowledge acquired in the context as described in (a) is knowledge through reading, but it is not knowledge through Lackeyan testimony.

That a specific text contains a lot of metaphorical expressions, or that it is a sonnet, or that it is humorous, as in cases (b), (c), and (d), is knowledge acquired through reading. But it surely isn't acquired through the author's *s*-testimony: the author's acts of communication aren't intended to convey the information that the text contains a lot of metaphorical expressions, or that it is a sonnet, and so forth. Nor is it acquired through the author's *h*-testimony: the reader doesn't take the author's acts of communication to convey the information that the text contains a lot of metaphorical expressions, or that it is a sonnet, and so on. This means that the knowledge acquired in these cases is not based on Lackeyan testimony.

Likewise, that the article contains an invalid argument, that the review is based on a misunderstanding, that the book is a warning call for people not to harbor grudges, or that the author assumes that *p* – as in (e), (f), (g), and (h) – is, in the contexts as sketched, known through reading. But that knowledge isn't based on either *s*-testimony or *h*-testimony. To write this out for (f): the reviewer certainly doesn't intend to convey the information that their review is based on a misunderstanding, so the review doesn't qualify as *s*-testimony; nor can a reader reasonably take the review's communicable content to express the information that the review is based on a misunderstanding, so the review doesn't qualify as *h*-testimony either. This means that the knowledge acquired just isn't based on Lackeyan testimony.

Likewise, that the author is intimately familiar with the Scottish Enlightenment, that what the Dutch did in the Caribbean was wrong, or that the square root of two is not a rational number – as in (i), (j), and (k) – is, in the contexts as sketched, knowledge acquired through reading. But it isn't knowledge based on Lackeyan testimony. To write this out for (k): when you come to know that the square root of two is not a rational number because you have read, followed, and comprehended the proof,

that the first line of *This Gun for Hire* reads "Murder didn't mean much to Raven" *is* based on Greene's *s*-testimony.

then your knowledge isn't based on *s*- or *h*-testimony since you now "see," intellectually, for yourself that this is true.

The conclusion of this section should be clear by now. The lack of attention that reading has received among analytic epistemologists cannot be explained by reference to the alleged fact that knowledge acquired through reading is just a token of the type *knowledge acquired through testimony*. What a reader may come to know through reading doesn't necessarily qualify as testimonial knowledge. I've shown that this is true given three different accounts of testimony. The list that I offered has things that someone may come to know through reading, while the knowledge thus acquired does not qualify as testimonial knowledge. I have indicated that we may come to know any of the things on this list *also* through testimony; but the point I have been eager to establish is that when we read texts, we can, in the appropriate circumstances, come to know things just through reading. I have thus argued that knowledge through reading isn't coextensive with knowledge through testimony. This counts in favor of the idea that reading is a source of knowledge in its own right – i.e., that it doesn't reduce to testimony.

Reading Isn't Simple Seeing

The second possible explanation of the inattention that epistemologists have paid to reading is that reading is just an instance of perception and therefore merits no special attention. The epistemology of reading is as much part of the epistemology of perception as the epistemology of, say, seeing horses is. *Reading* is just the name for the visual perception of a particular kind of objects, viz., words and sentences.[3] The fact that we have no special name for seeing horses but that we do have a special name for seeing words and sentences (viz., *reading*), this explanation says, should not seduce us into thinking that reading is in any principled way different from seeing horses. If reading is a source of knowledge at all, the explanation continues, it is only because *perception* is a source of knowledge, and perception encompasses reading. So, reading should not be thought of as a source in its own right, for the same reason that seeing horses is not a source in its own right.

This explanation, as I shall now argue, is implausible for reasons that I think are revealing. It is implausible, first, because *if* epistemologists thought that reading just is (a form or kind of) perception, they would,

[3] *Words* must be understood here as including numerals and proper names.

among the numerous examples of perception they discuss, occasionally slip in examples of reading. But they never do.[4] Epistemologists writing about perception have discussed, sometimes at great length, examples involving the perception of a green rectangular field, tiger lilies, wilting flowers, a hand, two hands, a computer screen, a large lake a few blocks away from the epistemologist's house, oneself in a mirror, an actor on the television, red buses, fake barns, identical twins, and more. But they never offer examples involving the perception of words or strings of them. This strongly suggests that epistemologists had and have no inclination at all to think that reading is just seeing and that, when they offered epistemological analyses and theories of perception, reading was not on their minds.

And there would seem to be an excellent reason for this: the objects of reading – words and strings of words like sentences or articles and books – are of a radically different nature than the green rectangular fields, tiger lilies, wilting flowers, and the other objects that I've mentioned. To a first approximation, the difference can be pinpointed by saying that, unlike the objects discussed in the epistemology of perception, the objects of reading *have meaning*. The notion *meaning* has many senses, and as I shall argue in Chapter 7, the objects of reading have meaning in many of those senses.

Another and related reason why reading wasn't and isn't on the epistemologists' minds might be this: simple seeing comes to us naturally, doesn't require special effort, and isn't the result of a conscious learning process. In this it contrasts with reading, which does not come naturally, requires special effort, and is the result of a conscious learning process.[5] Everybody with properly functioning eyesight can see green rectangular fields, tiger lilies, wilting flowers, and so on. It would be very odd if someone with good eyesight were to say, "I can't see green rectangular fields, for I haven't learned how to do that" or "I am terribly sorry, no one ever taught me how to see a tiger lily." But it wouldn't be at all odd if somebody with good eyesight were to say, "I can't read the *Summa contra gentiles* in the original language, because I don't know Latin" or "I can't read Kant because I can't read at all."

Of course, even if seeing a green rectangular field comes naturally and doesn't require having gone through some learning process, for someone to see *that* the field is green and rectangular, that person needs to have learned the concepts of green and of rectangular. Seeing comes naturally – seeing

[4] See Chapter 3, note 7. A really minor exception is Dretske (1969, 79, 157) who offers two or three examples that involve reading.

[5] Many issues related to learning to read are detailed by Dehaene (2009, chapter 5).

that does not. But this doesn't undermine the present point, which is that reading is not mere seeing, not just seeing, not simple seeing (I use these phrases as synonyms).

Although it is of course true that reading involves perception, there is more to reading than simply seeing words and sentences. (In what follows, I mainly focus on reading that involves visual perception, putting reading that involves touch to one side.) Reading is not just seeing a particular kind of object, viz., words and sentences, whereas seeing a horse *just is* seeing a certain kind of animal, and seeing Van Gogh's *Sunflowers just is* seeing a particular painting. One is just seeing something when one is having certain visual experiences of shapes, colors, and their relative positions in one's visual field. One may just see a horse, without knowing or believing that it is a horse one is seeing, without even knowing or believing that it is an animal one is seeing, without even knowing or believing anything at all about what one is seeing. What I have referred to as *just seeing* is what Fred Dretske initially called "object perception" (as contrasted with fact perception: seeing *that* the animal is a horse) and later on "simple seeing."[6] According to Dretske, simple seeing *X* is marked by the fact that it is compatible with having no beliefs about *X*.[7]

The reason why reading isn't simple seeing words and sentences, why it isn't just looking at what are in fact words and sentences, can be brought out rather easily. Suppose you don't know Greek but have opened a Greek edition of Homer's *Odyssey*. Then you are seeing words and sentences, but you aren't reading.[8] Moreover, if reading were simple seeing words and sentences, it would have to be compatible with forming no beliefs about what one is reading. But that seems wrong. One isn't reading unless one is forming, in a way to be qualified in a moment, such beliefs as that

- this sentence (referring to a particular sentence) is a statement
- that sentence (referring to another sentence) is a question
- the word *W* that is used here means *that*

[6] Dretske (1969, chapter 1; 2000, chapter 6). Audi (1998, 15) also calls this simple perception.

[7] Simple seeing *X* and having no beliefs about *X* are compatible, even if much simple seeing in actual practice is accompanied by beliefs about *X*. Fact-seeing normally builds on simple seeing in the sense that normally when one fact-sees that the animal is a horse, one also object-sees the horse. This is *normally* so, but not always. For example, I can fact-see that there is no horse in my study, but that is not built on my object-seeing a horse.

[8] Knowing a language is a graded phenomenon, since a language can be known to various degrees: one person can know a particular language better than another person. Reading too is a graded phenomenon: one person can be a better reader than another. And there is a relation between the two: the better one knows a language, the better a reader one tends to be. For an attempt to understand the metaphysics of graded phenomena, see Van Woudenberg and Peels (2018).

- the sentence *S* that is written here means *this*
- the point that the author is navigating towards seems to be *p*
- given what is said about her, the main character could be a hero, but also a villain
- this (referring to a particular passage) is an exhilarating passage

If reading requires all such beliefs to be occurrent, the requirement seems overly intellectually demanding. For when we read, we don't normally form explicit beliefs about words or sentences, what they mean, what their illocutionary force is, and so forth. Normally we find ourselves understanding what a sentence says or means without forming such explicit beliefs. When we read the sentence "During the second national bee count this weekend, over 19,000 bees were counted," we understand what it says without forming such explicit and occurrent beliefs as "*Second* is an ordinal number" or "*Bees* is a noun" or "This sentence is in the indicative mood." Readers who know what ordinal numbers, nouns, and moods are have a disposition to believe these propositions, but it is only on special occasions that we form such beliefs occurrently. Still, when we read, we do form many occurrent beliefs. Upon reading the above sentence about the bee count, a reader may form the occurrent belief that recently there was a bee count in the Netherlands. If we take the notion *belief* to cover occurrent and dispositional beliefs, as well as dispositions to believe, we must say that reading always involves believing – and that when one forms no beliefs at all, one certainly isn't reading.[9]

So reading isn't just seeing. Still, there is a relation (perhaps, there are even multiple relations) between reading and seeing. Reflecting on that relation, we should keep in mind that, as Nikolas Gisborne (2010, 118) has said, *see* is a massively polysemous verb. Three senses are especially relevant for present purposes. First, there is a sense that we have already encountered when we discussed the notion of object perception, which Gisborne calls the prototypical sense of *see*. In this sense, to see is to perceive visually. In such sentences as "I can see the queen from here" and "I saw the horse in the field," *see* is used in the prototypical sense. A test for

[9] I am here relying on Audi's distinction between dispositional beliefs and dispositions to believe. None of your beliefs is a dispositional belief unless, at an earlier time, you had the occurrent belief that *p*. But you may have the disposition to believe *p* even if you never actually (occurrently) believe or come to believe that *p*. For example, most people have the disposition to believe they weigh less than 450 kilograms, but few people have actually (occurrently) formed that belief explicitly. See Audi (1994).

identifying whether *see* is used in this sense is checking whether it is linguistically possible (whether it might make sense) to add prepositional phrases that specify the physical conditions of the seeing. If such an addition makes sense, then *see* is used in the prototypical sense; if not, then *see* is not used in this sense. The first example offered ("I can see the queen from here") already includes such a prepositional phrase, viz., *from here*. It could be substituted for other such phrases without the sentence becoming nonsensical – e.g., "I can see the queen through the window/ with my binoculars." On this test, *saw*, in the sentence "I saw the horse in the field," is also used in the prototypical sense, for a prepositional phrase may be added that specifies the physical condition of the seeing: "I saw the horse in the field in broad daylight/in a mirror."

Furthermore, *see* has two senses in which it is a knowledge ascription. There is, first, what Gisborne calls the purely propositional sense of *see* that we find in such sentences as "I see that the argument is valid" and "Frege saw that Russell was right." If you say of yourself that you see that the argument is valid, you thus ascribe knowledge to yourself: if you don't (think you) *know* that the argument is valid, you won't say that you see that it is. And when you say that Frege saw that Russell was right, you say that Frege *knew* that Russell was right. Here, *see* has no visual meaning whatsoever: it would be nonsensical to say "I see that the argument is valid through the window" or "Frege saw that Russell was right in broad daylight."

There is a further sense of *see* in which it has both a prototypical and an epistemic sense (which is not the purely propositional sense, for if it had the purely propositional sense, it couldn't also have the prototypical sense). Gisborne calls this the perceptual propositional sense of *see*, which we find in such sentences as "Jane saw that the child crossed safely" and "Harold sees that it is raining." In these sentences, *see* has a prototypical sense because we can, without the sentences becoming nonsensical, add prepositional phrases that specify the physical conditions of the seeing: "Jane saw through the window that the child crossed safely" and "Harold sees from where he sits that it is raining." But *saw* has an epistemic sense here as well. For when we say that Jane saw that the child crossed safely, we imply that the child did cross safely and that Jane knew this fact. As Craig French (2012, 122) has observed, in propositional contexts where it has a prototypical sense, *see* is evidential, by which he means that in such contexts *see* indicates that the source of the information in the that-clause is visual. If Jane came to know by sight, through seeing, that the child crossed safely, the source of her information was visual – she knew this not, for instance, through the testimony of others. Likewise, if Harold knows that it is raining through sight, by seeing, the source of his information is visual – he knew this not, for example, through hearing. In these cases, the word *sees* contains the answer to the questions "How did Jane know the child crossed safely?" and "How did Harold know it was raining?": they knew this through seeing (in the prototypical sense). When the word *see* is used in the perceptual propositional sense, the situation that is described by means of it is a case of what Dretske called fact perception. When *see* is used in the prototypical sense only (so, not in the propositional sense), the situation that is described by means of it is a case of what Dretske called object perception, simple seeing, or see_n (which stands for nonepistemic seeing).

Let us now return to the relation between seeing and reading. In doing so, we should keep in mind that the question we're considering is whether reading reduces to visual perception – i.e., to that source that takes as its input light that strikes the retina and that causes us to have visual experiences. If we keep this in mind, it is clear that for our purposes it is irrelevant that reading papers, articles, books, and so forth, often enables us to see things in the purely propositional sense. For example, when you read McTaggart's celebrated argument for the unreality of time and come to see that the terms of the *A*-series are entirely distinct from those of the *B*-series, nothing visual is involved in seeing the distinction. If the reduction thesis is to have any plausibility, the seeing to which reading should be reducible must have the visual at least as an essential component. This means that we can put to one side all the cases in which reading enables us to see things in the purely propositional sense.

We already noted that reading involves visual seeing (as announced, I am abstracting from reading braille). No one is reading unless they are seeing printed or written words and sentences – and now *seeing* is used in the prototypical sense. This states a necessary condition for reading but surely not a sufficient one. For, as already indicated, a person can see (in the prototypical sense) a copy of Homer's *Odyssey* in Greek and yet not be reading, due to that person's not knowing Greek. Or one may be seeing (in the prototypical sense) a book on the history of Portugal written in Portuguese and yet not be reading for a similar reason. Is there a sense of *seeing* such that reading just *is* seeing in that sense? If there is, it should be a sense that includes a visual component. The candidate here is seeing in the perceptual propositional sense. So, is reading seeing in this sense?

It may seem obvious that it is not. After all, seeing in the perceptual propositional sense is factive.[10] You can't see (in that sense) that the flowers are wilting unless they are in fact wilting – that is, unless it is true that they are wilting. But if reading is seeing in the perceptual propositional sense, reading should be factive too. And isn't it obvious that it isn't? For a person can truly be reading and yet form false beliefs. A person can read a book on honeybees (and thus be truly reading) and yet form the false belief that an adult queen bee has much larger wings than adult worker bees. One cannot *see* (in the perceptual propositional sense) that queen bees have larger wings than worker bees, but one can *read* that they have – for instance, because the author of the book was badly misinformed about bees. Seeing (in this sense) is factive, but reading is not – hence, the latter is not a case of the former.

Although seeing *that* is indeed factive and reading *that* is not, this argument goes too quickly, for it glides over the important question as to what the objects of reading are. We normally say that we read newspapers, articles (in those newspapers), letters and emails, contracts and advertisements, stories, books (textbooks, travel guidebooks, cookbooks, novels, philosophy books), poems – we have in fact developed a huge arsenal of terms by which we group, categorize, and label the objects of reading. But what all these objects have in common, and what makes them objects of reading, is that they are composed of words and sentences. As indicated before, I use *text* as the most general term for the objects of reading, and I will say that texts are composed of words and sentences – these are the parts of the wholes that texts are.

If reading is to instantiate seeing *that*, there must be a way to construe the objects of reading (texts) in a way that is analogous to the objects of seeing (in the perceptual propositional sense). How would that go? When Jane sees that the child has safely crossed the street, the object of her perception is the child, and what she comes to know through seeing is something about the child, namely, that it has safely crossed the street. The analogue for reading would be that the objects of reading are texts, and what a reader comes to know through reading (i.e., through seeing texts in the perceptual propositional sense) is something about the text.

[10] Dretske, and many others as well, endorsed the entailment thesis, according to which seeing that p entails knowing that p. The entailment thesis has come under some attack in Turri (2010) and Pritchard (2012). Ranalli (2014) argues – convincingly, it seems to me – that the attack is unsuccessful.

Does the analogue hold? The first thing to say is that it surely is possible to come to know something about a text through reading it. Through reading text *T*, you may come to know that *T* stages a conversation between a fox and a bird and that it warns us to beware of flattery, or that it contains an invalid argument, or that it is funny. However, these are not cases of seeing *that* (in the perceptual propositional sense), for there is nothing visual about *T* staging that conversation, and the reader who comes to know these things doesn't come to know them in a way that involves seeing in the prototypical sense. What a reader sees in the prototypical sense are printed or written words and sentences, not conversations or warnings. So the analogue doesn't hold. This indicates that reading is not seeing in the perceptual propositional sense. Seeing *that*, in the perceptual propositional sense and related to texts, amounts to no more than seeing that the sentences are set in italics or bold, or seeing that the text is printed in Times New Roman font. But this is not reading.

Moreover, most of the time readers don't form beliefs (and hence do not come to know things) about texts but about other things, such as bees, flattery, what happened to the Kurds in Turkey, Kant's argument for transcendental idealism, and the poetry of A. E. Housman. Forming beliefs about and coming to know these things just aren't cases of seeing *that* in the perceptual propositional sense. This reinforces the conclusion that reading is not identical to seeing *that*; it isn't seeing in the perceptual propositional sense. And it isn't simple seeing either.

Reading Is neither Acquired Perception nor Secondary Epistemic Seeing

The main argument in this chapter so far has been negative: reading doesn't reduce to attending to testimony nor to simple perception. In this section I continue the negative exercise by arguing that reading doesn't reduce to what Reid called "acquired perception," nor to what Dretske called "secondary epistemic seeing." I pay attention to these more involved notions of seeing because from a distance they may seem capable of enabling the reduction that I think should be resisted.

Here is how Reid ([1764] 1997, 171) introduces the notion of acquired perception:

> Our perceptions are of two kinds: some are natural and original, others acquired, and the fruit of experience. When I perceive that this is the taste of cyder, that of brandy; that this is the smell of an apple, that of an orange; that this is the noise of thunder, that the ringing of bells; this the sound of a

> coach passing, that the voice of such a friend; these perceptions, and others of the same kind, are not original, they are acquired. But the perception which I have by touch, of the hardness and softness of bodies, of their extension, figure, and motion, is not acquired, it is original.
>
> In all our senses, the acquired perceptions are many more than the original, especially in sight. By this sense we perceive originally the visible figure and colour of bodies only, and their visible place: but we learn to perceive by the eye, almost every thing which we can perceive by touch. The original perceptions of this sense, serve only as signs to introduce the acquired.

A few paragraphs further on, Reid says that "perception, whether original or acquired, implies no exercise of reason," by which he means that when we perceive things, we aren't engaged in reasoning, we aren't deriving conclusions from premises.

The idea behind the distinction is that whereas certain perceptions – the "original" ones – do not require a learning process on the part of the perceiver, other perceptions – the "acquired" ones – do require such a process. What we see without learning, Reid holds, is a two-dimensional array in which colored objects are displayed as having locations along the left-right and up-down axes, but not along the near-far axis.[11] The perception of a sphere is hence not original, because a sphere is three-dimensional. Seeing that something is a three-dimensional sphere requires that the perceiver has learned through experience that certain patterns of light and shadow are signs of distance and three-dimensional convexity. This learning process requires tactile sensations. Other instances of acquired perception require other learning processes; for example, when you see that it is your neighbor's cat who is roaming your garden. Here, learning through testimony will be involved, for you can't come to know through seeing alone that that particular cat is your neighbor's. The crucial mechanism in acquired perception, Reid holds, is association. Even if, contrary to what Reid thought, seeing that a globe is spherically convex is *not* an acquired perception,[12] the distinction between original perception and acquired perception is still a good one.

I should like to note that Reid holds that acquired perception is not really *perception*, although we speak of it that way (Reid [1785] 2002, 247):

> Acquired perception is not properly the testimony of those senses which God hath given us, but a conclusion drawn from what the senses

[11] An in-depth discussion of Reid on acquired perception is Van Cleve (2015, chapter 5).
[12] Van Cleve (2015, 483–485) discusses stereopsis, a mechanism not known in Reid's day.

> testify . . . . The appearance of the sign immediately produces the belief of its usual attendant, and we think we perceive the one as well as the other . . . . We are . . . authorized by language to call them perception, and must often do so, or speak unintelligibly. But philosophy teaches us, in this, as in many other instances, to distinguish things which the vulgar confound.

I take it that what Reid is pointing to is that purely phenomenologically speaking, we don't "see" (in the prototypical sense) that a globe is convex or that that is your neighbor's cat.

If we apply Reid's distinction to reading, the following picture emerges. Reading, of course, involves seeing that what is on the page are written or printed words and sentences. But this cannot be an original perception, since seeing that there are words on the page requires that one has gone through some learning process. Not everybody can see that there are words on the page (not everyone knows that, when looking at a page with words on it, it is *words* they are seeing), but everybody with normal eyesight *can* see two-dimensional patches of color (everybody can know, when seeing them, that they are patches of color). Acquired perception builds on original perception. What are the two-dimensional patches of color that are originally perceived? In the case of reading, the most plausible candidates are, of course, the curved and straight little lines that form words.

Suppose now that Agnes and Mercedes have an original perception of the following string of black shapes on a page:

> De zin is het zijn van alle creatuurlijk zijnde, de zijnswijze ook van onze zelfheid, en is van religieuzen wortel en van goddelijken oorsprong.

Suppose furthermore that Agnes is a native Dutch speaker, while Mercedes is a Spanish student who doesn't know Dutch. What then shall we say about them in terms of Reid's distinction when they perceive the string of shapes – what will they think, what will they believe, and why?

Mercedes, in all likelihood, will think that what she is seeing are words. She will think this because she recognizes that the shapes are letters, and she knows that letters are the materials that words are composed of. So she looks at the first little shape and thinks: "This is the letter *D*." We may also say: she sees that it is the letter *D*. This – i.e., seeing that it is the letter *D* – is an acquired perception. For Mercedes must have gone through some learning process (she must have learned the alphabet) in order to see that the shape is the letter *D*. A crude description of the learning process would be that Mercedes has come to associate the first black shape in the string with the thought that it is (or represents) the letter *D*.[13] And because she has learned to make this association, she is able to count five tokens of the letter *D* in the quoted sentence. As indicated, Mercedes will probably also think that each little string of letters separated from other strings of letters by spaces is a word, and so she will think that "De" is a word. We may also say that she sees that the first two letters form a word. This is again an acquired perception, for she must have gone through a learning process in order to be able to see that it is a word. A crude description of the learning process would be that Mercedes has come to associate a combination of letters surrounded by spaces with the thought that it is (or represents) a word. So Mercedes sees that the first two letters form a word. But she doesn't know *which* word, because she doesn't know what it means – she doesn't know that it means the same as the Spanish word *el*. She doesn't know this because she hasn't learned the meaning of the word *De*. Finally, she has learned that sentences start with a capital and end with a period. This enables her to see that the string of shapes she is looking at is one sentence. This too is an acquired perception.

Mercedes, then, has original perceptions as well acquired perceptions: she has the original perception of a string of straight and curved little black lines (she sees that there are straight and curved little black lines) and the acquired perception that there are letters, and that there are words, and even that there is a sentence. And yet, she isn't reading. (More cautiously put, she is not reading in the paradigmatic sense that I am interested in.)

Compare this to Agnes. We may presume that she has the same original and acquired perceptions as Mercedes. But thanks to a lengthy learning process she knows Dutch, which greatly expands the area of her acquired perceptions. She sees that the first word is the word *De*, the Dutch definite article, and the last *oorsprong*, which she knows is normally translated in English as "origin." Since Agnes knows Dutch – i.e., she knows (in some sense of *know*) Dutch words and, to some extent, Dutch grammar – she has some understanding of the meaning of the sentence (*some*, for the meaning of the sentence is, even for native Dutch speakers, somewhat opaque). So, Agnes is reading.

Now recall that according to Reid, acquired perception isn't really perception – i.e., it isn't seeing in the prototypical sense. If we follow

[13] Reading words poses what psychologists call the invariance problem: we need to recognize which aspects of a word do not vary, viz., the letter sequence, in spite of numerous shapes that the actual letters may take – they take on different forms in print and even more different forms in handwriting. See Dehaene (2009, 18–21).

Reid in this, as I think we should, we must say that, since reading involves various instances of acquired perception, it isn't really perception.

Up till now I have tacitly been assuming that when Agnes sees the words *De* and *oorsprong* and knows their meaning, she is instancing acquired perception. But this may well be doubted on the following ground: in the examples that Reid used, acquired perception is the association of what we originally perceive in one sense modality with what we have learned through original perception in another sense modality. In Reid's example, seeing that the globe is spherical is the association of what we originally see (distribution pattern of colors) with what we originally touch (shapes). But in the case of words there is no such association – that is, no association between what is originally perceived in two different sense modalities. For word meanings are originally perceived in no sense modality at all; and the same holds for sentence meanings. At this point, we may come to doubt that seeing the straight and curved little lines instances acquired perception.

We may, of course, expand the notion of acquired perception so that it encompasses the association of what is originally perceived in one sense modality with anything whatsoever. A particular array of straight and curved little lines may be associated with the word form C-A-T, and that word form can, next, be associated with a particular meaning. We may call this acquired perception with an asterisk: acquired perception*. These reflections reinforce the conclusion that reading doesn't reduce to Reidian original perception nor to Reidian acquired perception (which, as we observed, isn't really perception according to Reid).

For completeness' sake I add that we can say, Agnes sees the Dutch sentence expresses the proposition that everything that exists is dependent on something else. But then we are using *see* in the purely epistemic sense.[14] But this is not acquired perception either. What this shows, I think, is that reading is not (a form of) acquired perception either.

I started this discussion with the aim to clarify the relation between reading and seeing. Taking our point of departure in Reid's distinction and availing ourselves of Gisborne's distinctions, we can conclude that

[14] It is perhaps helpful to have some more illustrations of the use of *see* in the purely epistemic sense in the context of reading. When we read something and, as a result, say that we have come to *see* what the writer intended to say, then *see* is used in a purely epistemic sense. Likewise, when Frege read Russell's letter, he (as we say) *saw* that Russell was right; here, *saw* is also used in the purely epistemic sense. And when we don't know what *to procrastinate* means, consult a dictionary, and there *see* that it means "to put things off," *see* is again used in the purely epistemic sense.

although reading is a form of neither original nor acquired perception, it involves seeing in various ways. It involves

1. the original visual perception of colored shapes (usually black little lines and curves) at a particular place (normally a page); readers see these shapes in the prototypical sense of *seeing*;
2. the acquired visual perceptions* that the colored shapes are words and sentences, as well as the acquired visual perceptions that *this* colored shape is *this* particular word form (with *this* particular meaning or set of meanings); and
3. seeing that the sentences express thoughts (questions, affirmations, commands, arguments, etc.); readers see what is expressed by a sentence in the purely epistemic sense of *seeing*.

I now turn to Dretske's distinction between primary and secondary epistemic seeing.[15] Epistemic seeing, in contrast to nonepistemic seeing (seeing$_n$, as Dretske calls it), is seeing that yields belief. His analysis of primary epistemic seeing is this (the variables *S*, *b*, and *P* range over persons, things seen, and properties of things seen, respectively):

S sees that *b* is *P* in a primary epistemic way iff

(i) *b* is *P*
(ii) *S* sees$_n$ *b*
(iii) the conditions under which *S* sees$_n$ *b* are such that *b* would not look the way it now looks to *S* unless it was *P*
(iv) *S*, believing the conditions are as described in (iii), takes *b* to be *P*

There are many intricate points concerning this analysis, points that Dretske discusses at length but which I must forego. Instead, I walk through the analysis by means of an example, namely, Sander's seeing that the water is boiling. Which conditions need to be satisfied in order for this state of affairs to obtain? First, Dretske's account says, the water must be boiling. Unless the water is in fact boiling, Sander cannot see that it is boiling. Condition (i) ensures that primary epistemic seeing is factive. Of course, the satisfaction of this condition is insufficient for seeing *that*, for it may be satisfied and nobody believes that the water is boiling. The second condition requires that what Sander sees boiling is really water. He must have an object perception of water. If what he is looking at is, say, bubbling gasoline or a plateau of wet shiny rocks of somewhat uneven elevation, he is not seeing that the water is boiling. Still, the satisfaction of

[15] The account is developed in Dretske (1969), especially chapter 3, pp. 153–163.

(ii) is insufficient for the envisioned state of affairs to obtain, for Sander may object-see the water and the water may in fact be boiling without Sander forming the belief that the water is boiling. The reason for this might be that it just doesn't look to him that the water is boiling. Perhaps the lighting conditions are really bad, or perhaps his eyesight is troubling him. Condition (iii) therefore says that, for the envisioned state of affairs to occur, the conditions under which Sander sees$_n$ the boiling water must be such that the water would not look the way it looks unless it were boiling. This is still insufficient for the envisioned state of affairs to obtain. For the water may in fact be boiling, Sander may be seeing$_n$ the water, and the conditions under which he sees$_n$ the water may be such that the water wouldn't look the way it looks unless it were boiling, and yet Sander may not believe that the water is boiling. Perhaps Sander has a reason for being suspicious about the way the water looks given his current conditions; for example, his eyesight is very bad, or many things (including nonboiling things) look bubbling to him these days. Such reasons may withhold him from forming the belief that the water is boiling. That is why Dretske's condition (iv) states that, if the envisioned state of affairs is to obtain, Sander must believe that the conditions he finds himself in are as described in (iii) and that he, as a result of this belief, forms the further belief that the water is boiling.[16]

In Dretske's further explication of primary epistemic seeing, a crucial role is played by two notions that we shall need when we investigate the relevance of his account for the analysis of reading: *proto knowledge* (see Dretske 1969, 93–112) and *background beliefs* (see Dretske 1969, 112–126). To get at the first notion, compare the following two statements that I might make: (a) "I see that the water is boiling" and (b) "I see that this is boiling water." When I say (b), I am telling you that I know it is water I am seeing and that I know the water is boiling; in addition, I am telling you how I know these two facts, viz., through seeing. But when I say (a), I am telling you that I know it is water (but I am *not* telling you *how* I know this), and I am also telling you that I know it is boiling (and I *am* telling you how I know this; namely, through seeing). When I am saying (a) – so, when I am not telling you how I know it is water that is boiling – I am relying on what Dretske calls proto knowledge. Perhaps someone else informed me that the liquid I am looking at is water, or perhaps I made a prior chemical analysis of the liquid myself and found

[16] Dretske uses "takes *b* to be *P*" and "believes *b* to be *P*" as synonyms. See, for instance, Dretske (1969, 112).

out it is water. When seeing that the liquid is boiling, and knowing through some other route that it is *water* I am looking at, I can truly say (a). In that case, my knowing that it is water I'm looking at is my proto knowledge. It is because I already know that the liquid that is boiling is water that I can (say that I) see that the water is boiling. In general, proto knowledge is the knowledge perceivers have when they truly see *b* that is *P* but know that it is *b* they are seeing through another route than seeing.[17]

As to the notion *background beliefs*: condition (iv) includes the phrase that *S* believes that the conditions are as described in (iii). *S*'s background beliefs are *S*'s beliefs concerning whether the conditions are as described in (iii).

Seeing that the water is boiling in the situation as envisaged (Sander is seeing_n the water) is a case of primary epistemic seeing because the object about which the belief is formed is identical with the object that is seen_n. But the two often come apart. For instance, when we use a thermometer to measure the temperature of a patient, the object we form beliefs about is the patient, but the object seen_n is the thermometer; we see by the gauge that the car needs fuel; and we see by the way she limps that she has a broken leg. These are cases of what Dretske (1969, 153) calls secondary epistemic seeing, and his general account of it is this:

> *S* sees *b* is *P* in a secondary way iff
>
> (i) *b* is *P*
> (ii) *S* sees *c* ($c \neq b$) and sees primarily that *c* is *Q*
> (iii) conditions are such that *c* would not be *Q* unless *b* were *P*
> (iv) *S*, believing the conditions are as described in (iii), takes *b* to be *P*

Applied to the patient-thermometer case, this pans out as follows: *b* = the patient, *P* = having a temperature, *c* = the thermometer, *Q* = reads 39 degrees Celsius (say). If Sander is to see in a secondary way that the patient has a temperature, then Dretske's account requires (i) that the patient has a temperature; (ii) that Sander sees the thermometer (which is, obviously, not identical with the patient) and sees primarily that the thermometer reads 39 degrees Celsius; (iii) that the conditions are such that the thermometer would not read 39 degrees Celsius unless the patient had a temperature; and (iv) that Sander, believing that the conditions are

[17] More precisely, "*S's proto-knowledge* [is] that totality of information which *S* possesses about the identity or character of the *b* (which he sees to be *P*) at the time he sees that *b* is *P* minus only that increment in information whose *manner of acquisition* is described by saying that *S* can see that the *b* is *P*" (Dretske 1969, 96).

as described in (iii), believes (on that basis) that the patient has a temperature.

Let me now apply Dretske's account of primary and secondary epistemic seeing to reading, and begin with the first. Assuming that reading involves epistemic seeing, we should ask: What are the objects of primary epistemic seeing? In other words, what are the *b*s and *P*s that condition (i) speaks of when we are reading? The only plausible candidates for *b* are the straight and curved little lines that Agnes and Mercedes had original perceptions of. And the only plausible candidate for *P* is some such property as *being (a) written or printed word(s) or sentence(s) in a language.* Let us now assume that Agnes and Mercedes see$_n$ the straight and curved little lines; so, let us assume condition (ii) is satisfied. If this seeing is to be reading, condition (iii) requires that the conditions under which Agnes and Mercedes see$_n$ the straight and curved little black lines are such that they would not look the way they now look to them unless they were written (or printed) words (or sentences) in a language. I take it that normally this condition is satisfied. It hardly ever happens that something that is *not* a written (or printed) word (or sentence) looks like it: texts have a very definite look. Finally, condition (iv) requires that readers like Agnes and Mercedes, believing the conditions are as described in (iii), take the straight and curved little lines to be written words in a language.

It should be clear that the satisfaction of merely these conditions is, although presumably necessary, not sufficient for (the activity of) reading. For these conditions are satisfied when you are seeing$_n$ little lines in the mode of the Cyrillic script or runes or cuneiform – scripts that you don't master – and believe that what you are seeing$_n$ are written words in a language. Yet in these conditions you are not reading. Even if upon seeing these scripts you were to believe that they are written words not merely in *a* language but in the Russian, Sumerian or Akkadian, and a Germanic language, respectively, you still would not be reading. For the only thing you know when these conditions are satisfied is that the straight and curved little lines are written words in a language (or in this particular language). But that isn't reading. What prevents it from being reading, to a first approximation, is that the meaning of what is written is lost on you: you aren't grasping communicative content, not understanding what the words mean, not capturing what the text says, not getting at what the author wished to communicate.

Can Dretske's account of secondary epistemic seeing accommodate this element, viz., that it is crucial to reading that the reader (at least to some degree) captures the meaning of the text's content? Secondary seeing, as condition (ii) states, involves primary seeing, and in the case of reading the primary seeing, as I suggested earlier, must be seeing that the little lines (= *c*) are written words in a language (= *Q*). If the account of secondary seeing is to accommodate the grasp of meaning that is so crucial for reading, what then are plausible candidates for *b* and *P*? I will argue that there are no plausible candidates here and that thinking about reading as secondary epistemic seeing is therefore a dead-end street. Take any of the things that we can come to know through reading, such as that recently a bee count was held in the Netherlands, or that Kingsley Amis's *Lucky Jim* is funny, or that RMS *Lusitania* was torpedoed. If we apply the idea that reading is secondary epistemic seeing to the latter case and hence take *b* = RMS *Lusitania* and *P* = was torpedoed, we get the following:

> *S* sees that RMS *Lusitania* was torpedoed in a secondary epistemic way iff
>
> (i) RMS *Lusitania* was torpedoed
> (ii) *S* sees little lines ($c \neq b$) and sees primarily that the little lines are written/printed words (or sentences) in a language
> (iii) conditions are such that the little lines would not be written/printed words (or sentences) in a language unless RMS *Lusitania* was torpedoed
> (iv) *S*, believing the conditions are as described in (iii), takes it that RMS *Lusitania* was torpedoed

And this is wholly unconvincing. For it is irrational for *S* to believe that the conditions are as described in (iii). It is irrational for *S* to believe any of the following:

- That the little lines would not be written words in a language unless RMS *Lusitania* was torpedoed (after all, RMS *Lusitania* could be torpedoed even if the little lines were not words but just a random string of lines and curves, or if the little lines just weren't there [perhaps no one wanted to recount this nasty history]).
- That the little lines would not be written words in a specific language – say, English – unless RMS *Lusitania* was torpedoed (for reasons analogous to those just mentioned).
- That the little lines would not contain a meaningful message in, say, English unless RMS *Lusitania* was torpedoed (after all, RMS *Lusitania* could be torpedoed even if the little lines did not contain a meaningful message).
- That the little lines would not contain the meaningful message that RMS *Lusitania* was torpedoed unless RMS *Lusitania* was torpedoed (after all, RMS *Lusitania* could be torpedoed even if the little lines contained the meaningful message that RMS *Lusitania* returned home safely).

The conclusion that I think must be drawn from these reflections is that reading does not reduce to secondary epistemic seeing even though it involves it – just as reading involves primary epistemic seeing but cannot be reduced to it. This in turn suggests that reading needs its own place in epistemology; or, rather, that it needs its own epistemology. So far, I have been working with a somewhat intuitive notion of reading. Chapter 5 offers a formal analysis of it and aims to offer a comprehensive characterization of reading as a source of knowledge.

CHAPTER 5

Reading as a Source of Knowledge

This chapter aims to offer a comprehensive characterization of reading as a source of knowledge. The first section studies the use of the words *reading* and *reading that* and discusses the factivity of reading. I then offer a formal analysis of reading and of knowing through reading. Next, I take up the matter of how reading as a source of knowledge is individuated, referring back to the kinds of principles discussed in Chapter 3. The final section offers further characterizations of reading in terms of distinctions that epistemologists have used in order to structure the somewhat unwieldy field of sources of knowledge, and it sketches the many ways in which reading is connected to other sources.

Factive and Nonfactive Reading

Seeing *that*, or epistemic seeing, is factive. This is captured by the first condition in Dretske's analyses of both primary and secondary epistemic seeing. You can't see that the water is boiling if the water isn't in fact boiling. If you see that the water is boiling, then you know that it is boiling (and you know this through seeing). In this section I investigate whether reading *that* has this property of factivity as well.

Unlike seeing *that*, reading *that* could seem nonfactive. After all, although you cannot see that *p* and yet *p* be false, you can *read* that *p* and yet *p* be false. Here is an example: you can read in, say, the *Sun* that a statue of Elvis was found on Mars, although in fact there was no such statue found there. Many things we read are false. However, this doesn't all by itself show that reading can be nonfactive. Consider the following rejoinder: Well, if you have read *that* there was a statue of Elvis found on Mars, then it is a *fact* that you read *that* there was a statue found on Mars. So, contrary to what you said, reading *is* factive! This response says, in effect, that you can read *that p* and *p* be false, while at the very same time it is true *that you read that p*. You can read *that* there was a statue of

Elvis found on Mars, although no such statue was found there, while at the very same time it being true that *you read* that a statue of Elvis was found on Mars. The response is a good one in that it shows that we should make a distinction between two different kinds of situations that yet both qualify as situations in which you acquire what we might call *reading knowledge* (RK) – i.e., knowledge through reading.

- *Situation A*: You know that you have read *p*, but you don't know whether *p* is true. For instance, you have read a report in the *South Best Tribune* that a doctor at a local artificial insemination clinic has inseminated more than eighty women with his own semen. Given the kind of newspaper you think *SBT* is, you have your doubts about the report and are not inclined to believe the story is true. In that situation we should say that you don't know whether what the report says is true – so, you don't know whether the doctor inseminated more than eighty women with his own semen – but what you *do* know is that you read that *SBT* reported as much. Or you have read in *Reader's Digest* that the Vatican has been anxiously hiding from the public some old manuscripts that seriously undermine the content of the Catholic message. You don't know much about the Vatican, nor about old manuscripts, nor about the Catholic message, and you know only a little bit about *Reader's Digest*. You do the sensible thing and you suspend belief or move to disbelief. In that situation we should say that you don't know that the Vatican is anxiously hiding old manuscripts. But what you *do* know is that you read that the Vatican has been hiding manuscripts. In both of these cases you acquired a particular kind of reading knowledge, which I call RK_A.
- *Situation B*: You know that you have read that *p* (so you have RK_A), and at least in part based on that knowledge, you come to know that *p* is true. For example, you own an old sailing yacht and want to know what kind of paint they used in the old days for the boat's hull. You visit the maritime library and pick up a copy of *Old Sailing Ships Maintenance Manual*; there, you read that they used to paint hulls with a special sort of bitumen. You now know that you've read that in the old days yachts' hulls were painted with a special sort of bitumen (you have RK_A). But in addition you now also know that old ships' hulls were painted with a special sort of bitumen. This knowledge, which I call RK_B, is based on your knowledge that you *read* that old ships' hulls were painted with a special sort of bitumen. Your RK_A is, at least in part, the basis for your RK_B. (I say "at least in part" because it is

presumably also based on your background knowledge about yachts, sorts of paint, libraries and books, and more.)

By way of elucidation of the distinction between RK_A and RK_B, I offer three further remarks. *One.* RK_A is knowledge about the text, about what the words and the sentences mean: it is knowledge of textual content. To know that you read that *p* is to know that the text you have been reading says *p*. To know that you read in the *SBT* that a local doctor inseminated more than eighty women with his own semen is to know that the *SBT* says that the doctor did this – it is to know that that is (part of) the content of the report. Likewise, claims to the effect that you know that you have read that *p* in a text are claims to the effect that you know that the text says *p*. Your claim that you know you have read that the Vatican has been hiding old manuscripts from the public is a claim that the text you know you've read actually said that (had that content). I take it that these are plausible if somewhat unwieldy equations. But if they are correct, we should note that this means that reading *is* factive, for then it is impossible to know that you have read that thing about the doctor and the text not saying that thing about the doctor.

Two. In the two examples I provided, RK_A was really easy to obtain. In the first case, it was really easy to come to know that you read that a local doctor has inseminated more than eighty women with his own semen. In the second case, it was really easy to come to know that you read that the Vatican has been anxiously hiding old manuscripts from the public. For many people who are properly educated, it is often relatively easy to obtain RK_A. But it isn't always easy, especially not when we read difficult philosophical works, such as Plotinus's *Enneads*, Kant's *Critique of Pure Reason*, Adorno's *Minima moralia*, or Heidegger's *Unterwegs zur Sprache*. Nor is it so easy to obtain RK_A when we read poetry of such poets as John Milton, T. S. Elliott, Johann von Goethe, or Charles Baudelaire. Nor is it easy to obtain such knowledge when the texts were written by authors who lived in times and places far removed from where we are, such as the writers of the biblical texts, the *Epic of Gilgamesh*, or the *Mahābhārata*. Sometimes we don't know what a text means, and we are thus lacking in RK_A. Then we are in what I call a hermeneutical problem situation: due to ignorance of various kinds of things, we just don't know what a text means or says. The ignorance may be partial and temporal. There are in principle certain things we can do to try to reduce our ignorance. This is the topic of Chapter 8 in which I present an ignorance-based difficulty account of interpretation.

Three. Suppose we observe a speaker who starts out by claiming *p* and who in the Q&A session explains: "Well, I *read* that *p*." This will be perceived as a weak or weakening move. The question arises as to how we shall understand in this sentence the word *read*. It should be understood, I suggest, as being used in a factive and nonfactive way at the same time. When the speaker makes a backtracking move by saying "Well, I *read* that *p*," he uses *read p* in a nonfactive way – so, in a way that doesn't require or presuppose or entail the truth of *p*. At the same time, he uses it in a factive way, for he does claim that it is true that he has read that *p*. There is thus a distinction between factive and nonfactive reading.

To see the distinction more clearly, consider the following case. John gives a speech at a conference, in which he says: "I have been reading St. Augustine lately and read his defense of compatibilism.[1] Powerful stuff!" Eleonore, a formidable scholar of St. Augustine, stands up and urges: "Can you tell me *where* in St. Augustine's works you read this?" John begins by saying, "Oh well, of course St. Augustine doesn't use the label *compatibilism*, but what current friends of the position call by that name is Augustine's position." Eleonore repeats: "But *where* in his work do you read his defense of compatibilism?" John replies by making a reference to a passage in *De libero arbitrio*. Eleonore's response is that that passage is by no means a defense of compatibilism and that John misunderstood St. Augustine, that he read him wrong. Suppose they carefully go over the passage and Eleonore convinces John of the wrongness of attributing compatibilism to St. Augustine (and Eleonore, let us suppose, is right: St. Augustine is a libertarian). Having arrived at this stage, let us now return to John's claim that he read St. Augustine's defense of compatibilism. What should we now think of John's usage of the word *read*? We should now say, I submit, that John was making a false self-attribution. He has *not* read St. Augustine's defense of compatibilism, since there is no such thing. He *thought* he was reading such a defense, but he was mistaken; he *mis*read. Yet John had (really) been reading St. Augustine: that was true before he gave his speech and remained true after Eleonore convinced him of the wrongness of his claim. This reveals something important: one can be (said to be) reading and thereby be doing something that is nonfactive. John's reading in this sense is nonfactive in that he did not read *that* St. Augustine defended compatibilism (for that isn't what St. Augustine did), nor that compatibilism is true. John can be said to have been reading, while he cannot be said to have been reading that *p*. There is

[1] This paragraph is loosely inspired by Stump (2001).

thus a distinction between factive and nonfactive reading. The analysis of nonfactive reading – "*S* is reading" – must be different from the analysis of factive reading – "*S* is reading that *p*."

The Analysis of Reading

In this section I offer an analysis of "*S* is reading," by which I mean a specification of what must be the case if *S* is to be reading, or a bit more formally, a statement of the necessary and sufficient conditions that must be satisfied for "*S* is reading" to be true. *Reading* is a somewhat polysemous word, and my analysis aims to offer an analysis of what I take to be its paradigmatic sense. The analysis does not target a situation in which a person doesn't know Italian but can perfectly well articulate Italian words on a page: if that person reads aloud the words, his doing so is not the target of the analysis. Nor does it target the use of the word *read* in such sentences as "Read my lips" or "I was reading the lines on her face" or "She has read the situation well." The analysis, moreover, concerns reading through vision, not touch; the reason for this will become clear shortly. The analysis picks up points made in this chapter and Chapter 4. We already noted that someone may be just seeing words and sentences ($seeing_n$ or object perception) and yet not be reading, because they don't know that what they are seeing are words. This shows that (object-)seeing words and sentences (so, *seeing* is used here in the prototypical sense) is insufficient for reading, even if it is necessary for it.

We also noted that someone may fact-see words and sentences – so, see that the straight and curved little lines are words and sentences (which instances what Reid calls acquired perception and what Dretske calls primary epistemic seeing) or even see that they are Italian or Dutch words – but still not be reading. For example, you may know enough to be able to see that the words you are looking at are Italian or Dutch words, but since you don't know what the words mean and have no grasp of the syntax of these languages, you still aren't reading. One isn't reading in these cases because one doesn't know the language, or one doesn't know it well enough. This strongly suggests, first, that fact-seeing words and sentences is insufficient for reading, even if it is necessary for it; and, second, that knowing the language to which the words belong is necessary for reading – at least to some extent, for even if one has only a low proficiency in a language, one can be reading.

Fact-seeing involves believing. As we noted in Chapter 4, the belief that is involved in fact-seeing that is involved in reading need not be – and most of the time isn't – occurrent; usually, the belief is implicit and/or dispositional. When reading the previous sentence, you didn't form the occurrent belief that the first set of little lines is a word, or that it is an English word, or that it is the word *As*. Still, while reading, you believed these things non-occurrently, implicitly, dispositionally. (But now, having read the previous sentence, you presumably *do* believe them occurrently.)

Now, one may object-see the words, fact-see that they are Italian words, and even know this language (know what its words mean and know its syntax) and still not be reading. Working on the layout of the pages of a book, a graphic designer object-sees words, sees that they are, say, English words, and even knows the language, and yet they may not be reading; for example, because they are not focused on the text's content, they aren't trying to get a sense of what the words jointly mean. This shows that focusing on the content (trying to get a sense of what the words jointly mean) is also necessary for reading.[2]

This condition rules out a number of interactions with words as instances of reading in the intended paradigmatic sense. It rules out the person who can perfectly read out loud Italian words and sentences but doesn't know Italian. It also rules out the person who is reading aloud words that belong to a language they know but who does so "mechanically": they read the words all right, but they are not attending to the content, to what the words mean. That person is parroting – that is, they are articulating sounds that have meaning – but they are not reading. Finally, the condition rules out what so-called reading machines do: these pieces of assistive technology scan words and sentences and use a speech synthesizer to read them out loud.

The expression "what words jointly mean" is complex,[3] but I intend it to cover the meaning of sentences,[4] as well as the meaning of paragraphs or even larger textual units.[5] The meaning of these items can be understood or apprehended with greater or lesser accuracy and in greater or lesser depth. But *some* apprehension of the joint meaning of the words is required if one is to be reading. That is one reason why stones and cats are incapable of reading – they cannot and do not understand

[2] Like knowing a language, getting a sense of the content – or capturing what the words jointly mean – is a graded phenomenon too. One reader can have a much better sense of what the words jointly mean than another. So this condition, too, indicates a dimension in which one person can be a better reader than another. The condition suggests that the greater the reader's understanding of the joint meaning of the words is, the better the reader.

[3] See Chapter 7. [4] See Alston (2000), chapters 6 and 7.

[5] A still very informative discussion of the notion of what words jointly mean is Skinner (1969).

(or apprehend) the meaning of words. This is not to deny that certain animals can be trained to respond to words and sentences in ways that mimic the responses of humans, who do apprehend their meaning. Upon being confronted with a blackboard on which the words "Now stamp your right foot five times!" are written, both a horse and a person may respond by stamping their right foot five times. But only the person, not the horse, has *read* the words, as only the person, not the horse, has understood the joint meaning (the content) of the words. The horse is at best trained to behaviorally respond in a certain way to what are in fact words composing a sentence, but it doesn't understand the words because it doesn't see that they are words, doesn't know the language to which they belong, and doesn't form beliefs about the meaning of the words.

We noted that a person can be reading even when they *mis*apprehend the words, when they *mis*understand a text, as in the case of John who said he had read St. Augustine's defense of compatibilism. That is why, as we say, there are good, not-so-good, and bad readers. But even bad readers are readers, since they have *some* understanding of the text's content, *some* apprehension of what the units they are reading mean. To this we may add that a person is reading even when they are unsure about the precise meaning of certain words or passages.

The discussion suggests that the following conditions are individually necessary for reading. I submit they are jointly sufficient as well. So here is my proposed analysis:

S is reading iff

(i) *S* object-sees words and sentences
(ii) *S* knows the language to which the words and sentences belong; this includes acquaintance knowledge of word meanings[6]
(iii) *S* fact-sees words and sentences; i.e., *S* believes (mostly dispositionally) that what they are looking at are words and sentences that belong to this particular language, that this particular word means such and such, and so forth
(iv) through object- and fact-seeing the words and sentences, *S* acquires some understanding of what the words and sentences jointly mean – i.e., they grasp at least something of the text's content

These conditions should be understood liberally, because I should like cases such as the following to qualify as cases of reading: (1) a schoolgirl receives a text message from her friend, in what they between themselves

[6] This reflects what I argued in the second section of Chapter 1.

call "Backwards," that says "I etah loohcs," and she sympathizes with her friend; (2) you read a piece of paper with the following letter sequence on it: "Words the in sentence this are up mixed," and you get the thought. In these cases, conditions (i)–(iv), I submit, are satisfied. "Backwards" is a language, it is English with a little extra rule, and the mixed-up words are still words that belong to a language.

Three remarks should further elucidate the analysis. *One.* The analysis is in terms of seeing in the prototypical sense. However, blind people who have mastered braille can also read. Although they can't *see* words and sentences, they can *touch* them – and touch them in such a way that they acquire a sense of what the words and sentences jointly mean. Jeffrey Goodman therefore holds that reading by sight is a paradigm case of reading but is not "reading *itself*." He says (Goodman 2020, 53):

> Many blind people are capable of reading by way of feeling patterns of raised dots. But if vision and touch may facilitate reading, it seems chauvinistic to deny that reading using other sensory modalities may occur. Are there principled reasons for thinking that someone who has heard the audiobook version of *The Handmaid's Tale* . . . has failed to read that story? And if texts may be read visually or tactilely or audibly, what reason could there be for thinking that reading couldn't occur using taste buds or olfactory receptors?

These considerations find their way into his final analysis (Goodman 2020, 59):

> Person S reads text W if and only if S uses some sensory modality for the primary purpose of cognitively attending to the word structures embedded in W for the purpose of grasping the content of W, S does not relentlessly fail to grasp the entirety of W's content, and W is (partly) causally responsible for S's use of her sensory modality for that purpose (and not vice-versa).[7]

This account is unsatisfactory, at least when it is intended as an analysis of our ordinary notion of reading and not meant as a proposal in revisionary semantics. The account intentionally marks listening to an audiobook as an instance of reading. That doesn't sound right, for the simple reason that it entails either that there are virtually no analphabets or that analphabets (those that don't also have a hearing impairment) can read. The latter is a contradiction in terms, and the former is false: in 1820, 88 percent of the world's population could not read, and in 2016, 14 percent could not. In

[7] This "and not vice-versa" is included in order to exclude writing from being considered reading: in the case of writing, one's sensory modality *is* (partly) causally responsible for *W*.

fact, the account entails that most cases of listening to what someone is telling you should count as instances of reading. Suppose I am listening to your explanation of your unfortunate fall in the mountains. I then use my hearing capacity for cognitively attending to your words in order to grasp the content of what you are saying; I do grasp that content; and your speaking is (partly) causally responsible for my use of my hearing capacity. On Goodman's account I am reading – but I'm sure I am not. Hence the account is mistaken (at least when it is meant to analyze the commonsense concept of reading).

One problem with the analysis is that it aims to avoid chauvinism where there is none, and that in so aiming, it overgeneralizes. There is nothing inherently chauvinistic in saying that illiterate people cannot read. Saying that someone is illiterate doesn't by itself express any kind of moral (?) superiority over that person; it merely entails that that person cannot read. (On Goodman's analysis, it would be a silly thing for an illiterate person to say that he wants to learn how to read, for on Goodman's analysis, he is already able to read. But obviously this is not at all a silly thing to say for an illiterate person.) Nor is there anything inherently chauvinistic about saying that reading requires seeing. Saying this doesn't entail some kind of moral (?) superiority of seeing readers over blind people who use braille. Of course, it is entirely appropriate and fully standard to say that people who use braille can read. When we say this, we are using *read* in a slightly analogical sense, though. There is a historical argument for this. Braille is named after Louis Braille, a Frenchman who lost his sight as a result of a childhood accident. In 1824 he developed a code for the French alphabet as an improvement of night writing (*écriture nocturne*), which was a tactile military code designed by Charles Barbier in response to Napoleon's demand for a means for soldiers to communicate silently at night and without a light source.[8] As the code was further developed and entire books were coded in braille, their contents could be absorbed by blind people who had learned the code. When they were doing that, they could easily be said to be reading, even though they weren't doing the exact same thing as seeing people who are reading. The conditions for "*S* is reading" need rather obvious modifications if they are to apply to reading braille. But to require in the analysis of reading the unqualified "use of some sensory modality" is an overgeneralization.

[8] See the website of the American Foundation for the Blind: www.afb.org/blindness-and-low-vision/braille/what-braille.

Two. Gestalt psychologists have argued that when humans form a percept (a gestalt), the whole of what is perceived has a reality of its own: it is, in a way that I won't try to specify, independent of the reality of the perceived parts.[9] We can see a whole face even if we are only subsidiarily aware of the face's parts; the reality of seeing a whole face is, in some way, independent of seeing the parts that jointly compose the face. Reading also involves gestalt perception in the sense that at least experienced readers don't read texts by reading letter by letter and word by word. Rather they read by seeing larger wholes – not individual letters, but whole words; and often not even individual words, but entire parts of sentences, and even full sentences (when they are not too long). That is why condition (iii) explains *S*'s fact-seeing of letters and words *dispositionally*: even if, when reading, readers mostly don't form occurrent beliefs such as "This is the letter *e*" or "Here is the word *everything*," they do either dispositionally believe such things (in the way you dispositionally believe that Paris is the capital of France even when you're sound asleep or mentally occupied by other matters) or have a disposition to believe them (in the way you have a disposition to believe you are shorter than forty meters upon being asked whether you are, and you have never ever entertained the proposition "I am shorter than forty meters"). Object-seeing and fact-seeing must be understood as accommodating the gestalt element.[10]

Three. The proffered analysis isn't committed to any view on how reading and interpreting relate. It doesn't assume that reading always involves interpretation, nor that it never does, nor that it sometimes does. The proposed analysis of reading is supposed to be such that the activity picked out by it may yield knowledge.[11]

Two Kinds of Reading Knowledge

Reading, the analysis of which I have proposed in the previous section, may yield knowledge – reading knowledge, I have called it. In fact we already noted two kinds of it: RK_A and RK_B. In this section I propose their

[9] Fales (1996, chapter 3) is an in-depth discussion of gestalt-psychological aspects of seeing.

[10] See for many details Dehaene (2009), especially chapter 1.

[11] It may be objected that the account, focused as it is on *words* and *meaning*, implies that one cannot read the alphabet, because the letters of the alphabet aren't words and individually don't mean anything (except *a* and *i*). My response is that reading the alphabet indeed isn't reading – it fails to satisfy the reading conditions. So when we say "*S* is reading the alphabet," we use *reading* in an even further extended analogical way than when we say "*S* is reading braille."

analyses. Both of them include the analysis of reading, and the analysis of RK_B includes the analysis of RK_A, so that we have a nested series of analyses.

As said, RK_A is knowledge of what the text's words jointly mean, of the text's content, of what the text or its author says. We might as well call it *de dicto* knowledge as it regards knowledge of what the words that one reads mean. For the same reason we might also call it hermeneutical knowledge.

The object of analysis is "*S* knows through reading that what the text (or its author) says is *p*." Instantiations of this schema are "I know through reading *The Nature of Existence* that McTaggart argued for the unreality of time"; "Eleonore knows through reading *De libero arbitrio* that St. Augustine endorsed a qualified form of libertarianism"; "You know through reading *The Origin of Species* that Darwin saw a place for God in the biological evolution"; and "Susan knows through reading *A Christmas Carol in Prose* that Scrooge had a business partner named Marley." Here is my proposal:

> *S* has RK_A of *p* or, more precisely, *S* knows through reading that what text *T* (or its author) says is *p* iff
>
> (i) *S* has read *T*
> (ii) *T* (or its author) says *p*
> (iii) *S* believes that (ii) because (i)
> (iv) *S* has textual evidence for her belief that (ii)

I comment on these conditions subsequently.

RK_A requires that the knowledge acquired is the yield of reading, not of some other source. Condition (i) ensures this. Reading in this condition is the state of affairs described in the analysis offered above of "*S* is reading."

Knowledge is factive, and so knowledge of what a text (or its author) says is too. Condition (ii) ensures factivity – the analysis entails that a reader cannot know that a text says *p* unless the text indeed says *p*. As a comment on the use of the word *says* here, I note that this is a normal, albeit figurative, usage of the word, as texts don't speak literally – that is, they don't utter meaningful sounds.[12] Also, *says p* should not be taken to require that *p* is ever explicitly stated, although it might be. Aesop's fable doesn't contain the words "It is foolish to listen to flatterers," yet the fable

[12] In the development of his realist conception of truth, Alston initially also uses the word *say*: "A statement is true if and only if what the statement says to be the case actually is the case" (Alston 1996, 22). Eventually he shows a way to eliminate such figurative usage of *say*. I won't go so far as to show that this can be done in this case as well – but I think it can be done, and that there is value in doing it.

"says" (in the intended sense of *says*) that it is foolish to listen to flatterers. When readers get from reading text *T* to understanding what it (or its author) says, some form of interpretation may be going on. (This is a very loose statement; in later chapters I have much more to say about interpretation.)

The satisfaction of the first two conditions is of course insufficient for *S* having RK_A, for I might have read *T*, and *T* (or its author) may indeed say *p*, and yet I may not *know* that *T* (or its author) says *p* simply because I don't believe it (perhaps the thought did not occur to me, or perhaps I was absentminded, distracted, not sufficiently alive to the text). That is why condition (iii) requires that *S believes* that *T* (or its author) says *p*. This condition also requires that *S* believes this *because S* has read *T*. This is to rule out scenarios like the following: I already believe that for a short period of time after World War II, the Indonesian islands formed a political federation. Now I read a book that says as much. So conditions (i) and (ii) are satisfied, but (iii) is not, for I don't believe this *because* I've read it. The word *because* here signals a causal relation.

But even if conditions (i), (ii), and (iii) are satisfied, *S* may not have reading knowledge for the simple reason that, although *T* says *p*, *S* has no reason to believe *p*, or they have the wrong reasons for believing *p*, and hence *S*'s belief is true by luck. Condition (iv) should exclude this possibility. This condition is motivated by the same sort of considerations that motivate antiluck conditions on knowledge in general.[13] As indicated before, in many cases of reading this condition is rather easily satisfied; for instance, when we read travel guidebooks, cookbooks, or a manual on beekeeping, at least when they are of recent date and written in a language we know. But it can also be quite difficult; for example, when we are reading ancient texts written in styles and genres we're not familiar with, such as the *Mahābhārata* or the tracts of Duns Scotus, or, more recently, when we read modernist poetry, contemporary French philosophical works, or articles in scientific journals.

For RK_A nothing more is needed. The conditions mentioned are individually necessary and jointly sufficient – on the assumption, that is, that knowledge is indeed true belief that is justified. (This means that I am abstracting from Gettier problems that can arise in this context.)

Let's now move to the analysis of RK_B, which we might also name *de re* knowledge, or worldly knowledge, since RK_B concerns not what it is that is

[13] For this motivation, see Pritchard (2005).

written but whether what is written (and what we read) is true. The analysis incorporates, for obvious reasons, the analysis of RK_A, for you cannot know that *p* through reading unless *p* is indeed what the text (or its author) says. Here is my proposal:

> *S* has RK_B or, more precisely, *S* knows through reading that what text *T* (or its author) says (viz., *p*) is true iff
>
> (i) *S* believes that *p* because *S* has RK_A of *p*
> (ii) *S* is justified in believing *p* at least in part because *S* has RK_A of *p*
> (iii) *p* is true

By way of explanation, if through reading you are to know that *p* (and *p* is a worldly proposition), then you should believe *p*. Condition (i) requires this. It also requires that you believe *p because* you believe that *T* says *p* on the basis of your reading *T*. *Because* again signals a causal relation. The causal element is required, for you may believe *p* but, although the text also says *p*, you already believed *p* prior to reading; accordingly, you don't believe *p because* you read *T*, in which case your knowing *p* is not a case of reading knowledge.

Yet more is needed, for your worldly belief should be justified at least in part because you know that *T* (or its author) says *p*. The qualifier "at least in part" in condition (ii) is needed because all kinds of background knowledge are normally involved in justifying a worldly belief through reading as well. For instance, through reading *De bello Gallico* you can acquire justification for many beliefs about the Germanic peoples. But that justification is only in part due to what you read in Caesar's famous work. Many background beliefs are required as well, such as the belief that Gaul is a geographical area, that Caesar is a person (not a horse), that the text has an informational purpose and intends to communicate states of affairs (it is not a fairy tale), and many things more. Here we approach the epistemology of testimony.

It is possible that prior to reading *T* one already believed that *p* but that reading in *T* that *p* adds to the justification of one's belief that *p*. In that case (and if *p* is true), one's knowing that *p* is not a case of *pure* worldly reading knowledge – it is a mixed case. It is also possible that prior to reading *T* you already believed that *p*, but you learn through reading *T* that the justificatory basis for your belief was shaky, and that reading *T* provides a much better basis for it. In that case, you did acquire pure worldly reading knowledge.

Finally, as (iii) has it, *p* should be true, which is again an acknowledgment that knowledge is factive.

These, I claim, are the individually necessary and jointly sufficient conditions for worldly reading knowledge.

Having these analyses of reading knowledge before us, we must revisit the list of examples of things that can be known through reading (in the indicated contexts; see Chapter 4) but do not qualify as testimonial knowledge. The question to consider is whether the things on the list that I claimed are known by reading are instances of RK_A or RK_B.

Consider (a), coming to know through reading Greene's *This Gun for Hire* that its opening sentence reads "Murder didn't mean much to Raven." This case cannot be aligned with the base clause of either RK_A or RK_B; there is something wrong with filling out its base clause in the following way:

- *S* knows through reading that what *This Gun for Hire* (or its author) says is that the opening sentence of that book reads "Murder didn't mean much to Raven."

The same problem arises for (b), knowing through reading that the text contains many metaphorical expressions, as well as for some of the other cases: they cannot be molded into the base clause of RK_A. All of the following fill-ins are bogus:

- *S* knows through reading that what the text (or its author) says is that the text contains many metaphorical expressions.
- *S* knows through reading that what the text (or its author) says is that the book is funny.
- *S* knows through reading that what the text (or its author) says is that the article contains an invalid argument.
- *S* knows through reading that what the text (or its author) says is that it is based on a misunderstanding.

What goes wrong is this: the things on the list are known through reading *but not* because the text (or its author) says so. That was the reason the examples were constructed in the first place – so as not to be instances of testimony. This may mean that there is a further kind of reading knowledge that is instantiated in these cases. I address this matter in the next section.

The Source that Reading Is: A Third Kind of Reading Knowledge

I suggested in Chapter 4 that reading is a source of knowledge in its own right. The individuation of that source requires more attention. In this section, I discuss what the "something in the life of a knower" is that yields belief that can constitute knowledge in the case of reading – I examine what it is that knowledge "comes from."

At first blush, three initially somewhat plausible candidates present themselves:

A. words and sentences, or texts
B. the reading of words and sentences, or texts
C. the reader's emotive, logical, moral, and other kinds of responses to the reading of words and sentences, or texts

Candidate (A) can be written off almost immediately as words on surfaces *as such* don't yield beliefs, just as horses and paintings *as such* don't yield perceptual beliefs. Moreover, words, sentences, and texts are not processes; and sources of knowledge are processes – or so I have argued. It is the *reading* of words and sentences that yields belief, just as it is the *perception* of horses and paintings that may yield belief.

Yet we cannot simply settle on (B) as the best delineation of the source that reading is, for the following reason. One of the things that we may come to know through reading, I suggested in the first section of Chapter 4, per example (d), is that a particular book is humorous (Kingsley Amis's *Lucky Jim*, for example) or horrifying (Bram Stoker's *Dracula*, for example). However, we might need to be more specific here. For the question arises whether we come to know these things (assuming we do come to know them) (1) through reading these books or (2) through reading these books and through noticing our emotive responses to what we read. If the former, then (B) is a good description of that something in the life of a knower; if the latter, then a combination of (B) and (C) is.

An argument for (C) might be that we laugh (out loud or silently) when we read Amis and that we probably feel scared when we read Stoker, and that if we hadn't actually had these emotive responses, we wouldn't have known *through reading these books* that they are humorous and horrifying, respectively.[14] This suggests that the emotive responses we have while reading should be considered part of the something in the life of a knower that can yield belief constituting knowledge.

In the same vein, I suggested – per case (e) – that we can come to know through reading it that the article contains an invalid argument. But we cannot come to know this through reading unless we also attend to our

[14] It goes without saying that we could also come to know that these books are humorous and horrifying because some authoritative person reports this.

logic-sensitive responses to the argument presented in the article. This suggests that our logical response to what we read must also be considered part of the source of knowledge that is associated with reading. This logical response is also operative in (h): the reader comes to know that the author assumes that *p* because that is the inevitable though unobvious conclusion that the reader must draw, given what the author explicitly says. It is also operative in (k): the reader comes to know through reading the proof that the square root of two is not a rational number.

Moreover, I suggested that one can come to know through reading, as in (f), that the review is based on a misunderstanding. But in order to come to know this that way, one must remember what the work reviewed did say. So, to obtain the knowledge as described in (f), one must attend to what is stored in one's memory, which suggests that the memorial responses to what is read must be considered part of the source that is associated with reading. This memorial response also accounts for example (i), where the reader comes to know that the author is intimately familiar with the Scottish Enlightenment.

Also, coming to know by reading a "clean" statement of facts and figures that some of the things the Dutch did in the Caribbean were wrong, as in example (j), requires that readers have moral sensibilities. These sensibilities should therefore also be considered part of the source of knowledge that is associated with reading.

Likewise, we can come to know that words are aesthetically pleasing, beautiful, sublime, uplifting, grave, and the like; and again, in order to come to know this through reading, we must attend to the responses of our aesthetic sensibilities while reading.

The conclusion of this line of thought thus seems to be that the something in the life of a knower that is connected with reading and that yields beliefs that constitute knowledge is captured by (C). The source of knowledge that reading is, is the reader's emotive, logical, moral, and other kinds of responses to the words and sentences they read.

However, there is an argument for (B) that I think is better than the argument for (C). Consider (e) again – someone comes to know through reading that the article contains an invalid argument. Suppose now someone reads the article and does not see that it contains an invalid argument. That person may come to know through reading *what the argument is* (which is an instance of RK_A) even if they don't come to know *that it is invalid.* This suggests that in (e), reading works its cognitive wonders in conjunction with reason: through reading, the person comes to know what the argument is, and through reason, they come to know that it is invalid. But the former could happen without the latter.

Similarly, in (f) – coming to know through reading that the review is based on a misunderstanding – one can read the review and simply miss the point that it is based on a misunderstanding. Case (f) as described should therefore be analyzed as a case in which reading works its cognitive effects in conjunction with memory and reason: through reading, one comes to know what it is that the reviewer says about the book, and through memory and reason, one comes to know that what the reviewer says is based on a misunderstanding. But if one's memory was failing or one's reason not fully alert, one would not have come to know that the review was based on a misunderstanding. Yet one would or could have known through reading what the article said.

In a similar vein, one can come to know through reading the facts and figures related to the Dutch presence in the Caribbean and yet not come to know that what the Dutch did was wrong, although the person has surely read the facts and figures, even if his moral sense didn't work as it should. If, as described in (j), the reader comes to know *through reading* that what the Dutch did in the Caribbean was wrong, the epistemic benefit thus gained was worked by both reading and the reader's moral sense.

These considerations suggest that (B) should be preferred over (C) as the description of that something in the life of a knower that yields beliefs that can constitute knowledge. (B) more elegantly accounts for cases in which reason, memory, the moral sense, and presumably other sources as well do *not* work as they should or could but the reading is nevertheless as good as it should be. (B) thus describes more adequately the source that reading is. Reading works its cognitive effects (provides knowledge and understanding), as specified in the cases on the list, in conjunction with other sources.

This is the place to return to the topic of understanding through reading. One cognitive benefit of reading, I argued in Chapter 2, is understanding, and I distinguished various kinds of understanding that reading can yield. One of these is what I called a Type I understanding of a text – i.e., an understanding of how the text's parts hang together so as to work its effects. Another kind of understanding reading may afford is a Type I understanding of the text's Matter, in that reading may give insight into what Grimm calls the modal space around a focal event or state of affairs. What I again want to draw attention to is that when an understanding of a text or its Matter is gained through reading, reading works this wonder in conjunction with other sources, notably reason, as reason is the source that gives insight into what is possible, impossible, and necessary – it is reason that is at work when we form modal beliefs.

These reflections bring us back to the problem I mentioned at the end of the previous section, namely, that examples (a)–(k) are instances of neither RK_A nor RK_B, yet they are in crucial respects instances of reading knowledge. For in these cases there would not be knowledge unless the text at hand was read. We therefore need to distinguish a third type of reading knowledge, RK_C. Here is my proposal:

> *S* has RK_C of *p* or, more precisely, *S* knows through reading text *T* that *p*, where *p* is *not* something that the text (or its author) says, iff
>
> (i) *S* has read *T*
> (ii) *S* knows from other sources that *q*
> (iii) *S* believes *p* because (i) and (ii)
> (iv) *p* is true
> (v) *S* is justified in believing *p*

This analysis gives the right result for case (a) on the list:

> *S* knows through reading Greene's novel that it opens with "Murder didn't mean much to Raven" iff
>
> (i) *S* has read *This Gun for Hire*
> (ii) *S* knows from other sources (perhaps induction, reflection, reason) that texts have opening sentences
> (iii) *S* believes that Greene's novel opens with "Murder didn't mean much to Raven" because (i) and (ii)
> (iv) Greene's novel opens with "Murder didn't mean much to Raven"
> (v) *S* is justified in believing that Greene's novel opens with "Murder didn't mean much to Raven"

Condition (i) states that, if the knowledge that the base clause describes is to occur, *S* must at the very least have read the novel. Condition (ii) reflects the fact that some knowledge from other sources must be in place if the knowledge is to arise; in this case, the knowledge that texts have opening sentences. Condition (iii) is a causal condition that ensures that the belief that constitutes knowledge is due to the fact that *S* has read the novel and knows that texts have opening sentences. Factivity condition (iv) and justification condition (v) must also be satisfied if *S* is to have knowledge; and they obviously are. All these conditions are necessary, and jointly they are sufficient for *S*'s knowing that Greene's novel opens with "Murder didn't mean much to Raven." This looks good, then. Applied to case (f), the analysis gives a correct result as well:

> *S* knows through reading review *R* that it is based on a misunderstanding of the book under review iff

(i) *S* has read *R*
(ii) *S* knows the content of the book under review
(iii) *S* believes *R* is based on a misunderstanding because (i) and (ii)
(iv) *R* is based on a misunderstanding
(v) *S* is justified in believing that *R* is based on a misunderstanding

I submit that similar analyses can be given of the other cases on the list. Between them there are subtle and interesting differences, for instance, as to what is required for condition (v) to be satisfied. But I will not delve into these details any further, as I suspect that the above reflections and applications suffice to show the reality of RK_C and that at least some examples on the list are instances of it.

Further Characterizations of Reading as a Source

In this section, I offer further clarifications of the kind of source that reading is. I present some well-known distinctions that epistemologists have used to differentiate between kinds of sources and apply them to reading.

As I noted earlier, Ernest Sosa has said that "there are faculties of two broad sorts: those that lead to beliefs from beliefs already formed, and those that lead to beliefs but not from beliefs" (Sosa 1991, 225).[15] The former he calls transmission faculties, the latter, generation faculties. An example that he offers of the former is rationalist deduction: you believe that you are 1.94 meters tall, from which you deduce that you are shorter than 30 meters – which is a proposition that you also believe. An example that Sosa offers of the latter is visual perception: this faculty may generate the belief that the object you are looking at is round and yellow.

Sosa's distinction can be recast in terms of sources. Transmission sources have propositional output as well as propositional input; generation sources have propositional output but nonpropositional input. Applied to reading, we can see that reading often is a transmission source. For instance, I read your message that you will arrive at O'Hare airport next Tuesday at 6:00 p.m.: this is something you believe (and perhaps even know) and that I, through reading your message, now also believe (and know). There is belief input as well as belief output – belief that may amount to RK_A and even RK_B. However, reading is not *only* a transmission source, for as I have suggested, someone may come to know, by reading the book, that *Lucky Jim* is very funny. Coming to know this that

[15] Alston (1993, 6) makes the same distinction.

way, however, is not a matter of belief transmission; it is not, to repeat, a matter of testimony. It isn't that Kingsley Amis believed the book to be funny and made "This book is funny" part of the propositional content of the book, and that the reader picked up that proposition by reading the book. Reading the book didn't *transmit* that belief or knowledge – it *generated* it. The knowledge at hand is neither RK_A nor RK_B; it is RK_C. In a similar vein, one may come to know – as in (j) – that what the Dutch did in the Caribbean was wrong by reading a "clean" statement of facts and figures. Even if the author of the statement had no evaluative response to these facts and figures when they wrote them down, the reader may nonetheless come to know through reading the statement that what the Dutch did was wrong. In this case, reading is a transmission source (of RK_A and RK_B) and a generation source (of RK_C) at the same time. Generally speaking, reading can be both a transmission and a generation source. In this respect reading is like memory, if Lackey and Ginet are right.[16]

If we also consider acquaintance knowledge and know-how, it would seem that reading can be a generation source of the former and a transmission source of the latter. As I argued in Chapter 1, certain kinds of know-how can be transmitted through reading: reading a computer manual or cookbook can transmit knowledge of how to turn on your new computer or how to prepare a casserole, respectively. This is testimonial know-how. In addition, as I also argued in Chapter 1, reading can generate both knowledge by acquaintance of propositions and proxy knowledge by acquaintance of experiences.

Robert Audi (2002, 72) distinguishes between sources that are basic in the sense that they "[yield] knowledge without positive dependence on the operation of some other source of knowledge" and sources that are non-basic. Perception and reflection, he argues, are basic. One might know through perception that the flowers are yellow, and one might know through reflection that if two persons are first cousins, they share a pair of grandparents. In neither case does this knowledge positively depend on the operation of other sources. At the same time, a basic source may be *negatively* dependent on the operation of some other source in that one may acquire a defeater from other sources for a belief yielded by a basic source. If you believe, upon seeing them, that the flowers are yellow, but you also remember that the shopkeeper tends to manipulate the lighting, then your belief doesn't constitute knowledge, even if the flowers are in

[16] Lackey (2008, 251–277) and Ginet (1975, 148–153) argue that memory is a generation source.

fact yellow. This negative dependence on memory, however, doesn't compromise the basicality of perception.

Although one might doubt that perception and reflection are basic sources – after all, seeing movement and reflection both seem to require memory (of past place and of concepts, respectively) – there can be no doubt that reading is not a source that yields knowledge without positive dependence on the operation of some other source of knowledge. As argued in this chapter, reading is positively dependent on perception. It is also positively dependent on memory, for when one reads a paper or book, one needs to have some recollection of the previous parts of what one has been reading in order to get a sense of the content of the text. Reading is even more basically dependent on memory because readers must have some sort of memory knowledge of word meanings and grammar. Also, as was argued in the previous section, when we come to know through reading that the book is funny, that the article contains an invalid argument, that what is described is morally wrong, and so forth, reading is positively dependent on such sources as our aesthetic sense and moral sense, reason, and memory. There are many things we could not come to know through reading – things that we in fact *can* come to know through reading – without these other sources lending a helping hand.

Audi suggests a distinction between "essential" and "inessential" sources. He qualifies a source as essential if "what we think of as 'our knowledge,' in an overall sense, would collapse" without it (Audi 2002, 74). He argues that memory, while not basic, is an essential source. For without memory we would only know those parts and aspects of the world and of ourselves that present themselves immediately to our senses. We wouldn't recognize things; we wouldn't know past events; we wouldn't notice movement and development. Without memory, "'our knowledge,' in an overall sense," (henceforth simply referred to as "our knowledge") would collapse indeed.[17]

Inessential sources should thus be sources without which our knowledge would not collapse. Audi gives no examples, but might reading be one? In order to discuss this question, we should look into the notion of our knowledge as it can be fleshed out in various ways. The more relevant ones are

a. the totality of an individual person's knowledge acquired up to a particular time *t*

[17] BonJour (1998) is a forceful argument for the claim that reason (a priori rational insight) is an essential source.

b. the totality of an individual person's knowledge that is needed for basic survival
c. the totality of what the human race has come to know up to a particular time *t*
d. the totality of what the human race has come to know and that is needed for basic survival
e. the totality of what the human race so far has come to know and, in the future, will come to know

We should also look into the notion of collapse as it is used here in the context of our knowledge collapsing. This notion can be fleshed out in various ways as well; for instance,

x. it stops to exist
y. it gets truncated to some degree

This setup enables us to formulate the following question: If reading is not a source of knowledge, which of the following scenarios would be likely to obtain: (a/x), (a/y), (b/x), (b/y), (c/x), (c/y), (d/x), (d/y), (e/x), or (x/y)?

Prior to the invention of writing, reading was not a source at all, and a fortiori not an essential source. In those days, none of the scenarios obtained.[18]

Suppose now we go forth in time until after the invention of writing, but prior to the invention of book printing (Fischer 2004; Jack 2019). In that long era, most individuals didn't have any reading knowledge, and hence for them neither (a/x) nor (a/y) nor (b/x) nor (b/y) obtained: the totality of what they knew, or that subsegment of it that is needed for basic survival, didn't stop to exist, nor did it get severely truncated. For a select group of individuals, though, reading knowledge became part of the totality of their knowledge. If their RK_B was to be excised from it, some totality would remain, but in a truncated form. For them scenario (a/y) obtains, but not (b/x) or (b/y), for the knowledge needed for basic survival would remain.

Still focusing on the same era, if we next look to humankind as a whole, excising what was known through reading would truncate the totality of what was known to some degree – which means that (c/y) obtains – but it would not truncate the knowledge needed for basic survival; this means (d/y) would not obtain, and certainly not (d/x).

[18] Dehaene (2009, chapter 4) gives detailed information about the development of writing systems.

Let's now make a leap well into the twenty-first century. In large parts of the world, we must note the ubiquity and centrality of the written media and the expansion of libraries and of the World Wide Web. If what individuals living in the modern Western world know through reading were to be erased from the totality of what they know, that would be a serious truncation of what they individually know. Scenario (a/y) would obtain, although (b/y) would not, as the knowledge needed for basic survival could still be present. Shifting from the individual to humankind as a whole, we should say that the excision of what we have come to know through reading from the totality of what we know would be a very serious truncation of that totality – scenario (c/y) would obtain, but (d/y) would not, as the knowledge needed for basic survival can still be present. (But it should be noted that in the modern Western world it has become increasingly difficult to live your life above basic survival level if you cannot read.)

So far, I have left (e) out of consideration. But if we think of our knowledge as the totality of what the human race so far has come to know and in the future will come to know, then the inevitable conclusion appears to be that, if what is now known and will come to be known through reading were excised from the totality, there would be a near-total collapse of our knowledge. After all, if knowledge gathered in the past and the present may not be communicated through reading (so, only through speaking), vast stretches of what we now think we know would be lost. It would seem that without reading, our knowledge would collapse indeed. The conclusion then seems to be that, whereas reading once was an inessential source, as time went by it became for ever more people an essential one.

Finally, Audi defines a "unique source of knowledge" as a source that yields knowledge that "is not otherwise acquirable" (Audi 2002, 75). What we know through memory can normally also be known through perception: one may *remember* that the flowers are wilting, but one may also *see* that they are. This means that neither memory nor visual perception is a unique source.

Is *reading* a unique source of knowledge? In many cases it is not. Much knowledge acquired through reading can or could also be acquired through some other source. I may come to know that the Tate Gallery is open through reading as much in the newspaper; but I may also come to know this by just seeing that it is open. However, a case could be made that at least *sometimes* reading *is* a unique source, depending on the sort of text that the words one is reading belong to. Reading certain kinds of poetry, for instance, or reading elaborate historical narratives may yield in a reader beliefs that constitute knowledge that could not be yielded by any other source. The particular knowledge of human psychology that can be acquired by reading John Steinbeck's *Of Mice and Men* may, perhaps, not be yielded by any other source.[19] If this is correct, reading sometimes is a unique source of knowledge. In Chapter 6 I return to this topic when I develop the idea of creative-investigative writing.

By way of summary, then, in this chapter I argued, first, that there is a distinction to be made between factive and nonfactive reading. Next, I proposed an analysis of nonfactive reading (i.e., of "*S* is reading"). Based upon that analysis, I offered analyses of three kinds of reading knowledge. Finally, I argued that reading is both a transmission source and a generation source, a nonbasic source, and increasingly an essential source, and that sometimes it is even a unique source.

[19] A point in this direction is made by Gibson (2009).

CHAPTER 6

The Objects of Reading Are the Products of Writing

Reading has texts as its objects. These objects are the products of writing. This chapter aims to get a better view of these objects. It does so by comparing writing and speaking, for the question must have occurred to the reader whether there is any reason to focus the discussion in this book on *reading what is written* while abstracting from *listening to what is spoken*. After all, can't we also acquire knowledge (in all three varieties) by listening? Can't listening, too, bring us understanding of various types? And if my argument in Chapter 5 is any good, isn't there then a parallel argument for the conclusion that *listening* is a source of knowledge as well? I am not going to argue for it, but I take it for granted that these questions should be answered affirmatively: yes, through listening we can acquire knowledge and understanding; and yes, if my argument in Chapter 5 is any good, then there is a parallel argument for the conclusion that listening is a source too. Yet there is something special and unique about reading. It has to do with its objects: these have properties that the objects of listening lack – either entirely, or to some degree. The purpose of this chapter is to get a grip on the objects of reading by comparing them to the objects of listening. To be more precise, my aim is to get a grip on the *nature* of these objects, and this chapter delves, therefore, to a certain extent into the metaphysics of texts; in doing so, epistemological questions will temporarily recede to the background.

This chapter is organized as follows. In the first section, I highlight a number of important commonalities between speaking and writing. Next, I discuss some of Paul Ricoeur's thoughts on the distinction between speaking and writing, and I argue that Ricoeur doesn't actually grasp what he is reaching for. In the final section, I state what I think is truly special about writing – or rather, about a certain kind of writing.

The Fourfold Intentionality of Speaking and Writing

The first thing we should note about speaking and writing is that they are actions performed by persons. Nonpersons neither speak nor write, even if they communicate.[1] Bees, birds, dolphins, whales, and many other animals communicate with their likes, but they don't write (this seems obvious), nor do they speak in the specific sense that they don't employ a set of words and a system of grammatical rules that enable them to write down or vocally articulate an in principle infinite number of unique and meaningful sentences. Even though a number of attempts have been made to teach a language (with words and grammatical rules) to chimpanzees and dolphins and to communicate with them by means of these languages (notably American Sign Language and a system of visual symbols), the conclusion seems to be that nothing approximating human language capacity has been demonstrated in nonhumans.[2] Speaking and writing words that compose sentences, which in turn compose larger textual units, are uniquely acts of human persons.

Second, speaking and writing are personal actions of a special kind. They are *intentional* actions, in four different senses.[3] They are, first, actions that are normally performed intentionally; that is, they are not due to chance, they are not flukes or coincidences. Persons who speak or write normally have the intention, even the conscious intention, to speak or to write. Some actions that persons perform are *not* performed intentionally – for example, stumbling, knocking over a vase, and stuttering. Actions that are intentionally performed are actions that agents *set out* to perform. For this reason the following holds: when a person is performing an intentionally performed (in one word, an *intended*) action, they normally know what they are doing, what action they are performing. When you're speaking or writing, you can therefore normally answer the question "What are you doing?," for you normally know the answer, which is "I am speaking" or "I am writing," as the case may be (more specifically, it is "I am saying that . . ." or "I am writing about . . . ," respectively).

I said that speaking and writing are intentionally performed actions that you *normally* know you're performing. The qualifier is added to accommodate a number of phenomena: (i) One may be mumbling, which is a

[1] Sue Donaldson and Will Kymlicka (2011) and Donna Haraway (2007) stress the continuity between humans and nonhuman animals, among other things, in that all have rights. I stress that there is no obvious entailment from the inability to use a language to lacking rights.

[2] This conclusion is argued for by Clive D. L. Wynne and Monique A. R. Udell (2013, 277–296).

[3] In-depth studies of the notion of intention include Anscombe (1957) and Bratman (1999).

form of speaking, without having the intention to mumble, and without knowing that one is mumbling; one may mumble due to a psychological or psychiatric condition. (ii) One may be speaking without having the intention to speak and without even knowing that one is speaking; this is the case when one is talking in one's sleep. (iii) Persons suffering from Gilles de la Tourette syndrome may swear and curse – so, speak – without having the intention to swear or to curse. (iv) Deeply confused persons may write things without having the intention to write and without even knowing they are writing. (v) Finally, there is the phenomenon of *écriture automatique* that merits attention. This expression names, first, the phenomenon of writing down, without any policing influence of morality or political correctness, words and thoughts that spontaneously come to mind. It is the phenomenon that André Breton, an admirer of Sigmund Freud, was so enthusiastic about and that he used with Philippe Soupault in writing *Les champs magnetiques* (1920), a prime example of surrealistic writing. Here there is writing, and the authors even had the intention to write, but they did not have the intention to write anything in particular, for they didn't know (i.e., they didn't know in advance) *what* they were writing, or what they were writing *about* – if indeed there *was* something they wrote about. This is partly an exception to what is normally the case, since when a person is writing they normally know not only *that* they are writing but also *what* they are writing. There is a second, more involved form of *écriture automatique* in which one doesn't even know that one is writing. This is when one is writing in trance or under hypnosis. This is a clear exception to what is normally the case when one is writing.

The exceptions referred to do, however, testify to the fact that speaking and writing normally are actions performed intentionally; our performing them is no fluke, no coincidence, not a matter of mere happenstance.

The second way in which speaking and writing are intentional is that they normally are actions that target other persons; they are directed to others. When you speak or write, you normally want to communicate something to others: what you say or write is normally addressed to someone. This can be a very specific person or a well-defined set of persons (such as one's colleagues in the Department of Philosophy or one's co-members on the school board) but also less well-defined groups; Kierkegaard, for instance, addressed his contemporaries, Schleiermacher the cultured despisers of religion, and Churchill his then-living fellow Britons. The speech or text can also be addressed not to anyone in particular but to a hoped-for readership or audience (so, possible readers and listeners); for example, when you publish a book directed to no one in particular, or you give a radio speech directed to all and sundry. Other examples are a message in a bottle, and texts written in the hope that some future person will read and appreciate them (as in the case of Etty Hillesum's writings). Many actions are not intentional in this sense, as they don't target other persons: breathing is an example, and so are blowing your nose, riding a bike, smoking a cigarette, and watching the sun setting.

Again I added the qualifying word *normally*, this time to accommodate the following phenomena: (i) You can exercise or rehearse the delivery of a speech without anybody being present, and so without targeting or addressing anybody at that time. (ii) One can make notes for personal use only, thus not targeting other persons but oneself at a later time. Or one can write a diary only for oneself. Normally, however, when a person is speaking or writing, there are others who are targeted. In the interest of having as wide a notion of targeting as possible, we could say that speaking and writing are intentional in the sense that both are directed to persons, which may be other persons, your own person, God (if existent), or a combination of these.

A third way in which speaking and writing are intentional is that speaking and writing are normally about things. We speak and write about, say, the weather, politics, Napoleon's battles, Browning's poems, where we are going, why we did this and not that, when the game will start, who won the 2016 Nobel Prize in Literature, why William the Silent married four times, and what happened on the island of Utoya on July 26, 2011. Speaking and writing are intentional in the sense that what is said and written concerns things sometimes far removed, spatially as well as temporally, from where the speaker or the writer happens to be. Someone in Amsterdam can speak about the Swiss Alps, and someone living in 2019 can write about the First World War. These cases indicate and illustrate that speaking and writing normally have propositional content. Propositional content can be explained further by means of two other notions, which I borrow from Nicholas Wolterstorff (1995, 138–139), viz., the *noematic content* and the *designative content* of illocutionary actions. A fourteenth-century speaker who assertively utters "Regina mortua est," a late twentieth-century Dutchman who assertively utters "De koningin is dood," and an early twenty-first-century Brit who asserts "The queen is dead" say things with the same noematic content (they say in different languages the same thing, viz., that the queen is dead) but with different designative content, since they refer, we are assuming, to three different queens. Similarly, when Wolterstorff says "I have a cold" and his wife says "Nick has a cold" and someone else says "The 1993 Wilde Lecturer has a cold," then their utterances differ in noematic content but have the same designative content. Speaking and writing normally have propositional content, and thus they have noematic and designative content.

The qualifier (i.e., *normally*) accommodates cases of confused speaking due to, perhaps, Alzheimer's disease and cases of delightful nonsense poetry that lack propositional content, which accordingly are not *about* anything. A famous example of the latter is Lewis Carroll's poem *Jabberwocky* in *Through the Looking-Glass* (1871), which starts with these words: "'Twas brillig, and the slithy toves / Did gyre and gimble in the wabe; / All mimsy were the borogoves, / And the mome raths outgrabe." Many nursery rhymes fall in this category too. This goes to show that, normally, what we say and write does have propositional content.

The fourth and final way in which speaking and writing are intentional is that by (or by means of, or through) speaking and writing, persons normally attain, and intend to attain, a wide array of aims that are external to the speaking or writing. For example, speakers and writers may intend to inform their hearers or readers, motivate them, interrogate them, warn them, entertain them, convince them of something, or ask them a question. There is a contrast here with actions that are *not* means through which one intends to attain some goal that is external to the actions themselves – such actions are ends in themselves.[4] Examples include taking a stroll just for the fun of it, sitting on the beach just to see the setting of the sun, enjoying the taste of chocolate, reading John Betjeman's poetry just because you are curious, and listening to Mozart's Requiem or Brahms's First Symphony simply because they are so beautiful. These are examples of actions that aim to attain no particular goal, or perhaps better, these actions aim to attain no goal for which they are instrumental (see Anscombe 1957; Audi 1993). We might also say that these actions are aims in themselves. Normally, speaking and writing are not aims in themselves – they are, in the preponderance of cases, instrumentally aimed at the attainment of certain goals. This holds across the genres, so for newspaper reports as well as poems, for novels as well as scientific papers, for historical works as well as science fiction.

The qualifier is needed here in order to accommodate the following: (i) One may speak "just like that," without having any aim that is external to the speaking, as is the case when children are in the process of mastering a

[4] A very involved discussion of ends in themselves is Schlick (1927).

language and when actors and actresses vocalize their parts during rehearsals. (ii) One may write down words without intending any effect in possible readers. The writing down is an end in itself, performed "just for the fun of it"; it is done just to see what comes of it. Normally, however, there is something that speakers and writers aim to attain by speaking and writing. Normally, speakers and writers have perlocutionary intentions.

Having explained the fourfold sense in which speaking and writing normally are intentional, I now turn to a third communal feature. Both speaking and writing are normative activities in the sense that there are norms that speakers and writers should adhere to. These norms are of various kinds. There are norms having to do with grammar and lexicon: these norms specify which sentences are grammatical and which are not, and they specify word meanings, thus embodying norms for correct and incorrect language usage. There are norms appertaining to clarity, style, and tone, as well as norms having to do with structure and length. There are social norms: some words and turns of phrases display bad taste, while others ooze gentility; in certain circles, certain things had better not be said, or not said in this particular way, and so forth. There are also straightforward moral norms for speaking and writing: we shouldn't speak or write lies, make false accusations, or air slander and suspicions; rather, speakers and writers should aim to be reliable informants and honest communicators. Speakers and writers bear responsibility for their productions. There are also aesthetic ideals attached to speaking and writing, ideals having to do with elegance, word choice, sentence construction, use of metaphors, and so on.

So, speaking and writing have a number of communal features. But they are also different. In the next section I discuss Paul Ricoeur's take on the difference.

Paul Ricoeur on the Differences between Speaking and Writing

Differences can be of various kinds. The most fundamental distinction here is between *differences in kind* and *differences in degree*. Examples of pairs of items that differ in kind would be vertebrate/invertebrate, soccer/tennis, seeing/smelling, remembering/fantasizing, sonnet/limerick, and the word *utensil* used literally/the word *utensil* used metaphorically (as when Churchill referred to Mussolini as "that utensil"). Examples of pairs of items that differ in degree would be a pole of three meters/a pole of four meters, an IQ of 117/an IQ of 132, and a four-hour walk from Cambridge/a ten-hour walk from Cambridge.

If a difference between *A* and *B* is a difference of degree, it makes perfect sense to say that there is something of which *A* has more or less than *B*. For example, we can then say that one pole is taller than another, that one person has a lower IQ than someone else, and that Cambridge is nearer to Wellingborough than to Wolverhampton. Sentences like these have been called degree sentences (Van Woudenberg and Peels 2018). But where there are kind differences, degree sentences can't be used to express them. We can't say, for example, about two cows named Bertha and Gretha, that Bertha is more a cow than Gretha, or that Bertha is more a cow than a horse.

Of what kind is the speaking–writing difference? It doesn't seem to be a degree difference, for there isn't a quality or quantity such that speaking has more or less of it than writing. For instance, it makes no sense to say that speaking is "more" sender communication than writing, or vice versa. Is the speaking–writing difference then a kind difference? There are two reasons for answering in the affirmative. First, if I was right in saying that the most fundamental distinction here is the distinction between differences in kind and differences in degree, and if the speaking–writing difference is not a difference in degree, it follows that it is a difference in kind. Second, and more enlightening I think, we can see that this is so when we realize that the difference between writing and speaking is a difference in mode (or style) of sender communication. And this difference in mode (or style) is rather clearly a kind difference.

It goes without saying that speaking and writing are not the *only* modes of sender communication. There is also sender communication by flag semaphore, by Morse signs, by sign language, by smoke signals, and much more besides. These differences between styles of sender communication are also differences in kind, not in degree.

If two modes of communication are different in kind, then there is communality in that both are modes of communication, but there are also differences in that each is a mode of communication that differs from the other mode. The previous section dealt with the communalities. Let us now direct our attention to the differences and take our point of departure in Paul Ricoeur's thoughts on this topic.[5] A crucial term he uses to highlight the speaking–writing difference is *distanciation* (this is the way

[5] The context of Ricoeur's discussion is his critique of Gadamer. Gadamer maintained that humans always belong to a tradition. Ricoeur, by contrast, maintains that humans both belong to a tradition and can distance themselves from it. Ricoeur is motivated in saying this because he holds this is the only way to save a form of objectivity in the humanities. In my discussion of Ricoeur, I abstract from this context: the distinction between speaking and writing can fruitfully be discussed outside of it, and the way Ricoeur attempts to make the distinction is really independent of it.

Ricoeur spelled the word, and I keep to his spelling, thus signaling the fact that some technical usage is going on). In contrast with speaking, he says, there is a "triple distanciation introduced by writing: (1) distanciation from the author; (2) from the situation of discourse; (3) from the original audience" (Ricoeur 1973, 134).[6] Let us consider these distanciations in turn.

As to the first distanciation, Ricoeur (1973, 133) says that "writing makes the text autonomous in relation to the intention of the author. What the text signifies no longer coincides with what the author wanted to say, verbal significance and mental significance have distinct destinies." As this is supposed to contrast with speaking, Ricoeur must hold that when one speaks one's speech is not, or does not become, autonomous in relation to the intention of the speaker. What one's speech signifies coincides with what one wants to say, to use his phrase.

Now what might Ricoeur mean when he says that what is written is autonomous in relation to the intention of the author? First, what is it for one thing *X* to be autonomous in relation to another thing *Y*? One explanation is that it is for *X* not to causally depend on *Y*. So:

X is autonomous$_1$ in relation to $Y =_{df.} X$ is causally independent of Y.

For example, the death of Churchill was independent of the death of Hitler: the death of Hitler was in no way the cause, or part of the cause, of Churchill's death.

Now, what is written is certainly not independent of its author in this way. Texts are for their very existence causally dependent on their authors. But this is not decisive, for Ricoeur says that written texts are autonomous in relation to *the intention* of the author. Is this correct? Are texts independent of the intentions of their authors? To investigate this matter, we must return to the fourfold ways in which, I claimed, writing (and what is written) normally is intentional. First, it is intentional in the sense that the activity of writing (as well as its result) is not a fluke or mere happenstance; the activity was an intended one, as was the resulting text. Writing is also intentional in the sense that it is an activity that is targeted at other persons. Third, it is intentional in the sense that what one writes has a certain aboutness to it. Finally, writing is intentional in the sense that

[6] This is Ricoeur's own summary statement of his views. In his actual discussion of the speaking–writing difference, however, he mentions other distanciations as well, such as "the distanciation of the saying in the said" (1973, 132), the "distanciation of the real from itself" (141), and the "distanciation of the subject from himself" (141). I will let the summary statement structure my discussion.

authors intend their texts to do certain things: to inform others, to warn them, and so on. Given this fourfold distinction, is writing causally independent of the intentions of the author?

We should begin by noting that not all four senses apply here. The second and third senses of *intentional* do not apply, for it is plain wrong to say that a text is causally dependent on the fact that it is directed to others or on the fact that it is about something. But the other senses do apply. The first does so as follows: as I indicated, it is normally not a fluke or a matter of chance that a particular text exists, because normally, without an author having the intention to write, or to write something in particular, the text just wouldn't be there. And, as we saw, on this point there is no difference with speaking. For speaking too is not a fluke or mere coincidence; it is normally an intended action. The fourth sense also applies, as follows: normally, authors intend their texts to *do* something, to secure some effect (such as inform, warn, or amuse readers). A text is indeed autonomous in relation to the intention of an author in that whether or not it has the intended effects is independent of the author's intention. After all, an author may intend their text to do things that never happen, and their text may do things that they never intended it to do. But the same holds for speaking: a speaker, too, may intend their speech to have effects that just don't happen, and their speech may have effects that they never intended.

The upshot of this discussion, then, is that texts are not autonomous$_1$ in relation to the author's intention to write something (and even something in particular), but that they are autonomous$_1$ in relation to the intended effects that their authors envisioned for them. But this doesn't set writing apart from speaking.

In the quoted passage, Ricoeur also says that in a written text, what an author means and what a text means no longer coincide, and that when that happens, the text has become "autonomous in relation to the intention of the author." So here we face the following suggestion:

> X is autonomous$_2$ in relation to $Y =_{df.} X$ doesn't coincide with Y, where X = what an author wanted to say and Y = what a text means (or signifies).

Ricoeur suggests that in speech, what a speaker means and what a speech means *do* coincide.

For two reasons, however, it isn't clear that Ricoeur is convincing here – at least if we take Ricoeur's distinction to be roughly identical to Grice's distinction between author's meaning and sentence meaning

(Grice 1989).[7] First, consider the sentence "Is the window closed?" I take it for granted that this little bit of text has a definite meaning – the same meaning as the French sentence "La fenêtre est-elle fermée?" and the German sentence "Ist das Fenster geschlossen?" However, by writing any of these sentences with this specific meaning, an author may mean, or mean to convey, a variety of different things. The author may, for instance, ask a question, but they may also report that it is cold, or request that the window be closed; they may also report, by writing the very same sentence, that it is hot, or request that the window, if it is closed, be opened. So, there is a difference between the meaning of a sentence and what an author meant to convey through writing that sentence. But this distinction is of no help when the aim is to specify what sets writing apart from speaking. There is a perfect analogue here between writing and speaking: the distinction between author's meaning and sentence meaning has an analogue in the distinction between speaker's meaning and sentence meaning. Second, and more fundamental, utterer's (both speaker's and author's) meaning and sentence meaning are not merely different things – they are different *sorts* of things. They are different sorts of properties that can be had by different sorts of things. Sentence meaning is the property of a linguistic item – in my example, of a sentence – but utterer's meaning is not: utterer's meaning is the property of a person, for it is *persons* that mean to say things. For this reason, it is even impossible for a sentence meaning to be, or to be identical with, or to coincide with, an utterer's meaning.

Is there, we may ask, another sense of *autonomous* such that, whereas a written text is autonomous in relation to the intention of its author, a speech is *not*? I think there is, at least when the comparison is between speaking that is not electronically recorded or otherwise "fixed" (what I shall call *mere* speaking) on the one hand, and writing on the other. The reason for making the distinction this way is this: whereas it is essential for writing that the material carrier of what is written exists prior and subsequent to being read, it is not essential for speaking that the material carriers of the spoken words continue to carry the words prior and subsequent to being heard.[8] When a speaker is speaking and being listened

[7] Grice's distinction is in terms of utterer's meaning and sentence meaning. Both speakers and authors, on his account, are utterers. In the context of my discussion, I substitute *author* for *utterer*.

[8] Something of a limiting case here is the app Snapchat where the text vanishes after it is read. It is a limiting case because in the case of ordinary and traditional texts, the carrier exists before, and normally continues to exist after, reading, whereas a Snapchat carrier carries the text only before and up and until it is read, but not thereafter. I say this is *something of* a limiting case, because it isn't so much its being read that causes the text to vanish but its being clicked away (reading is even inessential, for the text may be clicked away unread).

to, he can "just like that" stop speaking (i.e., terminate the speech) or alter what he intended to say (e.g., summarize or skip an intended part, or improvise extempore a new line of thought). But when an author's text is being read, the author cannot just like that do anything that is analogous to what a speaker can do when they are speaking. A related point is that, once a text has been published, authors normally cannot control who will read what they wrote. To contrast, speakers can to a considerable degree, at least in principle, control who will hear their speeches. (*To a considerable degree*, for there are always the possibilities of being overheard and of eavesdropping.) And once they have spoken, speakers can prevent others from hearing their speech simply by not repeating what they've said – although they cannot prevent others from repeating what was said. This type of autonomy of the text in relation to the intention of the author can also be put in contrast with the nonautonomy of a speech vis-à-vis the intention of the speaker, as follows: even when an author has repudiated, abandoned, or otherwise distanced themselves from the views laid down in text T, T continues to be, since T is a material object that shares in the persistence conditions of material objects. T "has a life of its own," and its author has no (or only very little) say in how long its life will continue and how its life will sprawl. In the case envisioned, T doesn't carry the current views of its author and hence doesn't express what its author now would want to say. But still it is true that T carries the now-abandoned views of the author. We may put this as follows:

> X is autonomous$_3$ in relation to $Y =_{\text{df.}} Y$ has no significant control over X, where X = the material carrier of content (a book, or an electronic device on which content is stored) and Y = the intention of a communicator.

Speakers have significant control over the carriers of content, but authors lack such direct control once their texts have been published. That is to say, what is written is autonomous$_3$ in relation to the intentions of authors, whereas what is merely spoken is not autonomous$_3$ in relation to the intentions of speakers.

The first difference between speaking and writing that Ricoeur is making, then, boils down to this. Sender communication by writing involves, traditionally, the use of paper and the application of ink or pencil, and, since the dawn of the computer era, also screens and devices on which to save what one has written, whereas sender communication by mere speaking does not involve such things. Because of the kind of carrier it has, what is written has a permanence through time that what is merely spoken lacks. In order to be fully clear here, the expressions *what is written* and *what is spoken* should be disambiguated. They can be used to refer not only to the content of what is written and spoken, respectively, but also to the material carriers of that content. In the case of writing, letters, words, and sentences are carried by paper or by screens displaying what has been stored in electronic memory. In the case of speaking, they are carried by locutions, audible sounds, or sound waves. It is, of course, *the material carriers* of written content that have a permanence that the material carriers of merely spoken content lack. The former have much more staying power than the latter: material carriers of what is written can exist for hundreds and even thousands of years, while the material carriers of what is merely spoken exist only as long as their pronunciation takes.

To forestall possible misunderstanding on this point I should add that what is merely said can also "live on" in the hearts and brains of listeners, and that it can be repeated. However, in these cases the carriers are not token-identical with the carriers of the original speech. When I say that the carriers of what can be read have more staying power than the carriers of what can be heard, I have my eye on *token* carriers.

I should highlight that, without drawing attention to it, I have slightly changed the comparison that Ricoeur set out to make. He says that he wants to contrast speaking and writing; but since speaking, like writing, can be "fixed" on material carriers (e.g., tapes, recordings, videos, CDs, etc.) that can exist just as long as the material carriers of what is written, there is no contrast here. That is why I switched to contrasting *mere* speaking and writing. *Mere speaking* is speaking that goes unrecorded and that is, moreover, not speaking from a text nor the reading aloud of a prepared speech. *Writing* includes texts, but also recorded speech. Underlying this distinction, as I indicated, is the staying power of the material carrier and, hence, the possibility of unanticipated dissemination.

Let's move to Ricoeur's second distanciation: the distanciation in writing from "the situation of discourse." His thought here is that "the essence of a work of art, a literary work, or a work in general, is to transcend its psycho-sociological conditions of production and to be open to an unlimited series of readings, themselves situated within different socio-cultural contexts." To this he adds "the emancipation of the written material in regard to the dialogical condition of oral discourse, by which I mean that the relation between writing and reading is no longer a particular case of the relation between speaking and hearing" (Ricoeur 1973, 133).

This second distanciation has two rather different elements. One element is the distanciation in writing from the dialogical condition. What, according to Ricoeur, *is* the dialogical situation? It is, we may suppose, the situation speaker and listeners find themselves in when they are in dialogue, so when there is two-way communicative traffic. However, for at least two reasons this doesn't set speaking apart from writing. First, there are many situations that involve speakers but that don't qualify as dialogues: for instance, lectures and formal addresses by professors, preachers, and presidents often leave no space for dialogue. Second, it is entirely possible to enter into a *written* dialogue. Just think of Descartes's dialogues with Johannes Caterus, Marin Mersenne, Thomas Hobbes, and Pierre Gassendi on his *Meditations on First Philosophy*. Or think of the Leibniz-Clarke correspondence, or any epistolary correspondence for that matter. So there is no contrast to be found in this area between speaking and writing.

Another element of the second distanciation that Ricoeur mentions is that a written text transcends the psycho-sociological conditions of its production. Again, the thought is that this marks a contrast with speaking. But it is not obvious that it does. Let us first get clear on what those psycho-sociological conditions are supposed to be. Texts are produced – this much is uncontroversial. And they are produced under certain conditions – this is uncontroversial too. Those conditions, says Ricoeur, are of a psycho-sociological nature. The psychological conditions include, we may presume, the intention to write, the intention to write something in particular, and the intention to impact certain people, but also, presumably, emotional states and evaluative attitudes on the part of the writer. The sociological conditions likely include the group of people that the author belongs to and associates with, the societal arrangements that are in place (does the author live in a democracy or in a feudal regime?), dominant views and attitudes (does the author participate in a science-saturated culture, or in a culture with dystopic sentiments?), and the presence or absence of certain parts of culture (is there awareness of, say, the Russian Revolution, the Napoleonic Wars, cubism, or transcendental idealism?)

If this is more or less right, and if we assume with Ricoeur that these are indeed conditions of production, then we must say that *both* speaking and writing have psycho-sociological conditions of production. Speaking and writing as processes do not transcend these conditions. But perhaps we do face a difference when we focus on the *result* of the writing process – the text. For doesn't a text transcend the conditions of its production? The answer is a mixed bag. It seems relatively clear that texts can transcend the sociological conditions of their production if what we mean by that is that a text written in feudal times can continue to exist up until the present day, and that a text written in the favelas of Rio de Janeiro can be transported and read by the workers in Silicon Valley. On the other hand, a text can never escape being *this* particular text produced under *these* specific sociological conditions; in that sense, it can*not* transcend those conditions. A text written in an eleventh-century monastery will always and necessarily remain a text written in an eleventh-century monastery. It also seems clear that texts can transcend the psychological conditions of their production if what we mean by that is that a text can remain in existence even if its author changes their mind about it, even if they abandon the views laid down in the text, and even if the text has effects that they abhor. On the other hand, any text, once written, will always (and necessarily so) remain the product of the psychological conditions of its production. This cannot possibly be altered. A text by St. Augustine will always remain a text by St. Augustine, which is to say that it cannot possibly transcend that psychological condition of its production. As Joseph Butler famously said, "Everything is what it is, and not another thing." Cut to the current context: every text is what it is, and not another text.[9]

Charity of interpretation requires that we understand Ricoeur's claim about texts transcending the conditions of their production in such a way that it comes out true. This means we should understand it as a claim about the existence conditions of texts: texts continue to exist even if they are transported through times and places and even if their authors are dead or have changed their minds about what they wrote. For this is all true. The question now is: Does this mark a difference with speaking? It would seem not, for what a speaker says can also be transported through times and places; by an oral tradition, for example. And what a speaker says can "live on" in the minds of their hearers even when they have died or abandoned the views that they expressed. Hence, Ricoeur's second distanciation is not what sets speaking apart from writing.

Let us therefore turn to the third distanciation that is supposed to be characteristic of writing: distanciation from the original audience. This formulation is a bit enigmatic, for if writing is distanced in this way, how can there be an *original* audience? But I take it that a nonenigmatic formulation of Ricoeur's thought here would be this: when what a speaker

[9] This also holds for so-called living or evolving texts like the US Constitution, or, more humbly, study guides for university courses that are regularly updated. But to state this properly we need to introduce time indexes. For example, the US Constitution at t_1 is and will always remain the US Constitution at t_1.

says to a particular audience is written down and gets published, the written text gets distanciated from the audience to which the speech was originally directed. If this is what Ricoeur meant, it looks unobjectionable. However, it may not be the whole of what he meant. Consider the following quotation: "Whereas the vis-à-vis is given in advance by the colloquy itself in the dialogical situation, written discourse is open to an audience virtually understood as made up of whoever knows how to read" (Ricoeur 1973, 133). Ricoeur expresses the same thought also in the following way (as quoted earlier): there is "emancipation of the written material in regard to the dialogical condition of oral discourse, by which I mean that the relation between writing and reading is no longer a particular case of the relation between speaking and hearing" (Ricoeur 1973, 133). Here, the thought is slightly different from what I presented as my nonenigmatic formulation of Ricoeur's thought, for there is no original audience here. Rather, here it seems as if Ricoeur suggests that at least one difference between speaking and writing has to do with the respective receivers of oral and written communications. Suppose we divide receivers into audiences (listeners to speakers) and readerships (readers of writings). Then Ricoeur seems to suggest that whereas speakers have well-defined audiences, writers don't have well-defined readerships – they have the ill-defined, or open-ended, readership of whoever knows how to read (that particular language).

It may seem reasonably clear what Ricoeur is getting at. But in order to get a clear view of the lay of the land, we need to introduce a number of distinctions between receivers of communications, or ROC-groups, as I shall call them:

- intended ROC-groups: the people for whom the communication is intended
- actual ROC-groups: the people who have actually received the communication
- potential ROC-groups: the people who have not actually received the communication but who could, in principle, receive it in the future

Furthermore, we need to distinguish different ways in which ROC-groups can be defined. These definitions lie on a sliding scale between two extremes. At the one extreme end of the scale lie definitions of ROC-groups that are highly specific; at the other extreme end lie definitions that are wide open. Examples of specific ROC-group definitions would be "the persons who live on 50505 Hollyhock Road, South Bend," "all Swiss males who turn 85 in 2030," and "first-year students at the Vrije

Universiteit Amsterdam." Examples of wide-open ROC-group definitions would be "people who have a general interest in science," "people who feel concerned about the great problems of our time," and "cool people." The difference between the definitions on both extremes has to do with vagueness. With specific ROC-group definitions it is fully clear who falls in the extension of the definition. With wide-open definitions this is vague. By this I mean that even though there are people of whom it is clear that they fall in the extension of the definition, there are also many people of whom it is not so clear whether they do. In-between these extremes lie other ROC-group definitions. For our purposes, however, working only with the extremes suffices. I shall call these extremes *well-defined ROC-groups* and *open ROC-groups*. The two distinctions can be combined:

ROC-groups	Well-defined	Open
Intended		
Actual		
Potential		

One way to vindicate Ricoeur's claim about the third distanciation would be to show that some combinations that are possible for speaking are not possible for writing, or that some combinations that are possible for writing are not possible for speaking. Let us see whether we can establish that.

Speakers can obviously intend to reach a well-defined ROC-group. A father, for example, can speak to his children, who form a well-defined group. But writers too can address very specific ROC-groups. Manuals for computers and other electronic devices, for example, are intended to reach the users of those devices – again, well-defined groups. And codes of responsible research conduct are explicitly intended to reach researchers.

Authors can obviously intend to reach an open ROC-group. In writing *The Brothers Karamazov*, Dostoyevsky intended to reach a large readership, but it was not a well-defined group. Likewise, for all we know, when Shakespeare wrote the sonnets, he had no well-defined ROC-group in mind that was his target. It seems safe to say that this holds for many works of literature. But the same is true for speakers: they can intend to reach an ROC-group that is open and have no specific person or set of persons in mind to which their speech is directed. If a mayor gives a public speech on the occasion of the seven hundredth birthday of their city, then they intend to reach an open ROC-group.

Let's move on to actual ROC-groups. Whether a communicator's actual ROC-group is well-defined or open, it seems clear that both speakers and authors have actual ROC-groups. And it seems equally clear that for both speakers and authors their intended ROC-group may (but need not) coincide with their actual ROC-group.

So far, we have not seen a genuine difference between speaking and writing. Is that difference then to be found in the *potential* ROC-groups for speakers and writers? If we concentrate on mere speaking, it would seem that the potential ROC-group (whether it is well-defined or not doesn't matter) is much smaller for speakers than for authors. Speakers can communicate, without electronics, with at most a couple of thousand people, and only with people who are physically present at the time of speaking; this holds true for well-crafted venues like the Colosseum and St. Peter's Basilica in Rome, but often it is already quite a feat to speak to a few hundred people without electronic devices. For speaking, in Alvin Goldman's terms, is a synchronous mode of communication (Goldman 1999, 162). The potential ROC-group for authors is much larger, because books and articles endure through time and, hence, can be read by any number of future readers. This is a difference. It is not a difference in kind, however, but a difference in degree.

This must of course be nuanced if we no longer concentrate on *mere* speaking but take a number of technological advancements in consideration. Until not so very long ago, all speaking was mere speaking. It required the spatial and temporal nearness of speaker and listeners, their togetherness at the same place and at the same time. But this is no longer true. Microphone technology made it possible to speak to thousands of people who are both co-temporal and spatially near – for instance, people who are present in the same stadium as the speaker. Radio technology made it possible to speak to millions of people who are co-temporal but spatially scattered over the globe. And recording technology made it possible to speak to millions of people scattered over the globe at different times. Taking all this into consideration, we must say that the difference in degree mentioned in the previous paragraph more or less evaporates.

Is there, then, no serious distinction to be made between speaking and writing? Was Ricoeur all wrong? I don't think he was, even if he was not able to clearly pinpoint the differences. This is the topic of the next section.

Creative-Investigative Writing

The leading question for this section is whether everything that can be communicated (or done) through speaking can also be communicated (or done) through writing, and vice versa. I shall argue that the answer is no: there are some things that humans can only do by writing.

In order to get a proper grasp of this question, we should distinguish it from two other questions that it might be conflated with. First, it should not be conflated with the question whether every speech act that can be performed by speaking can also be performed by writing, and vice versa. Speech-act theorists seem to assume as much (Austin 1962; Searle 1969; Alston 2000). Alston articulates the consensus view when he says, "I follow current practice in using terms for speech in a broadened sense to cover any employment of language. Thus 'utterance' is to be taken to range over the production of any linguistic token, whether by speech, writing, or other means" (Alston 2000, 12n1). I don't intend to argue against the consensus. It seems plausible that each token speech act that can be performed by speaking can also be performed by writing, and vice versa – with the exception of mathematical and formal logic statements, many of which just cannot be talked about in the sense that they cannot, or cannot easily, be vocalized.

Second, my question should not be conflated with the question whether everything that is written can also be said in the sense of being acoustically vocalized, and whether everything that can be said (in the sense indicated) can also be written down. I suppose the answer to this question is largely yes. What is written can be read in the sense that it can be acoustically vocalized. And what is acoustically vocalized, assuming it is language, can be written down. Still, the qualifier *largely* is needed because intonation and "deliverance" of a speech may communicate or suggest things that are lost even when all the words are correctly penned down, and also because, as indicated, many statements of mathematics and logic cannot be vocalized.

My question is different. To get a feel for what my question is after, I question-wise note a few things. First, why is it that what counts in academia is publication of what is written (books, papers, articles, commentaries, annotations, etc.) rather than speeches, even if these speeches are recorded? Second, why is it that the reference lists of academic publications include almost exclusively *written* sources, and not speeches (unless they've been written down and published, of course)? Third, why is that new academic insights are mostly communicated through writing and not through verbal reporting (or that, if there is verbal reporting, it is usually based on what is or is about to be written and what has been or will be published)? Why is it that what academics *say* just doesn't substitute writing? Why is it that many academics can communicate their ideas much better – in a much more intelligible way – through writing than through speaking? And why do literary authors *write* – why don't they confine themselves to speaking?

Answers to these questions will refer to such considerations as the following. Whereas it is impossible to rehear what is merely spoken (even the echo of a speech is too short-lived for that), it *is* in principle possible to reread what is written – that is, in this possible world that is the actual world (perhaps there are possible worlds in which what is written fades away after being read by others than the author). This makes it possible for readers to carefully peruse what is written. At the same time, knowing that readers may do this, writers will be paying much attention to what they write, which often involves rewriting and reformulating their texts. Thus, writers reach a deeper level of thinking than is possible in speech. Writing thus enhances or makes possible deep forms of thinking and communication that would otherwise be unattainable.

Moreover, since writers can write without readers being present, they can reflect on what they want to say and how they want to say it in a much more protracted way than speakers can. This makes it possible for writers to communicate thoughts that are longer, more complex, more complete, more precise, more definite, and more rigorous, and they may do this with more subtlety and nuance than is possible by speaking – although there are also things that can and do get lost in writing. (For example, it is often inadvisable to make jokes in email messages, since tone tends to get lost.) And without others being present to hear and see us speaking, nonverbal cues cannot be picked up. Or perhaps I shouldn't say that these things "get lost" but, rather, that in writing we cannot and should not rely on tone and nonverbal cues. Experienced authors are alive to this and have found ways to not rely on them.

To further explain what my question is after, I should like to ask whether all writing can be described as *putting down thoughts one already had developed prior to putting them down*. To be sure, *some* writing can be accurately described that way. Writing an email to your friend to indicate that the dinner party will take place at the St. James Hotel is an example. Penning down a shopping list is another example, and so is writing a log book or writing a run-of-the-mill postcard on which you indicate your whereabouts. But not *all* writing is like that. St. Augustine and Wittgenstein, for example, both confessed to be doing their thinking while they were writing, and they were writing while doing their thinking. This describes, I think, a familiar phenomenon to people accustomed to writing. Writing often isn't merely putting down something one already knows or thinks or wishes or fears – rather, it is through writing that *one finds out* what one thinks, knows, or believes. Often, we may clarify our thoughts through writing. Alternatively, it is often through writing that we begin to form new ideas and begin to develop new thoughts about things. It is possible that through writing one may come to believe or even come to know things one didn't believe or know prior to writing them up. This kind of writing could be called novelistic writing – *novelistic* indicating that through writing, new, fresh, novel ideas are formed and developed. Since this may suggest that novels are the chief results of such writing, a better term would be *creative-investigative writing*. Outcomes of such writing also include, as I shall suggest, mathematical and philosophical texts. I first give a rough account of this category and, next, substantiate the claim that there *is* such writing.

The account is this:

> *S*'s writing of work *W* is creative-investigative if and only if *S* would not or even could not have formed the thoughts expressed in *W* if *S* had not engaged in writing *W*.

Suppose *S* is a mathematician, let us call him Theaetetus, who lived 2,500 years ago and who is interested in the problem of whether the square root of 2 is a rational number; or suppose *S* is Andrew Wiles living in the 1980s and ferociously working on a proof of Fermat's famous Last Theorem, which says that $x^n + y^n = z^n$ has no solutions for $n > 2$.[10] Neither Theaetetus nor Wiles, it would seem, could have formed the thoughts eventually leading to and constituting the proofs of these theorems without some form of writing (by hand or computer). Without writing, the proofs could not be given; they would not be cognitively accessible to them; they would not be able to know them. Had no writing techniques been developed and no writing devices been available to them, neither Theaetetus nor Wiles would have been able to provide the proofs. It would seem that in the actual world – that is, *our* world – the mathematical profession could not function without writing. That is, if not for writing techniques and writing devices, there would be no mathematics as we now know it, and no mathematical profession as we now know it. It is by and through writing that mathematicians develop their ideas and even come to know new things. Mathematicians engage in creative-investigative writing: they create *while writing*. They create ideas, concepts, and proofs while they are writing.[11]

[10] A highly readable and informative account of how Wiles worked on the proof is Singh (1997).

[11] Byers (2007) is one long argument for the claim that mathematical thinking is creative. He doesn't pay any attention to writing, though.

This is so even if mathematical Platonism were to be true. Mathematical Platonism is the view that the objects of mathematics exist independently of anyone holding beliefs about them, independent even of anybody having those objects "in mind." Platonism also maintains that mathematics is discovery rather than construction. This may seem to undermine the idea that mathematicians engage in creative-investigative writing. But that impression is wrong, for even if Platonism is true, mathematical truths need to be discovered, and discovery is a creative process. Hence, mathematical writing can still be creative-investigative: new mathematical concepts are developed by means of which mathematical objects can be described, and new mathematical arguments are construed so as to prove necessary and unalterable mathematical truths. This requires acts of creative mathematical imagination.

We may ask *why* this is so: Why do mathematicians in the actual world need writing that is creative-investigative? One answer might be that writing is needed *only* because of the imperfect rational and retentive powers of mathematicians. Actual mathematicians are indeed imperfect in these respects: they can "see," mathematically, only so far and remember only so much at a certain point in time. Therefore, they need writing as an aid to reason and memory. If this is the whole story, this entails that possible extraordinary persons like Anselm's god and Laplace's demon could be perfect mathematicians without engaging in novelistic writing. After all, these persons are supposed to be unlimited in their cognitive capacities: they have perfect ratiocinative and retentive powers, and they have mathematical knowledge without investigation – a fortiori, they never need to investigate anything through creative-investigative writing.

Related to this is reasoning by means of formal languages. We don't *speak* formal languages – we *write* them. Using formal languages is to manipulate symbols in accordance with certain transformation rules. Such languages, Catarina Dutilh Novaes has argued, "trigger cognitive processes that would typically not be triggered in their absence" (Dutilh Novaes 2012, 55). Referring to Sybille Krämer's concept of "operative writing,"[12] which contrasts with "phonetic writing," she says that "operative writing is not primarily about *communicating*: it is not meant to express something to *another* agent but rather to bring about within-agent specific cognitive processes"

[12] See Krämer (2003). This paper is a criticism of the so-called phonographic doctrine of writing, according to which writing is spatial, fixed speech. Krämer argues that many aspects of writing cannot be accounted for on the basis of this doctrine – for example, spaces between words; capitals, italics, and punctuation; headings; summaries; and footnotes.

(Dutilh Novaes 2012, 56). (This sides with my account that the writing is, initially at least, creative-investigative.) But whereas Krämer suggests that operative writing covers writing in formal languages only, I agree with Dutilh Novaes that it is a function of formal and nonformal languages alike: humans can engage in operative writing in formal as well as in natural languages.

Examples of the latter include, I suggest, the creative-investigative writings of literary authors. Without such writing, works such as Dostoyevsky's *The Brothers Karamazov*, Hardy's *The Mayor of Casterbridge*, Proust's *À la recherche du temps perdu*, and Musil's *Der Mann ohne Eigenschaften* simply would not and, likely, could not exist. It's not as if literary authors had the characters and plots and sceneries all thought out to the minutest detail prior to writing; nor, of course, had they thought out, prior to writing them down, all of the sentences that would eventually jointly constitute the work. Many literary authors have testified to the fact that the fictional characters of their works took on shape during the writing process. This suggests that literary writing too is novelistic writing in the sense explained earlier (at least, normally – there may be an author who is the odd one out and has it all in mind prior to writing). Literary authors would not and could not have formed the thoughts about their characters, plots, sceneries, and so forth if they hadn't engaged in writing. These works would not or even could not exist without writing, in contrast to shopping lists, recipes, central heating system manuals, and so on. In her biography of Thomas Hardy, Claire Tomalin indicates that Hardy had the daily habit of picking up his pen, and she quotes him as saying to a visitor: "I never let a day go without using a pen. Just holding it sets me off; in fact I can't think without it. It's important not to wait for the right mood. If you do it will come less and less" (Tomalin 2006, 358). And John Ruskin was hinting at this when he made a distinction between books of the hour, which are "essentially talking things," and books of all times, which are "essentially written things" (Ruskin [1865] 2002, 32).

The fact that both mathematical writing and literary writing are creative-investigative should not obscure the differences between them. First, whereas there are – at least on the Platonic view of things – objective, mind-independent mathematical facts, there are no objective, mind-independent "literary facts." Mathematical facts exist prior to any mathematician writing about them,[13] but the characters that populate *The Brothers Karamazov* didn't exist prior to Dostoyevsky writing about them. Second, whereas mathematical creative-investigative writing is, for humans, a ratiocinative and retentive aid to finding out things mathematical, literary creative-

[13] Most mathematicians are, in fact, Platonists (realists) about numbers.

investigative writing also is a ratiocinative and retentive aid to finding out things that are already there, but this way of finding things out may take the form of what-it-is-like experiences (as described in Chapter 1). By writing about, say, poverty, an author may be able to come to know, in a quasi way, what it is like to be poor. Literary novelistic writing, then, is the means by which characters, plots, and situations are created, and it can be investigative in that it can be a means to finding something out through quasi what-it-is-like experiences.

It isn't only mathematical writing and literary writing that are creative-investigative. Scientific writing in general has a novelistic aspect. It is not for nothing that all scientists write. Einstein has been quoted as saying, "My pencil is more intelligent than I" (Popper 1972, 225n39) – which suggests he engaged in novelistic writing. One reason for scientific writing having a novelistic aspect is that some things are just too complicated to be thought, or too complex for us to understand when they are merely said (literally). Writing is often *constitutive* in processes that are definitive of science. Here is an exciting illustration of this point taken from Andy Clark's *Supersizing the Mind* (2008, xxv):

> Consider this famous exchange between the Nobel Prize–winning physicist Richard Feynman and the historian Charles Weiner. Weiner, encountering with a historian's glee a batch of Feynman's original notes and sketches, remarked that the materials represented "a record of [Feynman's] day-to-day work." But instead of simply acknowledging this historic value, Feynman reacted with unexpected sharpness:
>
> "I actually did the work on the paper," he said.
>
> "Well," Weiner said, "the work was done in your head, but the record of it is still here."
>
> "No, it's not a *record*, not really. It's *working*. You have to work on paper and this is the paper. Okay?"

Clark comments that "Feynman's suggestion is, at the very least, that the loop into the external medium was integral to his intellectual activity (the 'working') itself. But I would like to go further and suggest that Feynman was actually *thinking* on the paper" (Clark 2008, xxv).

Similar things hold for philosophy. In the way it has been done in the Western world ever since Plato and Aristotle, philosophy involves and very often requires creative-investigative writing. The thoughts expressed in Plato's *Dialogues*, in Aristotle's *Metaphysics* and *Ethics*, in St. Augustine's *Confessions*, in St. Anselm's *Proslogion*, in Descartes's *Meditations*, in Locke's *Essay*, in Hume's *Treatise*, in Reid's *Essays*, in Kant's *Critiques*, in Husserl's *Ideen* – they would (or could) not have occurred to these men and could not have been developed by them had they not engaged in creative-investigative writing. The most elaborate description of this that I have come across is from Nicholas Wolterstorff. It is worth quoting in full (Wolterstorff 2019, 293–294):

> When I begin thinking about some topic, I write my thoughts down in longhand. I don't first have the thoughts and then write them down; I think while writing – or better, I think *in* writing. Perhaps there are some people who can develop a train of thought in their mind without writing anything down. I cannot. I think with fingers and pen – and with my eyes. I must have my thoughts in front of me where I can inspect them. I don't worry about rhetorical niceties at this point; much of what I write down consists of poorly composed sentences or sentence fragments. Nor do I worry about how I will put it all together. I write the thoughts as they occur to me, in whatever form and order they come. Worrying about niceties of rhetoric or style and about matters of order inhibits my brainstorming. I let thoughts come as they may.
>
> There comes a point when I sense that nothing more is to be gained by brainstorming. Up to this point, I have been alone with my thoughts. Now it is time to bring an intended audience into the picture by composing an essay or chapter with readers in mind. I do this at my computer. I don't prepare an outline in advance (I am incapable of doing that). I settle on a beginning and, with a vague idea in mind of how it should go from there, I let it happen . . ..
>
> Ideally, when I compose, I formulate the thoughts I have had into well-formed sentences and organize them into a sequence that will carry the reader along. But seldom does it go that smoothly. I cannot come up with a sentence that says what I want to say, a sure indication that I haven't reached clarity about what I want to say. Or the sentence is accurate but awkward. Or the writing becomes clotted and convoluted at a point, another sign that I have not achieved full understanding. Gaps in the argument appear. Or the whole thing is boring – and for me, being boring is an unforgivable sin. All this time I am thinking with the computer.[14]

[14] Another description of the phenomenon is due to Richard Menary, who explicates what is going on when he writes a scholarly paper. The description is offered to show how brain, body, and world are coupled in a way that makes it possible for us to consider them as a coupled system (Menary 2007, 629):

> Take the example of writing a scholarly paper by word processing. Which of the components play an active causal role? Presumably, thanks to the CPU, the keyboard and monitor are able to exert an effect on what I write next and the words I type, which come up on the screen, are an extension of short-term memory. In a stronger sense my reading and re-reading what I have written gives me new ideas about what I should write next. Thus, the keyboard and monitor play an important causal role in the production of the paper. There is, however, a sense in which this is the wrong focus of interest. Whilst it is true that tools such as keyboards and pens enable me to write, it is manipulating the written vehicles themselves that drives my cognitive processes. The sentences extend my working memory and are, of course, what can be re-written, erased, moved to another paragraph, etc. It is, moreover, precisely these kinds of manipulations that are not easily, if ever, achieved in the head.

I present this as a description as well as an illustration of creative-investigative writing and, moreover, as evidence for its reality.

What Wolterstorff writes implies that a thesis which on the face of it may commend itself as almost self-evident – i.e., the thesis that writing things down is *only* an aid to one's memory and that, if one's memory were much better than it in fact is, one would have no need for writing things down – is false. Of course, it is often true that what we write is an aid to our memory. We make notes of conversations we have had, we have agendas and calendars to remind us of our appointments, we make notes so as not to forget the numerous chores that await us, we make notes for papers and books that we should like to write, and so forth. But as the cases mentioned earlier suggest, there is also writing that is not merely an aid to memory, viz., novelistic writing. Such works are not written merely as aids to our limited capacity to remember things: they need to be written in order for the thoughts expressed in them to come into being. They wouldn't exist – they wouldn't be *there* – if there were no writing.

Creative-investigative writing has an aspect to it that I have kept back so far. Sometimes we think or feel that a certain idea is a *good* one, that it is an idea that we should work out, on paper or on screen. Sometimes, such an idea is the fruitful starting point of creative-investigative writing. But other times, it is not: when we try to work out the idea, we find that it doesn't work; there just is not enough "to" the idea. We can find this out, in an indirect way, through creative-investigative writing – *indirect*, because the fact that writing doesn't seem possible or promising indicates that the idea is not good after all.

If what I have suggested in this section is correct, this entails that within a community of agents with minds like ours there can be and often is, to use Alvin Goldman's phrase, veritistic gain through writing. There are things we just wouldn't know unless they were figured out through creative-investigative writing. This is what partly motivates this book's focus on reading: people may come to know things through reading texts – things that were figured out by their authors *through* writing.

Two further remarks are in order. First, it is entailed by what I said in this section that much writing is *not* creative-investigative: writing drug

Therefore, writing as an active and creative process is enabled by tools such as pen and paper or word processors. The written vehicles are then available for further manipulations such as restructuring, revising and re-drafting. Manipulating written vehicles is a kind of problem solving where a particular goal is aimed at: "how do I make this piece of writing clearer?" for example.

prescription manuals is not; writing letters and emails is (mostly) not; writing travel guidebooks and textbooks is not. Only some writing is novelistic. Hence, the conclusion of this chapter is not that speaking and writing, although they normally share fourfold intentionality, are nonetheless radically different. Rather, the conclusion is that a focus on writing can bring something to light about reading as a source of knowledge that might otherwise easily escape us. And even this conclusion must be qualified. For – and this is the second remark – novelistic writing seems to have some counterpart in speaking. Many philosophers, scientists, politicians, and so forth, indicate that they develop their thoughts (also) through speaking with others. There is such a thing as creative-investigative *speaking*. Socratic dialogues may be a point in case. Still, it seems highly probable that the content output of creative-investigative writing will be very different from the content output of creative-investigative speaking. Most of mathematics, most of philosophy, and most of what we now value as works of literature would not be there without creative-investigative *writing*: that is, most of these things would not be there if there was only creative-investigative *speaking*. What is special about writing is that many of the most interesting things written are due to novelistic writing. Again, this is what partly motivates this book's focus on writing, even though it is not exclusively, or even mainly, focused on reading the products of creative-investigative writing.

Where does this leave us with respect to the question of whether the distinction between speaking and writing is a principled or a gradual one? My discussion suggests that qua modes of communication, the distinction is a principled one: it isn't that we get writing if we add more of something to speaking. But both speaking and writing can enable creative-investigative thinking, which *does* have degrees (viz., depth of thinking). And I have suggested that novelistic writing typically has more potential for deep thinking than speaking has.

The reflections on creative-investigative writing can be seen as pointing to evidence in favor of the extended-mind hypothesis, according to which the manipulation of external vehicles can be part of cognitive systems.[15]

[15] Novelistic writing is one of the cases to which the following remark of Clark and Chalmers (1998, 9) applies: "In these cases, the human organism is linked with an external entity in a two-way interaction, creating a *coupled system* that can be seen as a cognitive system in its own right."

CHAPTER 7

Texts, Meanings, and Interpretation

The objects of reading result from writers' actions that normally have fourfold intentionality, or so I argued in Chapter 6. Intentionality is in great part responsible for the fact that those objects have or embody *meaning*, in a number of different senses that I will specify in this chapter. Reading and meaning hang together, for things that have no meaning cannot be objects of reading – at least, not of reading as I have defined it. The meaning of (and in) texts is one topic that this chapter takes up. It interweaves with a topic that so far has been conspicuously absent in this book: the topic of interpretation. The aim of this chapter is to clarify, in a very general way, the notion of interpretation, explaining what it is and how it is related to meaning (and hence to reading).

This chapter is organized as follows: first, I distinguish a variety of notions of meaning. Next, I discuss the question of how we know about meanings. Finally, I formulate a general account of interpretation in terms of meaning.

The Plethora of Notions of Meaning

Some decades ago, Jeffrey Stout (1982, 3) argued:

> What might we be asking for when inquiring about the meaning of a text? ... Are we, in a given case, interested in what the author planned to convey? In what might be called extrinsic intentions (such as the motive or aim of achieving tenure)? In propositions or messages the author intended to communicate? In the proper identification of a purposeful linguistic performance (like fomenting revolution or delivering a verdict)? In an intended reference? Or in something else? ... But in asking about the meaning of a text, our interest might also have little or nothing to do with author's intentions .... An interest in the meaning of a text might easily be a matter of its contextual significance .... We have, then, at least two clusters of topics that might motivate interest in something called "the

> meaning of a text." One pertains to the various kinds of thing that might be termed an author's intention, the other to equally various kinds of contextual significance.

Stout, I think, has it entirely right – *the meaning of a text* is a complex and slippery notion, as is the notion of meaning as such, as philosophers (Austin 1970, chapter 3) and linguists (Stampe 1968) alike have pointed out many times. However, while Stout concludes that we should give up on the notion of the meaning of a text (because, he says, we can say everything we want to say about texts without it), my approach is that our thinking about texts and textual interpretation is so fully saturated with it that we are pretty much stuck with it and that it is more fruitful to keep using the term, all the while staying alert to the different notions of meaning.

In this section I distinguish a number of different notions of meaning, or a number of different senses of the word *meaning*, or a number of different ways in which the word *meaning* is used. I use these phrases as equivalents. I am, thus, saying that *meaning* is a polysemous word. Let us now consider a number of distinct notions of meaning. My aim is not to offer analyses of them but merely to register their distinctiveness.

Sentence Meaning

Sentences have meaning. The English sentence "The earth revolves around its axis" has a particular meaning; it means the same as the Dutch sentence "De aarde draait om haar as." Sometimes it is difficult to tell what the meaning of a sentence is; for instance, when the sentence concerns a topic you are not familiar with, or when you don't know some of the technical terminology used in it. If we want to understand such a sentence, we try to find a sentence that expresses the same meaning but that does so, for us, *more clearly*.

William Alston (2000, part 2) has argued that the meaning of a sentence is its illocutionary act potential. His core idea is that for every sentence there is a "matching illocutionary act type": every sentence is such that it is especially fit for performing a particular illocutionary act type. The sentence "The door is open," for example, is especially fit for asserting that the door is open. The sentence "It is open" is especially fit for asserting that something is open. "The door of my house is open" is especially fit for asserting that the door of the house belonging to the sentence utterer is open. "Now start with it!" is a sentence that is especially fit for ordering the person addressed to start with something right after the sentence is uttered. And so on.

The meaning of a sentence, on Alston's account, is not its *perlocutionary* act potential. And this is surely correct. By uttering the sentence "The door is open," a speaker can perform all sorts of perlocutionary acts – for instance, they make the hearer feel nervous, or they make the hearer feel welcome, or they unwittingly put an idea into the hearer's head (the hearer happens to be a burglar). But none of these effects on hearers is the meaning of the sentence "The door is open."

Word Meaning

Words have meanings.[1] *To procrastinate*, for instance, means "to put things off." When we don't know the meaning of a word, we look it up in a dictionary.

When we specify of a particular word its meaning, and when we specify of a particular sentence its meaning, we do different things. When we specify the meaning of *to procrastinate*, we either provide synonyms for it or we point to examples and say, "*That* is an example of procrastinating." But when we specify the meaning of an indicative sentence, we can't provide synonyms, as sentences don't have synonyms, nor do we point to examples. Rather, when we specify the meaning of an indicative sentence, we specify what must be the case if the sentence is to be true. Hence, when we specify the meaning of the sentence "Because John procrastinated too long, he missed the boat," we indicate what must be the case if the sentence is to be true. This procedure cannot be followed in the case of words, since words have no truth-values. For the specification of the meaning of nonindicative sentences (questions, commands, etc.) we do other things, but none of them is of the same type as what we do when we specify the meaning of a word. For questions, for example, we specify what should be the case if something is to count as a correct answer to the question; for commands, we specify which actions would qualify as obeying the command.

It is a platitude that the meaning of a sentence is not the sum of the meanings of its constituent words. The sentences "Jack killed Jim" and "Jim killed Jack" contain the same words, but they have different meanings. Word order and syntax contribute as much to the meaning of a sentence as do word meanings.

[1] J. L. Austin has pointed out in his characteristic way numerous pitfalls surrounding the notion of the meaning of a word; see Austin (1970, 55–75). A thorough discussion of the notion of word meaning is Ullmann (1972).

Author's Meaning

In his book *Sesame and Lilies*, John Ruskin says that when we read authors, we should be animated "by a true desire to be taught by them, and to enter into their thoughts. To enter into theirs, observe; not to find your own expressed by them" (Ruskin [1865] 2002, 34). This, he continues, is a serious challenge, for

> very ready we are to say of a book, "How good this is – that's exactly what I think!" But the right feeling is, "How strange that is! I never thought of that before, and yet I see it is true; or if I do not now, I hope I shall, some day." But whether thus submissively or not, at least be sure that you go to the author to get at *his* meaning, not to find yours. (Ruskin [1865] 2002, 34)

Ruskin ([1865] 2002, 34) warns us that getting at the author's meaning is by no means easy:

> And be sure, also, if the author is worth anything, that you will not get at his meaning all at once; – nay, that at his whole meaning you will not for a long time arrive in any wise. Not that he does not say what he means, and in strong words too; but he cannot say it all; and what is more strange, will not, but in a hidden way and in parables, in order that he may be sure you want it.

As miners must dig to get the gold, so readers must dig to get the author's meaning.

Let us consider these thoughts more closely. The aim of reading, Ruskin avers, is to enter into an author's thought, as contrasted with finding our own thoughts expressed by the author; the aim is to get at the author's meaning, as contrasted with finding our own meaning. Perhaps Ruskin's point can also be expressed by saying that readers should aim to track down an author's meaning, as contrasted with projecting their own thoughts on the author. It is, I take it, a rather familiar phenomenon that readers sometimes read things that aren't there into a text. Readers may, for example, be convinced that a certain passage contains a hidden reference to Edgar Allan Poe's story "The Fall of the House of Usher," although the reference just isn't there. Or a reader may think that a text is a parable, while in fact it narrates a historical event. Or an anarchist, reading a certain passage in Hegel and driven by wishful reading, may misconstrue Hegel's thought by projecting their own thoughts onto Hegel's text. Or a confused reader may come to believe that in the fable of the fox and the crow, Aesop meant to say that flattery is a good thing, as it may bring you a fortune – thus ascribing to Aesop a view that is the exact opposite of what he actually intended to propound.

It goes without saying that we should not misread authors, or misconstrue their thoughts, or project our own ideas onto a text. But it should be doubted that the *only* aim we have when we read is to get at what Ruskin called *the author's meaning*. We may be interested, for instance, in finding out the extent to which an author is a child of their times. Or we may be interested in seeing whether or not the author correctly relates the facts surrounding, say, the killing of Crazy Horse. Neither of these aims fits the description of getting at the author's meaning, whatever that may mean exactly (more on this later).

To this it must be added that whatever aim we have when we read texts, truth must be our guiding value. When we read Thomas Jefferson with the aim of figuring out what views he held about slaves, we want to figure out what his views *truly* were (this is so, of course, even if we don't like those views or don't like them to be attributed to Jefferson); we don't want to misconstrue his thoughts or project our own thoughts on the topic onto Jefferson's writings. When we read Hegel with the aim of gauging the extent to which he was a child of his times, we want to gauge the *true* extent to which he was a child of his times. And when we read Virginia Woolf's *Mrs Dalloway* in order to find out in what percentage of the text Woolf applied the stream of consciousness technique, we want to find the *true* percentage. (Note that when these truths are known, they instantiate in the first two cases RK_A, and in the third case RK_C.)

It also need not be doubted that reading can sometimes be hard work. Sometimes, an author just isn't a very skillful writer; other times, the thoughts the author wants to express are so complex (or so bizarre) that it takes a lot of effort for the reader to capture them. We see this often in philosophy: it is hard work to follow and understand Plotinus's *Enneads*, Kant's transcendental deduction in the *Kritik der reinen Vernunft*, McTaggart's argument for the unreality of time, or Heidegger's *Unterwegs zur Sprache*. We see this too in certain fictional texts. Proust's *À la recherche du temps perdu*, for example, is a difficult read, and so is Bob Dylan's *Tarantula*. And introductions to quantum mechanics are also very difficult, and so are many elementary textbooks in many academic fields. Yet surely not all reading requires the hard work that Ruskin talks about. Newspapers are mostly easy to read, and so are cookbooks and concert tickets. I hasten to add that Ruskin would agree. The image of reading as mining, he holds, only applies to reading "books of all time," which he contrasts with "books of the hour."[2]

[2] Van Woudenberg's "Ruskin's 'Simple Thoughts' on Reading" (unpublished manuscript) is an attempt to make sense of this distinction.

Now, even if not all reading is reading to get at an author's meaning, it surely often is – or so I say. But what is an author's meaning supposed to be? In the rest of this section, I offer an account of this notion that is based on speech-act theory.

A core idea of speech-act theory is that when a person speaks (i.e., when they utter a sentence), they are, or can be, performing a number of different acts simultaneously. Suppose Bill utters the sentence "Tonight, there will be a spring tide." Then what he is doing can be variously described. Each description describes one of the many actions Bill is performing by uttering this sentence. Here is an incomplete list (you can think of each description as a true answer to the question "What was Bill doing?"):

a. Bill produced words.
b. Bill uttered a sentence.
c. Bill did a cockney accent.
d. Bill uttered the words "Tonight, there will be a spring tide."
e. Bill claimed that tonight there will be a spring tide.
f. Bill informed his audience that tonight there will be a spring tide.
g. Bill denied what Jack had claimed.
h. Bill explained why he wouldn't want to sleep at his aunt's house.
i. Bill tried to start a conversation.
j. Bill frightened the people.
k. Bill worked on my nerves.

The descriptions of what Bill did fall in certain broad classes that have been given different names. I use Austin's names, but Alston's characterization of the classes. The first few descriptions describe Bill's purely verbal actions. They don't describe *what* he said by uttering the sentence – they don't describe the *content* of his words – but merely *that* he said something, or that he said something in a particular way. The first few descriptions thus describe Bill's *locutionary acts*: they describe the simple fact that he spoke (or spoke in a particular way).

The middle few descriptions, by contrast, describe (in a way) *what* Bill said by uttering the sentence – they describe the sentence's content and, thus, Bill's *illocutionary acts*. They state that Bill *claimed* that there will be a spring tide tonight, and that he *informed* others that there will be a spring tide tonight. Illocutionary acts are usually analyzed as having two components: propositional content and a particular illocutionary force. Compare the following descriptions:

- Bill affirmed there will be a spring tide tonight.
- Bill asked whether there will be a spring tide tonight.

- Bill predicted that there will be a spring tide tonight.
- Bill suggested that there will be a spring tide tonight.

These are descriptions of illocutionary acts all of which have the same propositional content, viz., there will be a spring tide tonight. But they have different illocutionary forces: the first has the force of an affirmation, the second of a question, the third of a prediction, and the fourth of a suggestion.

The last few descriptions on the list describe (in a way) what Bill *did* by uttering the sentence; not by describing the utterance's content (not its propositional content and illocutionary force), but by describing the *effects* of what Bill said. He frightened people, or he worked on someone's nerves. Descriptions of this sort describe *perlocutionary acts.*

It seems entirely uncontroversial that authors, in writing texts, perform speech acts. They perform locutionary acts. After all, they produce words; they utter sentences (I use *utter* in a way that encompasses both speaking and writing). They also perform illocutionary acts. After all, they issue affirmations, requests, questions, commands, and so forth. Moreover, they perform perlocutionary acts. After all, they inform people, frighten them, warn them, entertain them, and so on. This is true of authors in general.

It is, I said, uncontroversial that authors perform speech acts. As I argued in Chapter 6, authors normally have intentions. And an important class of these intentions is the class of intentions to perform certain speech acts.

Ruskin's notion of author's meaning, I now suggest, encompasses the illocutionary acts the author performed by writing. "To get at the author's meaning" is to adequately capture these illocutionary acts. The basis underlying my suggestion is that Ruskin's notion of author's meaning involves the idea that authors mean things – more precisely, it involves the idea that they *mean to say* certain things (and not others), which is something that sentences and words cannot do, because they have no intentions. It is the notion we use when we ask: "What do you mean or intend (to say)?" It is the notion we use when we ask what Churchill meant or intended (to say) when he referred to Mussolini as "that utensil." It is the notion we use when we ask what erstwhile prime minister of the United Kingdom Benjamin Disraeli meant when he wrote, "I won't lose time to read your manuscript" – did he mean that he would read it immediately, or that he wouldn't read it at all? If he meant the former, then *that* was Disraeli's meaning. But if he meant the latter, then *that* was his meaning.

Ruskin's notion of author's meaning, I therefore suggest, also encompasses what Paul Grice has called *utterer's meaning*, a notion that he contrasted with *sentence meaning* (Grice 1989, 117–137). This is the difference between what a sentence means and what the speaker implicates (or implies, suggests, means to say) by uttering it. Consider the sentence "It is warm in here"; it has a meaning that everyone who reads these words understands perfectly well. For instance, when John utters that sentence in a particular context, he means that the window should be closed. But when Marie-Louise uses the same sentence in another context, she means that the window should be opened. This goes to show that it is one thing to know what a sentence means, but another to know what the user of that sentence means to say by using it. Most people who have read Disraeli's sentence know what it means, but not everyone who knows its meaning knows what Disraeli meant to say by using it.

Finally, Ruskin's notion, I suggest, also encompasses the author's perlocutionary act intentions. Writers often aim to secure certain effects through their writings: they want to inform people, warn them, entertain them, and so forth. Authors of textbooks aim at educating a readership, whereas the author of a love letter wants to convince the receiver of the letter of their love. Even if the authors fail in these aims, they still had the intentions.

Ruskin's injunction to get at the author's meaning (and not your own), then, can be paraphrased in different ways: to get at what the author meant to say; to get at what the author intended to communicate; to capture the author's thoughts and ideas; or to grasp the author's illocutionary and perlocutionary act intentions, as well as the author's intended conversational implicatures.

According to Richard Gaskin, talking about authorial intentions "is simply a roundabout way of referring to the objective meaning of the work" (Gaskin 2013, 218–219). The objective meaning of a work, he says, is its *original* meaning, which he describes as follows (Gaskin 2013, 219):

> The original meaning of a work of literature is a function of the meanings that its component words have in the language at the time of that work's promulgation, of the contemporary significance of the syntactic constructions into which those words are fitted, and of the work's historical and literary context. We may say that an author has the resulting or constructive intention to mean by his work what it objectively means in this sense.

Although this statement concerns literary works, I take it to hold across textual genres. My explanation of Ruskin's notion of author's meaning is virtually identical to Gaskin's notion of original meaning. The only difference is that, whereas Gaskin excludes speaker's meaning (as opposed to sentence meaning) from original meaning, I include it in Ruskin's notion. By my lights, Gaskin is not quite right in his exclusion, for speaker's meaning (in Grice's sense) is *also* part of the original meaning – it too is a function of the meanings of the component words, of the grammatical constructions used, and of the context of utterance.

It needs no argument that when we read, we often read for the author's meaning, understood in the way just explained.

Indicative Meaning (Including Subconscious Meaning)

Yet another notion of meaning is used in the following sentences: "The fact that the flag flies half-mast means that the nation is mourning"; "Mary is singing again; this means she feels happy again"; and "These specks mean you have measles." What we have here might be called the notion of *indicative meaning*, as certain things – the flag flying half-mast, Mary's singing, and certain specks – are indications of other things – people are mourning, Mary feels happy again, and someone has measles, respectively. Some symptoms are natural, while others are conventional. The specks are natural symptoms of measles, while the flag flying half-mast is a conventional symptom of mourning.

Sometimes, intentional human behaviors, or states of affairs resulting from those behaviors, are symptoms of something that the agent is or was unaware of. This also holds for texts and writing. Unbeknownst to herself, a writer may use only a limited number of sentence constructions, or mix metaphors, or select a relatively high percentage of words that have to do with warfare and battlefields. Other, more spectacular examples are what Freud has called *Fehlleistungen*, which the English translators of his work rendered as "parapraxes" – they are mistakes that betray something of the deep attitude of the person in question, such as miswritings, mishearings, misseeings, and slips of the tongue. One of Freud's examples is of a young man who ends his letter with *mit hässlichen Grüssen* (with hateful greetings) instead of *mit herzlichen Grüssen* (with cordial greetings). This, Freud avers, may look like a slip of the pen, but it may also reveal something of the writer's deep attitude toward the addressee – an attitude that the writer is unconscious of (Freud [1915] 1979, 50–110). In the latter case, the misspelling is a symptom of something else: it *means* something.

The rubric of symptom or indicative meaning also encompasses the rather elusive phenomenon that entire texts, in contrast to local misspellings, may express thoughts and ideas that go beyond what the author meant to say. In such cases, it wasn't the author's explicit illocutionary or perlocutionary intention or implicature to convey those particular thoughts and ideas. The author may be unaware of the very thoughts and ideas themselves – and this is *not* because of some false consciousness in the author. This sets the sort of cases I now have in mind apart from the Freudian cases mentioned in the previous paragraph, in which there *is* some sort of false consciousness. To substantiate the suggestion of the reality of this sort of symptom meaning, we may think, for example, of Shakespeare's *King Lear*. Certain thoughts and ideas in that drama may only become evident as the play is performed, thought about, criticized, and so forth. These thoughts and ideas may be latent in Shakespeare's text, and they may never have been explicitly contemplated by Shakespeare himself. Still, the drama, or the performances thereof, may be said to express (i.e., be a symptom of) those thoughts and ideas.

René Girard is a literary scholar who was rather keen on this kind of meaning. He argued that a number of novelists expressed important thoughts and ideas about desires and desiring that they had probably never explicitly contemplated.[3] The thought their works expresses, he argued, is that desires and desiring have a mimetic structure, by which he means that when person *X* desires something *Z*, *X* desires *Z* not because of *Z*'s own qualities but because some other person *Y* desires *Z* and *X*, unbeknownst to *X*self, mimics or imitates *Y*. Whether or not Girard is right is, of course, up for debate. But his approach to novels fits a general pattern, viz., that texts may express thoughts and ideas that their authors were unaware of. These texts have symptom meaning. For this specific subclass, a special term like *subconscious meaning* commends itself.

The rubric of symptom meaning encompasses yet another phenomenon, which is that texts are in different ways symptoms of cultural trends and social and societal arrangements that writers take more or less for granted and that certainly aren't the things they intended to write about (not the things they intended to communicate). Reading the seventeenth-century *Transactions of the Royal Society*, we are now struck by the personal nature of what we read there compared to what we read in, say, the latest issue of *Physical Review Letters*. Or compare the elaborate ways in which eighteenth-century writers conclude their letters to the current sober practice of ending even somewhat formal letters with "Best wishes" or "Yours." These modes of writing can be seen as symptoms or expressions

[3] René Girard discusses works by Proust, Stendhal, Flaubert, Cervantes, and Dostoyevsky. See Girard (1965).

of other things. Historians may regard them as signals of a particular cultural era or a particular social milieu, and of many other things as well. It is clear that when they do so, they aren't focused on author's meaning or sentence meaning or word meaning – rather, they are focused on symptom meaning.

Effect Meaning

Next, consider the sentence "The full meaning of the destruction of the Twin Towers dawned on him slowly." Here, the meaning of the attack on the Twin Towers is its significance, where the significance of an event is its relevance – i.e., a set of (alleged) unspecified or unspecifiable future effects or consequences of the item that has the meaning in question. I call this notion *effect meaning*, or *significance meaning*. Other sentences in which this notion of meaning is used are "The government has fallen, which means there will be elections" and "The sun shines, which means we won't have to bring our umbrellas."

It isn't only events that can have this kind of meaning: texts, too, can have it, for they too can be significant in the sense of being relevant and of having effects. When we say of a particular text that it is significant or meaningful, we may mean that it is likely to have future effects, but we may also mean that, looking back, we can see that it has had certain effects.

Functional Meaning

Humans make pottery, cutlery, ovens, tables, beds, clothes, and numerous other sorts of artifacts, such as laws and regulations, organizations, and societal structures. These things are made *with* a purpose and *for* a purpose. Pottery is intentionally made for the purpose of storing and cooking food in; cutlery is intentionally made for the purpose of civilized eating; laws and regulations are intentionally made for the purpose of structuring society; and so forth. These artifacts, we say, have meaning, their meanings being the functions they are intended to perform. I call this their *functional meaning*.

Texts too can have functional meanings. We speak of such meanings when we discuss the meaning of national anthems, or the meaning of Mao's "little red book" in contemporary China, or what the meaning is of the fact that some text was written by the prime minister and not by the king. Some texts are written with the intention that they perform a very specific function. Legal codices are written with the intention that they perform specific functions in jurisprudence and litigation; for instance, the function of reference source. Other texts are written or selected to perform specific and privileged functions in very specific contexts. National anthems, for example, are texts, sung on national days and at official ceremonies, whose function it is to affirm national identities. Churches have liturgical texts that are spoken or sung, the function of which is the attainment of some religious good. But there are also more humdrum functions that texts are sometimes intended to perform: shopping lists and to-do lists, for example, perform the function of aids to failing memories. Texts, then, can have meaning in the specific sense of being intended to perform certain very specific functions.

Value Meaning

There is one further notion of meaning to be distinguished. Consider the sentences "Nick's latest book means a lot to me" and "Hester's hike to Hannover was a meaningful experience for her." The notion of meaning used here is what might be called *value meaning*, since the meaning that the book and the hike are said to have is the *value* they have for some person.

Many things have value properties. Things mean something to us *because* they have value properties. Some acts mean much to us because they are acts of kindness; others, because they are acts of courage. Texts too have value properties. Certain papers mean much to us because the argument developed therein has intellective value: they are lucid, powerful, and original, and the conclusions are genuine insights. Certain letters mean much to us; we value them because they are expressions of genuine interest, or because we highly esteem its sender, or because its content is dear to us. Certain poems mean much to us because they are so beautiful. Texts of all genres can, for different reasons, mean much to us; we value them for something they have brought us.

These seven notions of meaning are distinct from each other. Of course, these meanings usually go hand in hand. For example, if a text has value meaning for you, you should at the very least know what the words composing the sentences mean, and you surely must know what the sentences composing the text mean. And it can be that a text has value meaning for you because of what the author meant to say, in which case value meaning is dependent on your grasping of the author's meaning. These relations notwithstanding, the notions are distinct and cannot be reduced to one another.

I have argued, then, that the objects of reading can have (or embody, or instantiate) a variety of meanings, and that we can read *for* these meanings; that is, read with the aim of grasping them.

How Do We Know about Meanings?

Having distinguished this variety of notions of meaning, we may ask: How do we *know* about meanings? How do we know word meanings, sentence meanings, author's meanings, and all the rest? In this section, I develop and defend the negative claim that we don't know about meanings through the natural sciences, and I will offer some very sketchy positive suggestions about how we do know about meanings.

There is no physical research, no chemical experiment, no biological evidence, no brain-science measurement we can turn to if we want to know or find out any of the following:

- what the word *Lusitanist* means
- what the sentence "During the second national bee count this weekend, over 19,000 bees were counted" means
- what Lincoln meant to say in the Gettysburg Address, what the original meaning of the address is
- whether a misspelled word is a slip of the pen or a parapraxis; so, whether it has symptom meaning
- what the future effects of the king's words will be; hence, what its significance meaning is
- what function the words *nihil obstat* have when printed on the mainly empty page at the beginning of a book
- what it meant for his father that Viktor wrote him that letter

When it comes to knowing any of the above meanings, what is needed is a kind of intelligence and reflection that just isn't "doing natural science." But then how *do* we know about meanings? Do we know them – assuming we *do* sometimes know them – through the operation of some of the sources mentioned in Chapter 3? Or do we know them through some kind of *non*natural scientific inquiry – through social scientific forms of inquiry, for example? Or are there yet other ways to know about meanings? Employing the notions of meaning presented in the previous section, I will discuss these questions and offer some suggestions.

We come to know word meanings in a variety of ways. First and foremost, there is the implicit testimony that we pick up from people who surround us and use words in certain ways. This is testimonial learning of a very specific sort: it is testimonial learning through imitation. The specifics of learning through imitation are intricate and subtle, and I won't try to analyze them here, but it surely needs to be mentioned as a major source of knowledge of words meanings. Second, there is the explicit testimony from dictionaries that we consult by reading them, which means that reading is a source of knowledge of word meanings. But we would not be able to learn the meanings of words through either implicit or explicit testimony if there wasn't a special source of linguistic knowledge in operation (perhaps the source that Noam Chomsky referred to as *linguistic competence*); a source that, as I stated in Chapter 6, animals lack. This source could be thought of either as a source in its own right or as a unique combination of more elementary sources such as perception, reason, and memory. We need not decide which way to go. But it surely looks as if the source through which we know word meanings is interwoven with memory, reason, and at least one of the sense modalities.

In the heyday of behaviorism, Leonard Bloomfield suggested that we know the meanings of words, as well as of more complex linguistic forms such as full sentences, in yet another way. The suggestion is based on a particular idea as to what meaning is: the "meaning of a linguistic form . . . is . . . the situation in which a speaker utters it and the response which it calls forth in a hearer" (Bloomfield 1935, 139). The thought here is that there is something common and peculiar to all the situations in which word *W* or sentence *S* is used, and there is something common and peculiar to people's responses when they hear or read *W* or *S*. If this is correct, then there would seem to be a social scientific way of figuring out the meaning of *W* or *S*. One would then have to identify the commonalities and particularities of the situations in which a particular linguistic form is used, and also identify the commonalities and peculiarities of the responses of hearers and readers to those forms. Knowing these situations of utterance as well as the behavioral responses to them *is* knowing the meaning of *W* or *S*. There are, however, many problems with this approach. I will highlight only one.[4] Consider the variety or responses that a parent's command "Come in now!" may elicit: no response (the child continues the activity engaged in as if no utterance was made); explicit refusal to comply; demand for justification; criticism of the parent for issuing a command; justification of noncompliance; plea for mercy; change of subject; running in the opposite direction; and compliance. The point is that there just doesn't seem to be a common response to "Come in

[4] This example is borrowed from Alston (1964, 27–28).

now!" and, hence, that on this account of meaning, this linguistic form has no clear meaning – or perhaps multiple meanings, both of which are incorrect. And imperatives are favorable cases for this account: for assertions, it is even more difficult to think of likely common responses. Think of all the possible behavioral responses to the advertisement "Jeff Koons exhibits in the Tate Gallery."

Next, consider the question of how we know what Lincoln meant to say in the Gettysburg Address. What is the author's meaning here? We can (come to) know this by a combination of (a) carefully reading the address, (b) finding out through investigation (or through attending to the testimony about such investigation) what the historical context was in which Lincoln delivered the address, and (c) acquiring some familiarity with Lincoln's character and the way he delivered speeches in general. We also need to know about (d) Lincoln's conversational implicatures, his perlocutionary intentions, and his illocutionary intentions, which we may know in part from the text and in part through historical inquiry. Likewise, we can (come to) know what Aesop's fable means by (a) carefully reading it and (b) becoming familiar with the genre of the fable, with how fables "work."

That a misspelled word is a parapraxis rather than a slip of the pen can be known only if Freud's theory is correct and the misspelling does in fact indicate the author's attitude toward the addressee. Whether Freud's theory is correct is an open question.

The significance meaning of a text can only be known if it has had some kind of effect; this can be studied by historians. Future effects of a text cannot be known, although they can be believed to be profound, due to, for instance, the social status of the writer, the communicated content, or the coverage that it is likely to receive. Believing that the significance meaning of a text will be thus and so, then, requires that one have access to grounds that make it likely that its significance will be thus and so. Social knowledge and reason will play key roles here.

The function of the words *nihil obstat* can be known through social and historical research, as well as through testimony.

What the value meaning of the letter to Viktor's father is can be known by Viktor's father through some form of self-observation. If others are to know this, they will have to rely either on Viktor's father's words or on a reconstruction of Viktor's family ties. But values cannot be known through the kind of research that is the business of the natural sciences. Values and what things *mean* to us are, rather, among the objects of the humanities. However, we know the value meanings of many things, including many texts, even without engaging in anything that qualifies as humanistic investigation.[5]

The general point I have been making in this section, then, is that meanings cannot be known through natural scientific research. This doesn't mean they cannot be known at all. Some meanings require social scientific inquiry; certain significance meanings, for example. But some meanings can be known independently of inquiry – for instance, many author's meanings, many value meanings, many word meanings, and many sentence meanings. To know these meanings often requires no more than a good modicum of common sense. Sometimes, however, it requires specialized skills, honed sensitivities, and knowledge that are characteristic of the humanities.[6]

General Account of Interpretation

If we assume, as seems utterly plausible, that there is a close relation between meaning and interpretation, the following, very general theory of interpretation commends itself:

> **General account of interpretation**: a statement, or a set of statements, is an interpretation of a text *T*, or of a part thereof, provided it attempts to specify the meaning or meanings of *T*, or of parts thereof.

This is only a first approximation. A number of comments should elucidate the account.

One. The general account, as its name indicates, is general. It is an "umbrella account," covering a number of much more specific accounts of interpretation that will be discussed in Chapters 8 and 9.

Two. The account says that an interpretation is an *attempt* to specify meanings. This is in recognition of the fact that interpretations can be misguided, incorrect, false, unjustified, implausible, or problematic in some other way. It is part of the account that interpretations are subject to standards of success, and also that it is possible for them to meet those standards – it is possible for interpretations to be well guided, correct, true, justified, plausible, or unproblematic.

[5] For more on this, see Van Woudenberg (2018b), where I argue that the humanities, in contrast with the sciences, study objects that have meaning that derives from human conventions, from human intentions, and/or from human purposive behavior.

[6] A thorough and fascinating historical discussion of the aims, skills, techniques, and results characteristic of the humanities is Bod (2015).

Three. Interpretations, the account says, are *statements* of meaning. But this must be understood somewhat liberally. Some interpretations are *explicit* statements; for example, the published specifications of the meanings of the words on the Rosetta Stone, the published specifications of the author's meaning of Shakespeare's *Macbeth*, and the published specifications of the effect meaning of the Declaration of Independence. But the interpretation of an entry in a cookbook, a humdrum newspaper article, or your uncle's email message telling you of his broken leg normally don't take the form of explicit statements – assuming that some form of interpretation is going on in the first place.[7] In these cases, and with this assumption, there is interpretation, but no explicit statement of meaning. These cases could be accommodated to the general account, however, by not requiring that the interpretative statement be made explicitly, but only implicitly. This can be done by taking recourse to counterfactuals, as follows. Suppose you read the newspaper article about the bee count. Also suppose that the following is true: if the question "What does the article actually say?" were put to you, you could accurately state an answer. My suggestion is that if the counterfactual statement is true of you, this means that you have made the statement, in the liberal sense of *statement* in which I intend the notion to be understood.

Four. The account must be understood in a somewhat qualified way in that there are specifications of meaning that do not qualify as interpretations. Statements to the effect that a text has value meaning for someone (e.g., "Nick's latest book means a lot to me") fall outside the scope of the general account. There is a principled reason for this. For word meaning, sentence meaning, author's meaning, indicative meaning, effect meaning, and functional meaning are all, in a way, *givens* – they are there for the reader to pick up. There are all sorts of interesting and subtle differences between the ways in which these meanings are givens; but the proper study of these differences will have to await another occasion. In the present context, the point is that value meanings fall outside the scope of the general account of interpretation because for readers, they are not givens. Of course, it can be a given that text *T* means a lot to person *X*. But the statement that *T* means much to *X* is not an interpretation of *X*. This means that, on the general account, all of the following kinds of statements qualify as interpretations:

1. The meaning of sentence *S* in text *T* is . . .
2. The meaning of word *W* in *T* is . . .

[7] In Chapter 8 I shall argue that this is indeed the case.

3. The author's meaning of *T* or of a part thereof (so, the illocutionary act intention and/or the perlocutionary act intention and/or the implicatures) is ...
4. Text *T* or a part thereof indicates that ... (which is *not* the author's meaning)
5. The effect that *T* had is ...
6. The function of *T* (in a particular era, in particular circles) is that ...

Interpretative statements of kinds (1) and (2) focus on the text, statements of kind (3) focus on what the author wants to communicate by means of the text, statements of kind (4) focus on what is unintentionally brought to expression by the author (in Chapter 9 I call them externalist interpretations), and statements of kinds (5) and (6) focus on two relational properties of the text. The accounts of interpretation that I shall be discussing target mainly interpretative statements of kinds (1)–(4).

Five. If statements of these kinds are made with a cognitive aim (so, if they are intended as truth claims), they should be buttressed by evidence. The kind of evidence relevant for one kind of interpretative statement differs from the kind of evidence relevant for an interpretative statement of another kind. Just compare the evidence needed to buttress the statement that *to procrastinate* means "to put things off" with the evidence needed to buttress the statement that the sentence "I'll be home for Christmas" is a promise and not a threat.

On the topic of interpretations being truth directed, I should like to insert a comment on Friedrich Nietzsche's famous statement, made in a short fragment in which he attacks positivism, that there are no facts, only interpretations (Nietzsche 1954, 458).[8] It may not be fully clear what Nietzsche is affirming here, but one take is that he denies there are objective facts; instead, there are only subjective interpretations. If Nietzsche means to say that there are no objective facts about, say, who composed "From the New World," who wrote *The Critique of Pure Reason*, whether the pressure of a volume of gas in a closed container that gets heated rises or not, or about how many moons are circling our planet, then there is no reason to do what he abhorred anyway – viz., to follow him.[9] For surely there are facts about these things (where I think of a fact as a state of affairs that obtains).[10] There are states of affairs that don't

[8] The German original reads: "Nein, gerade Tatsachen gibt es nicht, nur Interpretationen."

[9] He wrote, "Verhasst ist mir das Folgen und das Führen" (I hate to follow and I hate to lead); it is taken from the poem "Der Einsame" ("The Lonely One").

[10] My background here is Plantinga's metaphysics of modality as developed in Plantinga (1974, chapter 4).

obtain; for instance, the state of affairs consisting in Dublin being the capital of the United Kingdom, or the state of affairs consisting in Nietzsche being the author of the *Odyssey*. But many states of affair do obtain; for instance, the state of affairs consisting in Dublin being the capital of Ireland, the state of affairs consisting in Nietzsche being the author of *Also sprach Zarathustra*, and the facts mentioned earlier on in this paragraph. Moreover, some facts are known by us; for example, that every number greater than three is also greater than two, that the earth revolves around its axis, and that Franz Ferdinand, the pretender to the Austrian crown, was murdered in Sarajevo on June 28, 1914. Now, it is inessential for a fact's *being* a fact that it is known to be a fact by any human. There are many unknown facts, such as a fact about whether there is extraterrestrial life, a fact about what kills the novel coronavirus, and a fact about the number of trees in Costa Rica: these facts are currently not known by any human being.

Nietzsche contrasts facts with interpretations, and the way he does this suggests that interpretations are subjective: they are matters of mere preference or prejudice. Let me make this a bit more specific. His way of drawing the distinction suggests that, for any set of conflicting interpretations of what is assumed to be the same thing (a text, for example), there is no epistemically serious way to adjudicate between them. If this is indeed the view he propounded, then there is again no reason to follow him. For interpretations can often be known to be true (or false) – that is, they can often be known to state a fact (or not). When someone interprets the newspaper article about the bee count as being about beans, that person has a false interpretation of the article. Similarly, when someone interprets Aesop's fable about the fox and the crow as saying that flattery is a good thing because it brings its own reward, then that person's interpretation of the fable is false. But if someone interprets Robert Frost's poem "Stopping by Woods on a Snowy Evening" as being about the allure of death, then that interpretation may very well be true. If someone interprets a concert ticket with the text "Carnegie Hall, December 3, 1956, 8 o'clock" on it as indicating that the concert at Carnegie Hall on December 3, 1956, started at 8:00 p.m., then that interpretation is very likely true. Something's being an interpretation doesn't mean or entail that we are uncertain about it, or should be uncertain about, or should think of it as a mere opinion. Some interpretations are true; they are factive – others are false; they don't state facts. (I maintain this even if my interpretation of Nietzsche turns out to be false – even if, that is, his aphorism that there are no facts, only interpretations, should be interpreted differently from the way I interpreted it.[11])

These five remarks should elucidate the general account of interpretation given earlier. In the background of the account there is a leading idea about, as well as a certain "picture" of, interpretation. The leading idea is that to interpret a (part of a) text is to make sense of it (see, for instance, Lamarque 2000). When a text (or a part thereof) is unclear or doesn't make sense, the need for interpretation arises. It is not easy to state clearly and precisely what it is that one can when one *can* make sense of something, or what one cannot when one *cannot* make sense of it. But the broad contours will nevertheless be familiar to many. We read a passage and think, "So strange that the author says this; I expected the exact opposite"; or we think, "What the text says here conflicts with what it says there"; or we think, "I just don't get what the argument is supposed to be here"; or we think, "I just don't understand why what I read here is supposed to be obvious, which the author clearly assumes"; or we think, "Perhaps this makes sense against a certain background – but I just don't know what that background is!" We interpret in order to overcome obstacles that prevent us from making sense of what we read: we interpret in the interest of sense making. This is the idea on which traditional hermeneutics is based. Christian Thomasius, for example, has it that an interpretation is an evidence-based explication of what an author wanted his readers to understand but the understanding of which is difficult or dark.[12] In the same vein, Johann Martin Chladenius (1742, paragraph 180) tells us that the aim of interpretation is that dark passages become clear. Wilhelm Dilthey likewise articulates the traditional view when he says that interpretation is impossible when a text is completely alien to a reader, that it is superfluous when nothing in it is strange or dark to a reader, and that interpretation lies between these two extremes – interpretation is required where a text is somewhat strange to a reader, so as to make it understandable.[13] This idea about interpretation will recur in Chapter 8.

[11] I have been taking Nietzsche's aphorism at face value and have argued that, so taken, it is unacceptable. There is more to Nietzsche's views on facts and interpretations than this aphorism reveals, or so Schacht (1984) has argued. Particularly, Schacht avers that Nietzsche only rejects facts as positivists understand them; this may very well be true, but unfortunately Nietzsche doesn't explain what he takes that understanding to be.

[12] "Die Auslegung (interpretation) ist hier nichts anderes als eine deutliche und in wahrscheinlichen Muthmassungen gegründete Erklärung desjenigen, was ein anderer in seiner Schriften hat verstehen wollen, und welches zu verstehen etwas schwer oder dunkel ist" (Thomasius 1691).

[13] "Die Auslegung wäre unmöglich, wenn die Lebensäusserungen gänzlich fremd wären. Sie wäre unnötig, wenn in ihnen nichts fremd wäre. Zwischen diesen beiden äussersten Gegensätzen liegt sie

There is also, I believe, something of a picture, an image, that is attached to the notion of interpretation in general, at least when we leave out of consideration the notions that have to do with (musical or theatrical) performance and with the application of (legal or moral) rules. The picture is that some things are, as it were, *given* to us directly, but that sometimes, we want or need to go beyond what is directly given. Interpretation is going beyond what is directly given. In the case of textual interpretation, this works as follows. There are certain things that are given directly to us in the text. But often we do not stop there but want or need to go beyond these given things. In that case, we engage in acts of interpretation. Thinking about interpretation in this way requires a specification of these textual givens. Several options commend themselves here, as the textual givens can be described at different levels. The textual givens can be described as (a) straight and curved little lines; (b) written or printed words and sentences; (c) the content of the text as a whole; or (d) the text's message.

Depending on what one believes the textual givens to be, one will come down differently on where the process of interpretation starts. If one takes, say, in Aesop's fable of the fox and the crow, the textual givens to be (a) the straight and curved little lines, then one goes beyond what is directly given (and hence engages in acts of interpretation) when one says that the straight and curved little lines are English words – more specifically, that the first three sets of little lines are the words *A*, *crow*, and *having*. But when one takes the textual givens to be (b) the written or printed words and sentences (in a language), then one goes beyond what is directly given (and hence engages in acts of interpretation) when one says that the word *crow* means "passerine bird of the family Corvidae," and that the first sentence means that a bird of that family took a piece of cheese and flew into a tree in order to eat it – or when one says that it is an assertive speech act. And when one takes (c) the content of the text as a whole to be the textual given, then one goes beyond what is directly given (and hence engages in acts of interpretation) when one says that the fable's message is to beware of flattery and flatterers.[14] And the sequence doesn't end here, for one might take the textual given to be (d) the fable's message and then go beyond it and, hence, interpret it as an expression of ancient moralism.

also. Sie wird überall erfordert, wo etwas fremd ist, das die Kunst des Verstehens zu eigen machen soll" (Dilthey 1927, 225).

[14] This sequence resembles the application of Dretske's idea of secondary epistemic perception, discussed in the third section of Chapter 4.

Having thus presented the general account of interpretation, I move on, in the next chapters, to describe a number of *specific* accounts of interpretation. These descriptions are not intended as ladders to a platform where I can declare one the winner. For as will become clear, *textual interpretation* is a capacious notion, and all the accounts that I shall describe, however different they may be, are deserving of the name. This means that I won't be giving necessary conditions that are jointly sufficient for something's qualifying as textual interpretation – such conditions don't exist. Rather, each special account formulates only sufficient conditions. For each account, moreover, I shall discuss the epistemological aspects; that is, the factors that render an interpretation of the sort at hand justified or not.

CHAPTER 8

Knowledge through Interpretation (1)
Allegory, Difficulty, and Disambiguation

In this chapter, I discuss three specific accounts of interpretation that fall under the heading of the general account: first, the classical allegoresis account; next, the traditional difficulty account; and finally, the modernist account, according to which all reading involves interpretation. The focus is epistemological.

The Allegoresis Account of Interpretation: Two Kinds of Interpretation Knowledge

Hermeneutics is traditionally described as that field of investigation that aims to formulate rules or methods by which to interpret texts. One historically famous method is *allegoresis*. This is a method of nonliteral interpretation that is to be applied to some texts in order to unearth a deeper sense of the text, to expose its underlying, hidden meaning (Mantzavinos 2016). Allegoresis (or allegorical interpretation) fits the general account of interpretation because it is an attempt to specify the meaning of a text or of a part thereof. Allegoresis, moreover, clearly displays the element of going beyond what is given that, I suggested, is characteristic of interpretation: it goes beyond surface meaning. Doing this is at the same time an attempt to make sense of the text.

The allegoresis account of interpretation involves a notion of meaning – but which one? A little reflection can lead the way. The allegoresis account distinguishes between *surface meaning* and *deep meaning*. The distinction was made because it was felt that what authoritative texts such as Homer's *Iliad* on the surface mean, or seem to say, was inappropriate: what such texts seem to mean could not be what their authors really intended to convey. For this reason, the notion of a deeper sense, a hidden meaning, was introduced. The true meaning of these texts, it was urged, is the hidden meaning. In some cases, the hidden meaning is that which the author intended to communicate (so, what I have called author's meaning), which suggests that surface meaning is what I have called sentence meaning (or rather the totality of sentence meanings). In other cases, the hidden meaning is *not* what the author intended to communicate (i.e., not the author's meaning); in these cases, the surface meaning is the author's meaning, and the hidden meaning is a meaning that is projected onto the text or extracted from it by readers. In the former cases, the author intended his text to be an allegory; in the latter cases, he didn't. In this section, I focus on texts that are supposed to be intended as allegories.

One historically important example of allegoresis at work concerns Homer's account of warring gods in the *Iliad*. Being at each other's throats was felt to be unbecoming for gods and a most unedifying spectacle for humans to be confronted with. An allegorical interpretation of such texts has it that the wars as depicted are not between gods, but between elements. The war between Apollo and Poseidon, for instance, is really the battle between fire and water; the war between Athena and Ares is really the war between thoughtfulness and thoughtlessness; and the war between Aphrodite and Hermes is really the war between desire and reason (see Domaradzki 2017). It should not be assumed, however, that allegoresis can only take off when the surface meaning of a text is unbecoming. Practitioners of the genre can easily acknowledge the value of the surface meaning of a text, but consider it as not exhaustive.

An entailment of this is that if allegoresis seeks deeper meanings, then such interpretation is not needed to capture surface meanings. If some kind of interpretation is needed to capture the latter, it is not of the allegorical variety.

It goes without saying that not all texts have, and should not be supposed to have, a deeper meaning: regular travel guidebooks, cookbooks, course manuals, and business letters, for example, don't.

The epistemological question to be considered now is this: Under which conditions is an allegorical interpretation justified? For example, the satisfaction of which conditions would justify Theagenes of Rhegium's allegoresis that the hidden meaning of the war between Apollo and Poseidon is that it describes the battle between the elements of fire and water? It would seem that he must be justified in thinking, first, that a surface meaning of the text is that the gods are at each other's throats. He must also be justified in thinking that the text has a deeper sense. He finally must be justified in adopting the "interpretation key" that the god Apollo stands for fire and the god Poseidon for water. More generally and somewhat formally put,

S's allegorical interpretation of text *T* is justified iff

(i) *S* is justified in thinking that the surface meaning of *T* is that it says that p
(ii) *S* is justified in thinking that *T* has a deeper meaning: it says p^*
(iii) *S* is justified in adopting the interpretation key that gets him from p to p^*

These conditions need to be satisfied if Theagenes's allegoresis is to be justified. *Are* they satisfied? It seems rather clear that condition (i) is, for Theagenes knows the language. Whether (ii) and (iii) are also satisfied depends on a variety of factors. Theagenes assigned the *Iliad* a very high status, and this may justify him in thinking that Homer could not have wanted to say that the gods are at each other's throats. But what was his justification for assigning the *Iliad* such elevated status? To make a judgment on this requires interdisciplinary collaboration of classical scholars, historians, and philosophers. Classical scholars and historians can be expected to pronounce on what his reasons actually were, while philosophers can be expected to help decide whether those reasons justified Theagenes's belief about the elevated status of the *Iliad*. As I indicated in Chapter 1, there is no consensus among epistemologists about what justification *is*, nor about what is required for it. For present purposes I take an ecumenical view according to which justification comes in degrees and depends on a variety of factors, such as whether and the degree to which the target belief is internally coherent, coheres with other thoughts and beliefs of that person, and coheres with the thoughts and beliefs that were generally held at the time at that place. As a rule of thumb, the less coherence there is, the less justification, and the more, the more. We also need to consider whether the belief is based on what the person (at that time and place, and in that culture) thinks of as a good evidence; whether the belief results from what the person (at that time and place, and in that culture) thinks of as a reliable procedure. A very important factor is also the literary conventions that were in place at the time. Whether Theagenes was justified in thinking that the *Iliad* has a deeper meaning must be evaluated by reference to considerations of this sort.

In the ancient world, the Homeric texts were held to require allegorical interpretation. Within the Christian tradition, there has been an ongoing and incisive debate about its applicability to biblical texts.[1]

[1] A recent addition to the discussion is Carter (2018).

Epistemologically speaking, the point at issue is whether an allegorical interpretation can ever be justified – in other words, whether we can ever be justified in believing that a text has a deeper and hidden meaning. We should not assume that an allegoresis interpretation can never be justified, however. We are surely justified in believing that John Bunyan's *Pilgrim's Progress* (1678), Jonathan Swift's *Gulliver's Travels* (1726), and George Orwell's *Animal Farm* (1945) have deeper meanings and require allegorical interpretation.

Suppose now, if only for the sake of argument, that the allegorical interpretation of a particular text is justified, and, moreover, suppose it is true and that someone *S* believes it to be true. Then we should say that *S* has *interpretative knowledge* – that is, knowledge through interpretation. But we have to be more precise here. As we have distinguished two kinds of reading knowledge (RK_A and RK_B), we should also distinguish two kinds of interpretative knowledge. Interpretative knowledge of the *A*-variety could be described as knowing through interpretation that what *T* (or its author) says is *p*. Spelled out for Theagenes: he knows through allegoresis interpretation of the *Iliad* that what Homer says (means to say) is that there is a battle going on between fire and water.

This suggests the following general analysis:

> *S* has IK_A that *p* or, more precisely, *S* knows through interpretation (in this case, through allegorical interpretation) that what text *T* (or its author) says is *p* iff
>
> (i) *S* interprets *T*
> (ii) *T* (or its author) says *p*
> (iii) *S* believes that (ii) because of (i)
> (iv) *S*'s interpretation of *T* is justified

Condition (i) requires that the knowledge is acquired through interpretation, and not in some other way. Condition (ii) requires the factivity of interpretation, while condition (iii) requires that the belief is based on interpretation, and (iv) that the interpretation is justified.

Now suppose that Theagenes indeed comes to *know*, through allegoresis, that Homer says that there is a battle going on between fire and water, and let us say, if only for the sake of argument, that "There is a battle going on between fire and water" means "Water can extinguish fire, and fire can make water evaporate." Suppose furthermore that, intellectually serious as he is, Theagenes wants to know whether what Homer says is actually true. Now finally suppose that prior to reading and interpreting Homer, Theagenes didn't know that water can extinguish fire, nor that fire can make water evaporate. Can we then say that *through interpretation* of the *Iliad* he acquired interpretation knowledge of the *B*-variety, that is, knowledge through interpretation that water can extinguish fire and that fire can make water evaporate? If we can, this suggests the following analysis:

> *S* has IK_B that *p* or, more precisely, *S* knows through interpretation that what text *T* (or its author) says (viz., *p*) is true iff
>
> (i) *S* believes that *p* because *S* has IK_A of *p*
> (ii) *S* is justified in believing *p* because *S* has IK_A of *p*
> (iii) *p* is true

As with the two analyses of reading, this second analysis builds on the first, which is included in (i). Condition (ii) ensures that the justification is due to interpretation, which is as it should be, since the knowledge at hand should be *interpretative* knowledge. Condition (iii) ensures factivity.

The question remains whether we *can* say that Theagenes acquired interpretative knowledge that water can extinguish fire. I think we can *if* we think that all the conditions are satisfied. But are they? Any doubts we may have, I suspect, can be traced to doubts about whether (ii) is satisfied. Can Theagenes's belief be justified simply because (or simply in virtue of the fact that) he has the interpretative knowledge that Homer said that water can extinguish fire? What this boils down to is whether we can think that allegoresis is a reliable method. And this is a question I propose to put aside. But the crucial point to see is that if it *is* reliable, then the analysis of "*S* has IK_B that *p*" tells us what more is required for such interpretative knowledge.

The Difficulty Account of Interpretation

I now move on to an account of interpretation that differs from allegoresis in that it doesn't necessarily look for deeper and hidden meanings. But the allegoresis account can be viewed as a special case of it – at least in cases where the text at hand makes for a difficulty if it isn't understood allegorically. On the difficulty account, as I shall call it, interpretation is required when we encounter difficulties while reading a text – difficulties that are due to ignorance on the part of the reader.[2] I take this to be, at least in part, the traditional view on the relation between reading and

[2] I adopt the so-called new view of ignorance, according to which ignorance is the lack of true belief. I detail my reasons in Van Woudenberg (2009).

interpretation, held by (as we saw in the previous chapter) Thomasius, Chladenius, and Dilthey. In this section I discuss a number of specific ignorance-based difficulties that readers with epistemic interests may encounter, and how readers should try to resolve them. These difficulties must be distinguished from difficulties that are *not* based on ignorance on the part of the reader but on what I call textual opacity. Textual opacity can be due to holes in arguments and plots, illogical connections, intertextual inconsistencies, blurred lines of thought, and fuzzy thinking or confusion on the part of the writer. I will return to opacity-based difficulties in Chapter 9. For now, the focus is on difficulties based on reader's ignorance.

On the difficulty account, interpretation has a number of characteristics. First, since readers, if they encounter the difficulties I am about to discuss, are *conscious* of these difficulties, their interpretative efforts (assuming their aims are epistemic) will also be *conscious* undertakings. Hence, if there is such a thing as unconscious interpretation (a topic I shall take up in the next section), it falls outside the scope of the account. A further characteristic is that the difficulties it points to could, normally at least, be resolved by the author at the time that they composed their text. *Normally* – for authors can be confused about what they intend to write, their texts can be obscure to themselves, and in cases of *écriture automatique* they may not know *what* they have written (and in cases of hypnosis not even *that* they have written). A final characteristic is that this kind of interpretation is person relative: one reader may experience a difficulty where another does not and, accordingly, one reader may have to engage in interpretation where another may not.

Difficulties about What the Words Are

Some hindrances to reading are of a rather elementary and prosaic nature. First, it may be that the surface that carries the words has been damaged or deteriorated over time so that the words have become illegible. The causes of this may be that holes have fallen into scrolls, papyri have partly crumbled, handwritten letters have partly decomposed, electronic files have got jumbled, or ink from pen or printer has lightened over time. These causes of damage are purely physical. Or it may be that words have "traveled" from one surface to another: they have been manually copied, as was a standard procedure up until the Renaissance. It may so have happened that copyists made small mistakes and so produced a partly corrupted text. Or, if they didn't unintentionally make mistakes, they sometimes intentionally "corrected" the text in a bad way. Finally, it may be that an author misspelled a word or misused it, perhaps assuming that it means something it doesn't mean.

On the proposed account, resolutions of such difficulties qualify as interpretations. Examples are statements such as "The word that has become illegible is the word *W*" and "This is a corrupt passage – it should read thus and so" and "That is a printing mistake."

Over the ages a lot of intelligence and ingenuity has been brought to solving difficulties of this sort by graphologists, stemmatologists, book scientists, and others. How these difficulties are sometimes overcome is a technical matter that I don't intend to enter into. But, depending on the nature of the difficulty, proposed solutions are justified to the extent that they are based on such evidence[3] as knowledge of handwriting practices in different eras (which abbreviations were in use; what forms letters take over time) and of individual authors; of copying practices; of printing and typesetting practices; of the language at the time of writing (certain words, or words used in specific senses, may not yet have been available at the time of writing); and of the intellectual milieu of the writer (which makes it likely that he used certain words and expressions, but unlikely that he used others).

If a reader has successfully solved difficulties in a justified way, they have acquired knowledge of *what the text is*. Put this way, what we have here doesn't strictly qualify as *interpretative* knowledge, since it is not a specification of a meaning of the text or of a part thereof. However, such knowledge is normally based on interpretation. For example, when a word has become illegible, the hypothesis that it is word *W* that has become illegible can be justified by the fact that it makes most sense of the sentence's meaning. This suggests the following, somewhat more capacious, account of interpretative knowledge:

> *S*'s knowing that *p* is *interpretative* knowledge iff *p* is a proposition that either specifies meaning or is *based on* propositions that specify meaning.

Correct resolutions of difficulties as to what the words are, on this more capacious account, qualify as instances of interpretative knowledge.

[3] Evidence, as I use the notion, is whatever is relevant to the justificatory status of a belief. Evidence can consist of things we know and of experiences, but also of things we have good reason to believe. To avoid cumbersome locutions, I only mention *knowledge* in the body of the text, but this should be understood in a wider sense.

Ignorance of the Meaning of a Word

Even when one knows what the words one is reading are, one may be ignorant of their meaning. For example, you read William Wordsworth's poem "I Wandered Lonely as a Cloud," a poem that narrates a walk along the side of a lake. At one point, the poem's narrator sees a host of daffodils and exclaims, "A poet could not be but gay, / In such a jocund company." Suppose your difficulty with this line is that you don't know what *gay* means. You take up a historical dictionary to find that one of its meanings is "joyous," and that in Wordsworth's day, it did not yet mean "homosexual." Given this fact and given the fact that in the larger textual unit in which the word occurs it makes sense to think that it means "joyous," you draw your conclusion.

Difficulties about word meanings should be solved on the basis of evidence; wishful thinking or projection won't do. Relevant evidence includes what relevant dictionaries list as meanings of a word; whether the sentence containing the difficult word makes sense if the word is used in a particular meaning; knowledge of grammar as functioning at the time of writing; and cultural-historical knowledge of which words, in which meanings, were available, and which were unavailable, at the time of writing.

A reader who has resolved a difficulty of this sort has, in fact, specified meaning – i.e., the meaning of a word. Hence what the reader does fits the general account of interpretation. If the specification is correct and justified, the reader has acquired interpretative knowledge of the *A*-variety; that is, knowledge of what a particular word means. With respect to word meaning, there is no interpretation of the *B*-variety.

Ignorance of the Reference

Another difficulty that readers may face concerns *reference*. One may never have heard the proper names Kipchoge and Mariana Alcoforado, and one may not know whether these names have bearers, and if they do, who they are or were, where they live or lived, and so forth. The same holds for rigid designators – singular terms that uniquely pick out one object from among all other objects – like "the tallest man in South Dakota" or "the instrument that Schumann loved most": someone reading these expressions may not be able to pick out that tallest man or that beloved instrument. It also holds for plural referring expressions like "the early Roman kings" and "the members of the college" – a reader may not know who falls in the extension of these expressions.

Not knowing the referent of a name or other rigid designators, or of plural referring expressions, *may* prevent one from more fully understanding a text or a part thereof. An illustration of the point is the story, related in the biblical book of Acts, chapter 8, of an Ethiopian who was an official to Queen Candace and who was reading the words from the prophet Isaiah: "Like a sheep he was led to the slaughter, and as a lamb before its shearer is dumb, so he opens not his mouth." The Ethiopian official was wondering whether Isaiah was referring to himself or to someone else. When the apostle Philip tells him that the referent is Christ, he gets a more adequate grasp on what he has been reading, a better understanding – or so the Christian tradition has maintained.

That said, we mustn't assume that ignorance of reference always or inevitably forestalls a more adequate understanding of what one is reading. Upon reading Shakespeare's sonnet "Shall I Compare Thee to a Summer's Day?" one may wonder who has been so fortunate as to be compared by Shakespeare to a summer's day. Is it a specific woman, or, as is widely held, is it a specific man (Bryson 2008)? It doesn't seem to matter much here: the poem can be understood, its meaning grasped, even by a reader who doesn't know the referent of *thee*, and even if the second personal pronoun never had a flesh-and-blood referent.

The epistemological question arises as to how to fix the referent of a name or of a definite description that one is ignorant of (assuming there is one). Relevant evidence may be found in the text itself but can also come from other sources, like testimony from the author and from historical, geographical, and other research.

Suppose one has found a justified and adequate solution to a reference problem and one believes in the solution – does one then have *interpretative* knowledge? If one has, then (given the general account of interpretation) "Shakespeare compared Mr./Ms. *X* to a summer's day" should be a statement of meaning. Is it? Well, yes, for in this case *thee* means "Mr./Ms. *X*." (Compare "Who do you mean?" "I mean you!")

Not Knowing What a Sentence Means

Next, readers may not know what a sentence means even though they know all the words. Two distinct phenomena fit in this class. First, a sentence can be ambiguous because some of the words it contains have multiple meanings. Consider, for example, the sentence that Noam Chomsky used in this context, "The fish is ready to eat," or the sentence that Benjamin Disraeli used when someone sent him a manuscript,

"I won't lose time to read your manuscript." Ambiguity can best be explained by means of the sentence-proposition distinction: in each of these examples, one sentence can be used to express different propositions.

Overcoming difficulties of this sort requires, first, disambiguating the sentence – so identifying the various propositions that the sentence might be used to express – and, second, settling on which of these propositions the author most likely intended it to express. Such interpretations, if they are to be justified, should be based on evidence. Knowledge of the situational and textual context in which the sentence is used will often settle the matter.

Second, a reader may also be ignorant of the meaning of a sentence because it is not clear to them whether a sentence is an endorsement of something or the mere reporting of a fact, whether it is a question or a request, whether the question is genuine or rhetorical, whether it is a compliment or an insult, a promise or a threat, a joke or a serious proposition. Ignorance about which of these alternatives is the most likely may impede a proper grasp of the meaning of the sentence. The difficulties are unclarities about the kind of speech act that an author performs, or *intended* to perform, by writing the sentence at issue.

Evidence helps readers to overcome such difficulties, such as evidence concerning the direct context of the sentence and concerning the general thrust of the text that the puzzling sentence is a part of, but also intelligent reflection on what makes most sense, and knowledge of the shared beliefs and convictions of the community to which the author belonged.

Proposed solutions to these difficulties qualify as interpretations – they are specifications of meanings, viz., sentence meaning and author's meaning. Such solutions thus fit the general account of interpretation. And in a relevant sense they go beyond something that is directly given, and they are ways of making sense of what one is reading. If the interpretation is accurate and based on evidence, the reader has interpretative knowledge of the *A*-variety.

Ignorance of Authorship

Another difficulty that readers may meet – and that readers on the Internet increasingly will meet – is not knowing who authored the words they are reading. This will not always pose a difficulty, but it surely sometimes does. For example, it has recently been argued that the ancient Greek work known as *De mundo* was authored by Aristotle himself. For fully appreciating Aristotle's full views on the soul, this is a claim of some moment, for if it is true, a number of passages about the soul in the *corpus Aristotelicum* have throughout the centuries been misunderstood (Bos 2003).

Another example is that some websites contain serious libel, disinformation, outright falsehoods, and bald lies. Many of these pages cannot be traced to authors who can be held responsible for them. Such texts pollute entire channels of communication. There are two general and related points to be made here. First, ignorance of authorship keeps readers from the often-important business of making responsibility ascriptions. Second, it is, in general, a matter of great import who says what. It matters a great deal whether the president of the United States says that North Korea must comply or else be eliminated, or your local shopkeeper says it. Ignorance of authorship can, in some cases, hinder assigning the proper weight or significance to the words that we read.

All of this is compatible with the fact that sometimes, anonymity is a good thing; for instance, when it protects writers against unjust retaliation. It can forestall shooting-the-messenger dynamics and may protect whistleblowers.[4]

Finding out about authorship should be based on such evidence as knowledge concerning the milieu and context in which the text was produced – that is, knowledge concerning which ideas were prevalent at the time of writing (if the time is known) and familiarity with the writing style and other idiosyncrasies of candidate authors – and knowledge of who could have profited from anonymous publication, and how. In the absence of these kinds of evidence, authorship may remain unknown.

If readers have accurately and with justification found a solution to an authorship problem, they have acquired knowledge. Is this *interpretative* knowledge? Yes, it can be, when *T*'s style and content characteristics indicate that *X* authored *T*, which is a statement that explicates indicative meaning and hence qualifies as an interpretation. When authorship is established in other ways, it will most likely be based on interpretative knowledge.

Not Knowing Why the Author Wrote It

Even if none of the difficulties discussed so far arise, or if they have been solved to the reader's satisfaction, a reader may still not understand *why* an

[4] As Bouter and Hendrix (2017) have shown, whistleblowers play an important role in diagnosing research misconduct, but they often experience severe negative consequences. Bouter and Hendrix argue that even though anonymous whistleblowing should be discouraged, under certain conditions it can be legitimate.

author wrote what they wrote. Since why-questions can ask for motivations (or causes) as well as for purposes, readers may be doubly puzzled: they may not understand *what motivated* the author to write the text, but they may also not understand *to what purpose* the author wrote it. We should not suppose, however, that there is an airtight distinction between the two, because purposes can be motivators at the same time: for example, your purpose in writing a specific email is to make contact, but that purpose itself can motivate you to write it. But the two can come apart.

As to what motivated someone to write something, there is no dearth of possibilities: the wish to become famous, the need to make ends meet (in combination with the belief that writing pays), the urge to creatively express oneself, the hope that by writing one will attain clarity in thinking, and so on. These are what Jeffrey Stout called extrinsic motivations. Writers also have intrinsic motivations; for instance, to show what is right or wrong in Edmund Burke's views on conservatism, to explain how to operate the new type of lawn mower, or to explain how Houdini did his dangerous tricks. Intrinsic motivations are mirrored in an author's illocutionary and perlocutionary act intentions. Some of these intrinsic motivations, as we can see, are aims. Not knowing why an author wrote what they wrote is the same as lacking a Type II understanding of an author (see Chapter 2).

If readers have accurately and with justification solved a puzzle about why an author wrote what they wrote, they have acquired knowledge. Justification in cases like these depends on evidence consisting of textual cues and concerning the psychological makeup and intellectual profile of the author, other works written by the author, knowledge of the views of the author about the work at issue, and so forth.

Is such knowledge *interpretative* knowledge? Yes, it is, for statements like "*X*'s motivations and purposes in writing *T*" are statements of illocutionary and perlocutionary act intentions and hence statements about author's meaning – thus, they qualify as interpretations on the general account of interpretation.

Ignorance of Genre

A final group of difficulties that readers may experience and that I want to mention are difficulties due to ignorance of the literary genre to which the text belongs. Between literary genres, differences exist in the conventions (techniques, rules) constitutive of the genres. The reader's expectations and genre should make a good fit. If one doesn't know whether the text is popular science writing or science fiction, one won't be able to know its author's meaning.

If a readership expects the first chapter of the biblical book of Genesis to provide historical information about what once happened during a particular week some 6,000 years ago (much in the way Anne Frank's diary provides historical information about what happened to her during a particular week in the Second World War) whereas the author(s) of Genesis worked from assumptions that don't match these expectations, then misunderstanding will ensue.[5]

A reader may find difficulties in reading a text on the assumption that it belongs to genre *G*. But suppose the difficulties disappear on the hypothesis that the text belongs to genre *G**. Then this may be evidence that the text belongs to genre *G**. Informed decisions about how to understand a text, if they are to be justified, should be based on evidence that may consist of knowledge of the characteristics of the various genres, knowledge that the author intended to write in a particular genre, and so forth. The default assumption should be that the author did not write – and did not intend to write – nonsense, or wildly incoherent ideas, or things that fly in the face of accepted common sense. That is, readers should heed the default principle of charity of interpretation.

Suppose now that a reader correctly and with justification comes to believe that the text at hand belongs to genre *G*. Then the reader has acquired knowledge. Is it *interpretative* knowledge – is it a statement that specifies meaning? In a somewhat indirect way, I suggest, it is. For knowing that *T* belongs to genre *G* tells you how to approach or interpret *T*. Perhaps we could say it is a higher-order level of the meaning of *T*. But I won't pursue this any further.

This ends my discussion of the difficulty account of interpretation. I don't claim completeness for the list of difficulties, but it should give a decent sense of the kind of difficulties involved. To have a proper understanding of the account, two more things need to be said. First, I emphasize again that the account concerns interpretation that is needed due to ignorance on the part of the reader, not due to textual opacity. Second, it may be that readers experience none of the difficulties discussed in this section – or that they did but solved them all – and that nonetheless the reader remains ignorant of the central message of the text. I discuss this matter in Chapter 9 under the heading of *holism*.

[5] This argument is made by Walton (2009).

An Objection to the Difficulty Account

The difficulty account as I have presented it has an implication that may seem counterintuitive if not outright false to many. It can be put as follows. Suppose two persons, Ms. *X* and Mr. *Y*, read *T*. Ms. *X* experiences none of the difficulties discussed in the previous section, whereas Mr. *Y* experiences, and overcomes, several of them. Then this account entails that whereas Mr. *Y* has engaged in acts of interpretation, Ms. *X* has not. This may look problematic for various reasons.

It may look problematic, first, because Ms. *X* and Mr. *Y* have in the end (let us assume) reached the same epistemic goal – they both understand what the text, or its author, says. But if they've reached the same goal, they must have traveled the same way; perhaps the one traveled unreflectively and the other reflectively, but it is the same way nonetheless. Second and related, the account depicts interpretation as an affair that is much too self-conscious and self-reflective, failing to acknowledge the fact that much interpretation goes on implicitly, unreflectively, in subtle and unconscious ways. Ms. *X*, who experienced no difficulties, surely interpreted what she read in implicit, unreflective, subtle, and unconscious ways.

These objections could be reinforced by considering cases in which a reader initially faces difficulties in reading a text but overcomes them step by step so that reading it becomes easy, in the end proceeding even more or less automatically. Is this reader initially engaging in acts of interpretation, but later on no longer so, simply because the proceeding has become smooth and unreflective? That looks strange. Compare Wittgenstein's reflections on following a rule, such as following a recipe (Wittgenstein 2009, sections 185–242). When someone follows a recipe for the first time, it will be a self-conscious, self-reflective, and time-consuming affair. But after following it twenty times it becomes easy and automatic. Is, after those twenty times, the person no longer following the recipe, simply *because* it has become easy and automatic? That seems wrong. Likewise, readers should be thought to engage in interpretation even when the reading is easy and poses no particular problems.

And then there is the related point that some difficulties are much easier to overcome than others. Ignorance of the meaning of a particular word can be overcome by consulting a dictionary. Is that really difficult? Ignorance of authorship can, in some cases, be overcome by rather intricate literal-historical inquiry – *that* is difficult. What the account as stated overlooks is the fact that difficulties come in degrees and that overcoming them therefore requires various degrees of effort. But then the picture that naturally suggests itself is that interpretation is something that can be represented on a scale, the one extreme of which represents automatic, unself-conscious, and implicit interpretation, and the other conscious and self-reflective interpretation.

By way of response, I first note that it is correct that the account reserves the notion of interpretation for self-conscious and self-reflective dealings with reading difficulties. This was explicitly so defined. But I left open the possibility that there is a sense of *interpreting* such that both Ms. *X* and Mr. *Y* interpret when they read. *Is* there such a sense? this Chapter I shall argued that there is.

Before getting there, I offer some reflections on the other elements of the question. The following-a-recipe thought is that this is something that initially may be really difficult but that can become smooth and easy, but that all the time, the recipe is followed. So the difficult–easy distinction is irrelevant when it comes to following a recipe. Likewise, the objector says, for interpretation. This raises two questions. First, can we say in general that the difficult–easy distinction is irrelevant for making distinctions between *X*s and not-*X*s? And secondly, is interpretation relevantly *like* following a recipe?

As to the first question, consider a child who is learning how to do simple additions, let us call him *X*, and a professional mathematician that we shall call *Y*. Suppose both must add 316 and 434. *X* puts the second number below the first one, then adds 4 to 6, making 10, and writes, below a line that he drew, the number 0; then he adds 1 to 1 and 3, making 5, which he also writes below the line, to the left of the number 0; finally, he adds 3 and 4, making 7, which he also writes below the line, to the left of the number 5. In this way *X* has calculated that the addition of 316 and 434 makes 750. But *Y* need not make these or any calculations – she "sees" the correct sum immediately. What *X* did was on the difficult side of the difficult–easy distinction, whereas what *Y* did was on the easy side of it. If the following-a-recipe thought is mimicked here, we should presumably say that *X* and *Y* did the same thing – they performed calculations – and add that whereas *X* did so self-consciously, explicitly, and with some difficulty, *Y* did so implicitly, automatically, and easily. However, many epistemologists will say that this is wrong, because *X* and *Y* did not travel the same cognitive route: *X reasoned* his way toward the sum, whereas *Y intuited* the sum. It is phenomenologically unsatisfying to say that *Y* reasoned "implicitly." *X* and *Y* came to know the sum via different ways, through the operation of different sources. This difference was at issue in Chapter 3, where I discussed the twofold office of reason.

Saying that *Y* intuited the sum doesn't entail that when she considered the addition in her tender years, she then intuited it too – we may assume that at one time she had to make the calculation in much the same way that *X* did. But this shouldn't seduce us into thinking that now that she is a professional mathematician, she *still* must calculate the sum, albeit that the process now is quicker, easier, and unconscious.

What I intend this to show is that, if a result *R* is reached by persons *A* and *B* such that *A* reaches *R* in a way that involves overcoming ignorance-based difficulties while *B* reaches *R* effortlessly and immediately, we must *not* conclude from this that the process operative in *A is the same* as the process operative in *B*, albeit disguised because it works unconsciously and automatically. Calculation of and direct insight into the sum are different things. If this analogy is to be relevant to the concerns of this chapter, there should be a result *R* that reader Mr. *Y*, who faces a difficulty, and reader Ms. *X*, who does not, both aim to reach. It would seem that the result that both aim at is something like a basic understanding of the text, some sense of what the words jointly mean. Toward that end they do different things. We cannot conclude that what Ms. *X* does in order to reach that result is an implicit or unconscious version of the process that was operative in Mr. *Y*, who reached the same result only after having solved difficulties. I called the latter process *interpretation*. I take it that this classical distinction is plausible and helpful. But it remains an open question whether the easy reader doesn't engage in something that merits the appellation of interpretation as well – but as indicated, I will get to that later on in this Chapter.

Apropos the second question, I think we should be skeptical about the idea that interpretation is relevantly like following a recipe. A recipe is an algorithm, a set of rules such that following them ensures an intended result. For interpretations of the sort covered in this section, however, there doesn't seem to be an algorithm. If there are rules that guide difficulty-overcoming interpretations, they are rules of thumb at best. Such rules don't ensure a correct result.

The objector also pointed out that some difficulties are much easier to overcome than others. And this, the objector continues, means that interpretation comes in degrees. This, however, is not so much an objection as a welcome implication of the view. For it matches, phenomenologically speaking, the experience that it is much harder to reach a basic or ground-level understanding of some texts than of others: it is much harder to understand Kant's *Critique of Pure Reason* (or a part thereof, such as the "Transcendental Deduction of the Concepts of Pure Reason") than Robert Herrick's poem "To the Virgins, to Make Much of Time," and it is much easier to reach a ground-level understanding of the bee-count newspaper article than of a recent paper in *Physical Review.*

The Modernist View: No Reading without Interpretation

The view pushed by objectors to the difficulty account of interpretation is that readers, even when they don't have to overcome difficulties in order to get a ground-level understanding of a text, engage in interpretation. Here is a recent rough and sketchy statement of the view:

> Reading is an interpretative act and this is not simply the case when it comes to what we think of as more complex writing – religious scriptures, philosophical texts, legal documents, or literary works. The simplest language can need interpretation. If, when driving, we see a sign saying "Heavy Plant Crossing," this minimal communication needs consideration; we need to be able to understand "plant," in this context, as meaning not a living thing that grows in earth, water, or on other plants, but rather as meaning a large, heavy machine or vehicles used, for example, in road-building. We expect large lorries and earth-movers, not triffid-like monsters. (Jack 2019, 94)

This quotation contains two somewhat different suggestions. It starts out by saying that reading is an interpretative act, which sounds like a characterization of what is essential to reading, but in the very next sentence it articulates the weaker view that language (by which, I take it, is meant the written words that we read) "can" need interpretation, which sounds like some language doesn't need that, in which case reading is not always – hence, not necessarily – an interpretative act. Let us call the first view the essentialist view, the second the accidentalist view. The modernist view is the essentialist view. It is the view that all reading involves interpretation, and that this is not just a matter of happenstance, a perhaps interesting but in the end contingent fact about humans or about human psychology. The modernist view makes a *modal* claim: we *can*not read without interpreting; it is *impossible* to read and not engage in acts of interpretation. Chief proponents of the modernist view include Hans-Georg Gadamer[6] and Paul Ricoeur (see Bleicher 1980; Westphal 2009; Zimmermann 2015).

[6] Here I make a wide gesture to Gadamer's papers in Gadamer (1976). What I have called the modernist view is nowhere explicitly stated, nor is it named by that name (I suspect Gadamer would disown the term, as in many respects he represents traditionalist tendencies; but in the particular respect that I am focusing on, he does strike a distinctly nontraditional, modernist pose), but it seems presupposed or entailed by many things that he writes.

The quoted passage contains an example of interpretation. The words "Heavy Plant Crossing," in order to be understood properly, must be interpreted. And they must be interpreted because *plant* has multiple meanings. It can mean, as a noun, "a young tree, vine, shrub, or herb" but also "the land, buildings, machinery, apparatus, and fixtures employed in carrying on a trade or an industrial business" (*Merriam-Webster*). And to interpret, in this case, is to select from among various alternatives the presumed correct meaning of *plant* in the context. Many sentences are like this in that they contain words with multiple meanings. The sentence "The bishop pair is a powerful weapon, since two bishops working together can control many squares from a distance, which is useful in both attack and defense" contains the staggering 10^{12} possible combinations of word meanings.[7] In order to understand it properly, a huge amount of disambiguation must take place.

This suggests that when we read sentences that contain words each of which has only one meaning, we don't or even can't engage in interpretation. If this is correct, it means that the sentence "John Henry Newman's corpse was exhumed more than once" needs no interpretation in order to be understood – or, better, it *can*not be interpreted, because all the words in it are semantically unambiguous (*corpse*, unlike *corps*, has only one meaning, viz., "dead body"). Still, we could say that if we are disambiguating words in sentences, we are engaging in interpretation. We could state:

> **Interpretation qua lexical disambiguation (IqLD)**: a sentence is interpreted if it contains at least one word that has multiple meanings and that needs to be disambiguated in order for a reader to arrive at what is supposed to be the proper understanding of the sentence.

Lexical disambiguation can be a self-conscious and reflective affair, but it can also be smooth, unreflective, and automatic. For this reason, this is a notion of interpretation that applies both to easy-reading Ms. *X* and to difficulty-facing Mr. *Y* (if the difficulty concerns word meaning). What is key is that both engage in lexical disambiguation and hence in acts of interpretation – the one self-consciously, the other not.

[7] The example is taken from Postma (2019, 5) where the following calculation is offered: The bishop (3) pair (4) is (13) a powerful (5) weapon (2) since two (1) bishops (3) working (27) together (6) can (2) control (8) many (1) squares (8) from the distance (6), which is (13) useful (2) in both attack (9) and defense (12) $\rightarrow 3 \times 4 \times 13 \times 5 \times 2 \times 1 \times 3 \times 27 \times 6 \times 2 \times 8 \times 1 \times 8 \times 6 \times 13 \times 2 \times 9 \times 12 = 10^{12}$.

IqLD does not capture the modernist view of interpretation fully: the modernist holds that *all* reading involves interpretation, whereas IqLD allows for reading without interpretation. To obtain a better view of the modernist notion of interpretation, we should take a cue from the idea of disambiguation. We could say that a reader interprets a text (or a part of it) if they engage in any kind of disambiguation (i.e., in any kind of selection from among genuine alternatives). And since texts (or parts thereof) can be ambiguous in different respects, interpretations can differ with respect to the item disambiguated. Disambiguation is taking place when we read sentences like "The oak was felled" – is *oak* used literally or metaphorically? If it is used literally, the sentence is about a particular tree of the genus *Quercus* of the Fagaceae family. If it is used metaphorically, it is, or can be, about a deceased person who was a stronghold in their community. Likewise, many sentences can be used to perform different speech acts, and so for a reader to pick out the intended one requires disambiguation and, hence, interpretation. Examples are the abovementioned Disraeli and Chomsky sentences. Disambiguation is also going on when we read personal pronouns and indexicals. *I* can refer to anybody who can write or speak, and *you* and *he/she/they* can refer to anybody. *Here* can refer to any place where there are human beings who are speaking or writing, and *there* can refer to any place. *Now* can refer to any time at which humans utter that word. *Then* can refer to any time. So, in order for a reader of pronouns and indexicals to pick out the intended persons, places, and times, disambiguation (and, hence, interpretation) is required.

We may therefore distinguish, in addition to IqLD,

> **Interpretation qua mode disambiguation (IqMD)**: a sentence is interpreted if, in order for it to make (the most likely) sense, a reader must select from a multiplicity of possible writing modes the one that the author has likely availed himself of (literal, metaphorical, cynical, tongue-in-cheek, sarcastic, etc.).

> **Interpretation qua speech-act disambiguation (IqSAD)**: a sentence is interpreted if, in order for it to make (the most likely) sense, a reader must select from a multiplicity of possible speech acts the one(s) that the author has likely performed by means of it.[8]

[8] This formulation is too general and should be appropriately narrowed down. It is too general, because one and the same sentence that is written down can be a locutionary, an illocutionary, and a perlocutionary act at the same time – in which case no selection is needed. However, one and the same written-down sentence can be used both as a threat and as a promise, *but not at the same time*. IqSAD should be understood as taking care of this.

> **Interpretation qua reference disambiguation (IqRD)**: a referring term (definite description, proper name) is interpreted if, in order for the sentence or larger textual unit to make (the most likely) sense, a reader must select from a multiplicity of referents the one to which the term likely refers.

There are likely other kinds of ambiguities in texts. Generalizing over them, we can state:

> **Interpretation qua disambiguation (IqD)**: to interpret a word, or a sentence, or a text, is to disambiguate it – i.e., to select from a multiplicity of possibilities the most likely one, the one that makes the most sense.

If all reading is to involve interpretation, as the modernist view has it, and if interpretation is disambiguation, then everything we read should contain at least one ambiguity. Whether this is the case is a factual matter. But it surely seems that something like disambiguation takes place very often.

The IqD account of interpretation is epistemologically relevant in a threefold way. First, it is veritistic in nature: disambiguations can be correct or incorrect, and often they can be *known* to be correct or incorrect. Second, on this account interpretations can be justified to any degree, and the relation between truth and justification can be thought of in BonJour's way: the more justification one has for an interpretation, the more likely it is that that interpretation is true. Third, readers can obtain interpretative knowledge of the two varieties that I distinguished in Chapter 7: knowledge of what a text or a part thereof (or its author) says (what I have called IK_A) and knowledge that what a text (or its author) says is true (what I have called IK_B).

The justification of an IqD is dependent on a variety of factors. There doesn't seem to be any hard formula that covers all these factors, nor one that specifies their relative weights. Generally speaking, factors that are relevant include

- the ordinary meanings of words at the time they were used;
- the genre conventions that were in force at the time the text was written;
- what we know from other sources of the author's views, intentions, aims, and purposes; and
- whether the text makes more sense, is rendered more intelligible, when interpreted this way rather than that way.

The epistemology of IqD has structural parallels with the widely discussed epistemological principle according to which knowing that *p* requires the elimination of all not-*p* possibilities. The intuition behind this principle, as put by David Lewis (1996, 549), is this:

> It seems as if knowledge must be by definition infallible. If you claim that *S* knows that *P*, and yet you grant that *S* cannot eliminate a certain possibility in which not-*P*, it certainly seems as if you have granted that *S* does not after all know that *P*. To speak of fallible knowledge, of knowledge despite uneliminated possibilities of error, just *sounds* contradictory.

The intuition, then, is that one cannot know that the person one is seeing on the street is Abasi when the possibility cannot be ruled out that the person one is seeing is Abasi's identical twin brother Abayomi. You cannot know that the animal in the pen is a zebra unless you can eliminate the possibility that it is a cleverly painted mule, to borrow one of Dretske's examples. It hardly needs pointing out that if knowledge that *p* requires the elimination of all not-*p* possibilities, skepticism looms (see Pritchard 2005, chapter 1). Certain possibilities just cannot be eliminated. That we are deceived by evil demons, as in the Cartesian scenario, cannot be eliminated. Neither can it be eliminated that we are brains in vats hooked up to a computer that is operated by a superscientist who manipulates our brains in such a way that although we say to ourselves, for example, "I see a stork flying over the haystack," we don't really see this, because we don't have eyes. Such radical scenarios cannot be eliminated (see, e.g., Pritchard 2005, chapter 2). This means that if the epistemological principle is correct, we just don't have any perceptual knowledge.

Disambiguation is like the elimination of alternatives. To be justified in adopting one of the disambiguated options is to eliminate the other alternatives. Must *all* alternatives be eliminated? Critics of the epistemological principle mentioned in the previous paragraph think not. Not all alternatives are equally relevant to consider; for knowledge, these critics say, only relevant alternatives need to be considered – in other words, knowing *p* requires only that *relevant* not-*p* alternatives are eliminated. An early proponent of the relevant alternatives theory of knowledge – even before it was baptized with that name – is J. L. Austin. In his paper "Other Minds" (in Austin 1970), he discusses a case in which someone, let us call her Aegli, declares, pointing to a particular bird, "That is a goldfinch." An interlocutor asks, "How can you tell?" (or "How do you know?"). Aegli replies, "By its red head." The interlocutor responds: "But that's not enough: plenty of other birds have red heads. What you say doesn't prove it. For all you know it may be a woodpecker." Suppose Aegli has a good response to this and similar challenges. Suppose she says, "Well, the bird has also the characteristic eye-markings of a goldfinch, as well as characteristics *XYZ* of goldfinches." Then at some point, says Austin, it becomes silly or outrageous for the interlocutor to go on saying, "That's not enough." For, he continues, "Enough is enough: it doesn't mean everything. Enough means enough to show that (within reason, and for present intents and purposes) it 'can't' be anything else, there is no room for an alternative, competing, description of it. It does *not* mean, for example, enough to show it isn't a *stuffed* goldfinch" (Austin 1970, 84).[9] We are supposed to envisage a situation in which the issue of the stuffedness of the goldfinch is just not a relevant one. For knowledge, it is only *relevant* alternatives than need to be eliminated.

Applied to IqD this means that, in order to arrive at likely and proper disambiguations, we don't need to eliminate each and every alternative that is incompatible with what we take to be the likely and proper disambiguation – only the relevant ones need to be eliminated. This leads us to the question of when, in the case of reading, an alternative is relevant and when it is not. I don't think there is a general answer here. Relevance is context dependent. The article on the bee count appeared in a Dutch newspaper. Given what we know about what gets published in newspapers, the alternative interpretation according to which the word *bees* refers to busy people, not to social insects that live in beehives, is an irrelevant alternative. No reader should lose time to eliminate that possibility. However, if we change the context, the alternative may become relevant. Consider, for instance, a context in which it is a live option that certain terrorist cells communicate with each other via public media in a coded way. In this context, the following alternative interpretation of the newspaper article becomes relevant: the word *bees* refers to a particular virus, and the message is that terrorists have so far been able to infect over 19,000 people with the virus, whose lethal effects will reveal themselves within a few months. (The code could be this: the first number that appears in an article on bees in that particular journal on a specific day is the number of people infected with the virus.) In that context, it is very important for public officials to take that possibility into consideration. But in ordinary contexts it surely is out of bounds to say that readers of the article have not got its message unless they have been able to exclude the possibility that the article is about virus-infected people.

[9] The relevant alternatives theory is further developed by Dretske in his paper "Epistemic Operators" (in Dretske 2000).

Similar things could be said about lexical meanings, modes, and speech acts. In order to know whether a word is used in sense *S*, or whether a textual part is used in mode *M*, or whether it is a vehicle of speech act *SA*, one doesn't have to eliminate *every* conceivable alternative to *S*, *M*, or *SA* – only the relevant ones. Whether an alternative is relevant or not is context sensitive here, too; and hence, whether it needs to be explicitly and self-consciously eliminated in order for a reader to get a proper understanding of the text is context sensitive. But anyone engaging in the explicit and self-conscious elimination of possibilities engages in acts of interpretation. And so does any reader who does so unreflectively. Here, then, do we have a notion of interpretation such that we can engage in interpretation reflectively and self-consciously, but also without explicit awareness.

Outstanding Issues: Relations

In this final section, I take up two outstanding issues that need clarification: first, the mutual relations between the three accounts of interpretation discussed in this chapter; second, the relations between reading and interpretation.

Concerning the relations between the three accounts of interpretation discussed in this chapter, I make three, rather obvious points. *One.* Disambiguation can proceed consciously and self-reflectively, but it can also proceed more or less automatically. If it proceeds consciously and self-reflectively and we apply relevant alternatives epistemology to IqD, what we have is part of the difficulty account of interpretation. The difficulties that I mentioned do not constitute a fixed but an open set, and ambiguity-based difficulties can be viewed as elements of this set. *Two.* Allegorical interpretations can be viewed as covered by the difficulty account when those interpretations are offered as resolutions of difficulties that we face when we try to get at the author's meaning. *Three.* Allegorical interpretations require prior IqD of what is supposed to be the surface meaning of the text.

Concerning the relation between reading and interpretation, I again make three points. *One.* There can, obviously, be reading without allegorical interpretation. *Two.* There can also be reading without the reader having to explicitly and self-consciously overcome reading difficulties of the various sorts discussed earlier. Some reading is easy, and some readers are properly educated and well trained. *Three.* The modernist view is that all reading involves IqD: when we read, we engage in IqD at the same time. The modernist view, I said, is an essentialist claim, a modal claim, namely, the claim that we cannot read without engaging in IqD. Given that so many linguistic items are ambiguous, this claim certainly looks plausible. This raises the following question: Should we think of IqD as part of the reading activity, or should we think of the two as distinct acts that always go together? If the former is the correct view, this means that engaging in IqD should be a part of the analysis of reading; but if the latter is the correct view, it should not.

An argument for why the latter view should be preferred over the former could be this. It seems at best a contingent feature of languages that many of its elements are ambiguous. There are possible worlds in which a language exists without ambiguities. If we moreover suppose that that language exists in written form, this entails that reading, in that world, occurs without IqD. This shows that reading and interpreting are distinct processes. And they remain distinct processes, even if in the actual world reading is *always* (let us assume this to be the case) accompanied by disambiguation.

It bears noticing that it happens more often that in the actual world, one thing is as a matter of empirical fact always accompanied by another, without this entailing that the latter is a part of the former – thus, without the latter being an element in the analysis of the former. Vertebrates with a heart, as a matter of empirical fact, are also vertebrates with a liver, and vice versa. Yet *having a liver* is not an element in the analysis of being a vertebrate with a heart; nor is *having a heart* part of the analysis of being a vertebrate with a liver. At each moment of a stone's existence, it is as a matter of empirical fact always located at some particular place; yet *being located at a particular place at a time* is not part of the stone's existence, nor an element in the analysis of the stone's existence.[10] Likewise, even if reading is always accompanied by IqD, this doesn't necessarily mean that the latter is a part of, or an element in the analysis of, the former.

This line of thought can be resisted, though. One might think that the analysis of reading given in Chapter 5 offers a reason for thinking that the process of IqD *is* part of the reading process – at least, of the reading process as it occurs in the actual world. For condition (iv) of that analysis states that the reader must acquire some understanding of what the words and sentences jointly mean, and since so many language elements in the

[10] It also bears noticing that even if one thing is, not as a matter of empirical fact but *necessarily*, accompanied by another thing, this doesn't entail that the latter is part of, or an element in the analysis of, the latter. *Being triangular* is necessarily accompanied by *having three sides*, yet the latter is not part of, or an element in the analysis of, the former.

actual world are ambiguous, in order for the reader to acquire the understanding that (iv) speaks of, disambiguation must be part of reading.

However, I believe there is a compelling argument against this. Consider the Disraeli and the Chomsky sentences. You can read them (indeed, you *have* read them) even though you don't know – and can't know (at least, not from the ways I have introduced them) – which of the alternatives that these sentences can be used to express should be deemed the correct one. In such a situation there is reading on your part, but no IqD.

I therefore conclude that IqD must *not* be included in the analysis of reading. This outcome entails that condition (i) of the analysis of RK_A should be modified into (i*) *S* has read *T and* engaged in IqD.

In Chapter 9 I explore the epistemology of four more kinds of interpretation.

CHAPTER 9

Knowledge through Interpretation (2)

Holism, Reconstruction, Externalism, and Reader Response

In this chapter I discuss four more kinds of interpretation, and the epistemology thereof. First, I present what I call holistic textual act interpretation. This account is motivated by the assumption that authors perform actions through the production of entire texts. In the wake of this, I briefly identify a kind of interpretation that is a response to textual opacity, viz., interpretation as reconstruction. Third, I discuss what I call externalist interpretations of texts – that is, interpretations that are not directed at author's meanings but mostly at indicative meanings. Finally, I discuss an account that gives pride of place to reader response in the interpretative process.

Holistic Textual Act Interpretation and Interpretation as Reconstruction

One of the notions of meaning that I identified earlier in this book is the notion of author's meaning. The account of interpretation that I shall develop in this section is best thought of as being geared toward author's meanings. The point of departure here is speech-act theory. The illocutionary and perlocutionary acts this theory identifies are normally performed by relatively short strings of words – most often complete sentences, but regularly also strings that aren't complete sentences, and even single words, such as *aha*, *indeed*, or *pardon*. In this section I argue that there are holistic textual acts, as I shall call them – acts that are performed by the production of textual wholes such as entire articles, chapters, books, poems, and essays, and that specifications of such acts qualify as interpretations – holistic textual act interpretations. To acquire an initial sense of what I am trying to get at, we may remind ourselves of some elementary insights from the theory of action (see, e.g., O'Brien 2015).

Action is often distinguished from mere behavior in that actions are intentional doings, whereas mere behaviors are not. Actions form a subclass of behaviors: the subset of intentional behaviors. Tics, stuttering, inadvertently kicking over a vase, and so on, are unintentional behaviors; hence, they are not actions. Many actions are performed by performing what can intuitively be thought of as more basic actions that jointly compose the complex action.[1] For example, the action that can be described as "climbing Mont Blanc" is composed of a large number of such ground-level acts as putting one's left foot in spot s_1 at time t_1, putting one's right foot in spot s_2 at time t_2, and so on, catching with both hands a particular rock at a particular time, and so forth. Similar things are true of such (higher-level) actions as singing Dylan's "Changing of the Guards," driving a car, raising one's children, teaching a class, writing a book, whistling, and going on vacation.

These phrases indicate action types, as opposed to action tokens. Singing Dylan's "Changing of the Guards" is a *type* that has been "instantiated" in the many actual performances of the song by Dylan as well as by others, each performance being a *token* of the same act type. The type-token distinction allows the same action type to be realized in concrete action tokens that can differ between themselves in many ways.[2] The action type of singing Dylan's "Changing of the Guards" is realized when a person sings it in a different key than the original key, with or without the background vocals, and presumably even when some of the lyrics have been changed or even entire stanzas are left unsung.[3]

An implication of the type-token distinction is that one and the same token series of events can be, and in fact virtually always will be, a realization or instantiation of a number of different event types. For instance, one particular token performance of "Changing of the Guards" is a token of all of the following action types: singing "Changing of the Guards"; singing a Dylan song; singing a song; and using one's vocal cords. This means that if one wants to answer the question of what person *S* is doing, one must select a level or mode of description from a number of available alternatives. Suppose Casimir is climbing Mont Blanc, and you are asked to describe what Casimir is doing. Then you might truthfully answer any of the following: he is moving; he is moving his limbs; he is

[1] Action theorists usually hold that some actions are *not* performed by means of performing other actions. Plausible examples of such basic acts – as they are usually called – are waving one's hand, nodding one's head, or contracting one's biceps.

[2] Types can be thought of as universals, and universals as items that can be "instantiated" in particulars. See Armstrong (1989) and Loux and Crisp (2017, chapters 1–4).

[3] Some action types are not multiply realizable, for instance, the action type *Vincent van Gogh's committing suicide.*

climbing; he is mountain climbing; he is climbing Mont Blanc; he is enjoying spectacular sights. Now suppose you ask Casimir himself what he is doing. If he thinks of what he is doing "under the description" of climbing a mountain, then he will say that he is mountain climbing. It is possible that Casimir doesn't know that the mountain he is climbing is in fact Mont Blanc. In that case, he won't think of himself as climbing Mont Blanc, but he will, as indicated, think of himself as climbing a mountain. He will presumably not think of himself as realizing tokens of the act type *moving*, even though he won't disown your description of him when you describe him as moving. But saying that he is moving is, although correct, "underdescribing" what he is doing, as it is possible to give a much more informative description of what he is doing, such as the description that Casimir himself gives of his action.

A corollary from this is that two rather different kinds of description of what someone is doing are possible: external and internal descriptions. *Internal descriptions* are descriptions that actors themselves would give, from an internal perspective. Casimir will say he is mountain climbing (that is what he has been training for), not that he is moving his limbs (that is *not* what he has been training for). The latter, however, is an *external description* that truthfully could be given of what Casimir is doing, for he *is* moving his limbs.

There seems to be a conversational maxim (or principle) that we observe – at least, if we want to be cooperative – when we are called upon to say (i.e., to give an internal description of) what we are doing. The maxim is as follows: Give an *informed* description of what you are doing – that is, a description that fits what you believe you are doing and what you are intentionally doing. For example, when you're sitting in a chair reading Kant and someone asks you what you're doing, the principle tells you not to say "I am sitting in a chair" or even "I am reading." Such answers will make the person asking the question feel that you're evading the question, that you're opting out (see Grice 1989, 24–31), for the simple reason that it is already obvious to the interlocutor that you are sitting in a chair and that you are reading. The principle also tells you that, depending on the specifics of the circumstances, each of the following *would* be an appropriate answer: "I am trying out this chair in order to find out whether I can comfortably read in it, because if so, I will purchase it"; or "I am reading *Kant*" (the tacit contrast being that you are *not* reading Reid or Moore); or "I am waiting for Marilou, and so as to use my time efficiently, I am also reading the chapter of Kant that is to be discussed in next week's class." The principle tells us to answer the question of what we are doing by providing the most informed description "under which" we are acting, the one by which we would describe to ourselves what we are doing.

External descriptions of what person *S* is doing can, in principle, be of two different kinds. They can be descriptions offered by others that purport to state what *S* thinks *S* is doing, or they can be descriptions that have no such intent. Descriptions of the first kind, if correct, will in the main be descriptions that *S* will be happy with, since *S* will feel understood (I say *in the main* because sometimes it is no occasion for happiness when one is understood, or seen through). If someone gives an external description of *S*'s behavior of the second kind, then *S*, when apprised of the description, may be surprised, annoyed, moved, disturbed, or uplifted by it. But – and this is a point I shall be exploiting later on – even if *S* doesn't, as we say, recognize themselves in the description offered, the description may nonetheless be adequate. And we may say that someone recognizes themselves in a description of their behavior provided that description is the description under which they acted or a description under which they could think of themselves as acting.

These insights from action theory are relevant for singling out the kind of interpretation that I propose to delineate in this section. For speech acts are *actions*; some of them are ground-level ones, others higher-level ones. Locutionary acts, like writing words on a page, are the lower-level acts that compose higher-order acts such as illocutionary acts; alternatively, the latter are performed *by means of* the former. Illocutionary acts are normally performed by producing sentences. Texts often consist of many sentences. This gives rise to the question of whether there is some action performed by producing *the whole* of the text "over and above" what is performed by means of the individual sentences. This question is analogous to asking whether someone who is putting their left foot here, their right foot there, their hands on that spot, and so forth, is doing something "over and above" the things just described, or is doing so *by* doing the things just described. Are they, for instance, climbing Mont Blanc, or are they warding off an attack? To deny this option for the writing of texts is to affirm that what a writer does by producing the text *just is* the conjunction of the speech acts that they perform by producing the individual sentences. It is no doubt possible that some texts are like that. But there are at least two considerations that make it plausible that an author, by producing a text, can perform an action over and above, or by means of, the actions performed by the individual sentences – an action that is not just the summation of the speech acts performed by individual sentences.

First, it is a standing practice among readers to try to get at the "core" of what they read, to grasp the main point, the central message. Teachers and professors train their students in this practice when they give them assignments to summarize what a writer wrote, to describe the gist of a book, to identify the main claims that are made, to pinpoint the central argument that seems to be offered, or to formulate what (the students think) a writer meant to say. They also train their students in this practice when they urge them to distinguish main issues from subsidiary ones and admonish them to dig deeper when they feel their students haven't yet got to the heart of the matter. This practice of trying to get at the central message suggests that writers are normally held to have *holistic textual act intentions*, or *holistic intentions* for short. Attempts to summarize a text, thereby capturing the heart of it, are attempts to state the holistic textual act intentions of an author. Such attempts I call *holistic textual act interpretations.*

Texts across genres have, or can have, this holistic quality, as I will demonstrate in a moment. But first I should like to point out that some texts *lack* this holistic quality: in such a text, there is no speech act that its writer performs over and above or in virtue of the speech acts performed by the individual sentences that compose the text. A sure mark of the lack of this holistic quality is that such texts defy summary. Examples include old-fashioned telephone books, dictionaries, manuals, shopping lists, and inventories: they cannot be summarized; they have no core or no main points that can be distinguished from peripheral matters.

The second reason to believe that writers normally have holistic textual intentions is that many texts seem to have a value or significance that transcends the sum of the value and significance of their individual sentences. The value or significance of Thomas Gray's "Elegy Written in a Country Churchyard" (1751) as a whole transcends the value and significance of any of its parts. The same holds for newspaper articles like the one about the national bee count, for Merleau-Ponty's *Phénoménologie de la perception* (1945), for Herman Hesse's *Siddhartha* (1922), and so forth.

These two reasons are connected: authors write holistic texts *because* such texts are the vehicles of holistic textual acts. And they want to perform holistic textual acts because holistic texts have a value and significance that transcends the value and significance of its parts. And because a text is a whole, it has a core and can be summarized.

In order to get a sense of reality in the midst of these perhaps somewhat airy reflections, I offer some examples of holistic textual actions as well as of holistic textual interpretations. For each of the cases I shall explicate what the relevant justifying evidence is.

Consider once again the newspaper article on the bee count in the Netherlands. If it has a holistic feature, a summary of it must be possible, a statement of its core. I suggest that the following is a good one: Deemed unreliable due to the weather conditions, the recently held bee count has been extended. By contrast, none of the following are adequate summaries:

- In the recently held bee count, fewer bees were counted than in the previous bee count.
- The bees spotted most often during the recent bee count are the honeybee, the bumblebee, and the red mason bee.
- During this year's bee count, temperatures were lower than during last year's count.

Although none of the statements are false, they fail as summaries. Why? Because they leave out the core message. If the first summary is adequate (as I claim it is), this means that the holistic interpretation of the article is that the writer of the article is *reporting that the recently held bee count, deemed unreliable due to the weather conditions, has been extended.* The interpretation is that the italicized words capture the holistic textual act that the writer performed by writing the article. In terms of the conversational maxim discussed earlier, the interpretation offered amounts to the claim that the author, when asked what he was doing when he was writing (and assuming he conformed to the principle of cooperation), would answer by saying – exactly, or almost exactly – what the italicized part of the sentence says.

There are no hard-and-fast rules of evidence concerning this kind of interpretation. But all of the following are evidentially relevant considerations: (1) word and sentence meanings; (2) the genre to which the article belongs: it is a *newspaper* article and hence purports to report facts; (3) the fact that the summary offered *looks* adequate: it captures what seems to be the core of the article – and it is a general epistemological principle that what *seems* to be the case is prima facie, or defeasible, evidence for its *being* the case;[4] and (4) the fact that there is nothing in the text that defeats the summary's adequacy.

My second example is Aesop's fable of the fox and the crow. The core of the fable has been admirably captured by the following quartet, quoted in the introduction:

[4] A thorough exposition and defense of this principle – often called the principle of credulity – is Swinburne (1991, 254–271).

> *"It is a maxim in the schools,*
> *That* Flattery's the food of fools:"
> *And whoso likes such airy meat*
> *Will soon have nothing else to eat.*

The summary can, in fact, even be shorter: Flattery is the food of fools, meaning, it is foolish to listen to flatterers. None of the following adequately summarizes the fable: Flattery pays; animals carry on social lives; crows love cheese.

Over and above the speech acts performed by means of the individual sentences that compose the fable, Aesop performs the holistic textual act of warning against flattery. That means that I take it that if Aesop had been asked what he was doing by writing the fable (assuming that he was cooperative and that the conversational maxim that I alluded to is correct), he would have answered: "Showing that it is foolish to listen to flatterers."

What is the evidence for thinking that this is a correct holistic interpretation of Aesop's fable? Evidentially relevant considerations include the following: (1) the text is a fable, which makes it clear that Aesop never wanted to affirm that a fox and a crow were carrying on a conversation; (2) fables, generally speaking, have moral content; (3) the summary offered *looks* adequate (it looks vastly better than the alternatives that I mentioned), which, given the principle of credulity, gives it prima facie justification; (4) nothing in the fable undermines the summary's adequacy; and (5) the summary brings out a point that we can easily see is something that people might want to communicate or endorse – certainly if we take into consideration the moral opinions of Aesop's time and place.

We should not think that holistic textual act interpretations can only be of the illocutionary variety. The case of Aesop's fable can illustrate this point, for it is not unlikely that Aesop had the intention to convince his readers that flattery is the food of fools. This holistic interpretation is of the perlocutionary variety.

Let us consider as a further example Steve Turner's verse "Everything" (in Turner 1982, 137):

> Looks aren't everything.
> Luxury's not everything.
> Money's not everything.
> Health is not everything.
> Success is not everything.
> Happiness is not everything.
> Even everything is not everything.
> There's more to life than everything.

In the first six lines Turner performs six distinct illocutionary acts – he makes six assertions. The seventh line is an assertion as well, albeit a seemingly paradoxical one, for how can *everything* not be everything? A little reflection, however, teaches us that the word *everything* is used here in two different meanings. In its first occurrence it means "the set of all things" (which includes such things as looks, luxury, money, and health) or, alternatively, it means "everything you want." In its second occurrence it means "all-important" or "something that trumps everything else qua significance." Thus, the air of paradox vanishes. The final line is another assertion, and again one that at first sight looks paradoxical, for how can there be more than everything? A little reflection suggests that *everything* means something like "everything you want," and this removes the air of paradox – at least, if we assume the message of the last line to be that there is more to life than having the things you want to have. But the poem doesn't say what that "more" might be.

Should we say that Turner's poem is a mere conjunction of eight assertions, or should we say that Turner, over and above making eight assertions, performs a further act by means of the text *as a whole*: a holistic textual act, an act that is not performed by any of the text's parts individually, nor by the sum of the acts performed by the parts? I suggest, unsurprisingly, the latter. Can we state what that act is? Well, can we summarize the poem, specify its core? Various possibilities present themselves; for example, (a) "It is so easy to say that this or that is not all-important, but it is very difficult to state what *is* all-important" and (b) "We often speak of what is not all-important, but seldom or never about what *is* all-important." I take it these summaries are going in the right direction. Going in the wrong direction, I suggest, are (c) "Looks, luxury, money, health, success, and happiness are all-important," (d) "There are true paradoxes," and (e) "It makes no sense to ask for what is all-important."

Assuming that (a) or (b) – or something in the neighborhood – is an adequate summary, we can say that the holistic textual act that Turner performs by this poem is *asserting (a) or (b)*, which is an illocutionary act. Assuming that Turner wants readers to reflect on what is all-important and what is not, we may also say that he had the holistic textual act intention to *make readers reflect on (a) and (b)*, which is a perlocutionary act intention.

The italicized phrases constitute holistic textual act interpretations. They are epistemically justified insofar as they are based on evidence, such as evidence pertaining to word and sentence meanings, especially knowledge of the ambiguity of the words *not everything*, and the rationality of the principle of charity,[5] according to which we should interpret the words of others in a way that makes them look most rational (the principle entails that we should not ascribe contradictions to Turner).

Or consider case (j) from Chapter 4, a text consisting of "clean," neutral statements about what the Dutch did in the Caribbean. It offers detailed facts and figures, containing neither evaluative nor loaded language, that is, no words like *self-serving*, *injustice*, *rape*, or *exploitation*. The writer is thus performing a number of illocutionary acts of the kind *reporting*. Now suppose the intention of the writer is to accuse the Dutch of exploitation by means of the report. In that case the writer had a communicative intention for the text as a whole – a holistic textual act intention. The writer performs the holistic act of issuing an accusation. Yet none of the sentences composing the text and instantiating illocutionary acts instantiates an accusation. Accusing the Dutch of exploitation is an act that is performed by the writer by means of the text as a whole, and the phrase is a sort of summary of the text; it gets at its core. Had the writer been asked what they were doing when writing (and if they were cooperative), they could have said, "I am accusing the Dutch of exploitation in the Caribbean."

"Accusing the Dutch of exploitation" constitutes a holistic textual act interpretation of the report. If it is to be justified, it should be based on evidence, such as knowing what the report says (RK_A), and knowing that exploitation is unjust and that exploiters deserve to be charged.

Or consider the following example, taken from chapters 38 through 41 of the biblical book of Job where God is described as putting a series of questions to Job: "Where were you when I laid the earth's foundation? . . . Who marked off its dimensions . . .. Who stretched a measuring line across it? . . . On what were its footings set, or who laid its cornerstone?" And so the questioning goes on and on. Each individual sentence issues an illocutionary act of the type *asking a question*, or *interrogating*. But over and above asking questions, or interrogating, God is, in effect, described as *asserting Job's ignorance*, or even as *accusing Job* of not having a proper view of the divine majesty. By producing the text, the writer issues tokens of the illocutionary act type of asking questions, or interrogating. But over and above this, by means of the text as a whole, the writer asserts Job's ignorance, or even accuses him of being ignorant. This is the holistic textual act that is performed by the text as a whole. Or at least, this is a plausible interpretation of these chapters. Whether it is justified depends

[5] A classic discussion of this principle, with twists and turns, is Davidson (1984, chapters 9 and 11).

on the quality of the evidence on which it is based. Relevant evidence includes knowledge of the context of the chapters and their contents, knowledge of Hebrew modes of expression, knowledge of genre, and knowledge of texts and of modes of expression therein from surrounding and related cultural milieus.

This should suffice as a presentation and explanation of the idea of holistic textual act interpretation. Some concluding remarks are in order. First, the textual act interpretations given earlier were chiefly for expository purposes, so as to get a sense of the kind of interpretation that I have in mind. Much more can and should be said about each individual interpretation. Second, holistic interpretation is a kind of interpretation that we engage in rather often; in fact, we engage in it every time we try to answer questions like "What is the core of what I have just read?" This is a question about what Ruskin called author's meaning. Third, holistic interpretations fit the general account of interpretation: they are specifications of meaning, they display to various degrees the feature of going beyond what is given, and they try to make sense of the whole of a text. Fourth, there doesn't seem to be an algorithm that we can follow so as to faultlessly arrive at a text's correct holistic textual act interpretation. This doesn't mean that there is no rationality to this kind of interpretation – we noted the principles of credulity and charity. Fifth and finally, holistic interpretations admit of degrees: some interpretations are better than others, for they capture the core of a text more adequately than others.

It is possible to acquire knowledge of the holistic textual acts of authors. Such knowledge qualifies as interpretative knowledge, and it is knowledge of the *A*-variety; in other words, it is knowledge of what the text, or its author, says. Spelled out more fully:

> *S* has IK_A that *p*, that is, *S* knows through interpretation (in this case, through holistic textual act interpretation) that what text *T*, or its author, says is *p*, iff
>
> (i) *S* holistically interprets *T*
> (ii) *T*, or its author, says *p*
> (iii) *S* believes (ii) because of (i)
> (iv) *S*'s interpretation is justified

And this may in turn be the basis for knowledge of the *B*-variety.

I should now like to get back to the phenomenon of textual opacity, which I mentioned in Chapter 8. Sometimes, it is very difficult to grasp a text's holistic meaning, to get a good sense of its larger message, even though the reader faces none of the difficulties covered by the ignorance-based difficulty account of interpretation, or if there were such difficulties, the reader solved them all. Difficulties of this sort fall outside the difficulty account of interpretation presented in Chapter 8. Such difficulties can again be due to the reader's ignorance, but they can also be due to the opacity of the text, or so I have suggested. Let me offer some examples. In his *Essay concerning Human Understanding*, John Locke upholds the general adage that reason should be our guide in everything. But when he works out his views in minute detail, he develops views that are at odds with the general adage (see Wolterstorff 1996). Bernard Williams, in his essay "Deciding to Believe," presents an argument for the conclusion that it is conceptually impossible to believe at will (Williams 1973, 148–149). Different interpreters, however, have given rather different reconstructions of what the argument is supposed to be.[6] Basically the same holds for the passages where Kant argues that space and time are forms of the intuition, the passages where McTaggart argues for the unreality of time, the passages where Putnam argues for internal realism, the passages where Wittgenstein argues for the impossibility of a private language, and so forth. When it comes to identifying the structure of these arguments, readers face difficulties – difficulties that are due, I aver, to textual opacity (in combination with difficulty of subject matter) rather than to reader's ignorance. Other cases that fall under the rubric of textual opacity are, for instance, first versions of student papers that contain underdeveloped thoughts and are ill-structured, which forestalls understanding of the papers' direction. This failure isn't due to ignorance on the part of the professors who read these papers, but rather to textual opacity. And works of literature are also sometimes textually opaque in a way that makes it difficult to clearly see what their overall message is. As an example I offer Bob Dylan's *Tarantula* (1969).

Texts that are opaque with respect to their main point or core message invite interpretation in yet another sense. Suppose we want to know from McTaggart's opaque text what his argument for the unreality of time is. Opacity invites interpretation. But it isn't allegorical interpretation that is invited here, for McTaggart's text is not an allegory, and so it is not supposed to have a deeper and hidden meaning. Nor is it interpretation of the sort that the difficulty account is concerned with, for I am assuming that all such difficulties (about word and sentence meanings, reference, authorship, genre, and why the author wrote it) have been solved. Nor is it

[6] Different interpretations have been given by Govier (1976), Winters (1979), and Van Woudenberg's "On the Modal Status of the Claim That Belief Is Involuntary" (unpublished manuscript).

interpretation qua disambiguation, for I assume that ambiguities have been properly solved too. No, the kind of interpretation that opaque texts invite is interpretation *as reconstruction*. A somewhat formal account can be stated as follows:

> **Interpretation as reconstruction (IaR)**: a proposition *p* is a reconstruction of the core message, or the holistic meaning, of opaque text *T* iff *p* is a possibly complex statement that (i) covers most or all of the statements in *T* that are relatively clear, (ii) does not cover opaque statements, (iii) does not cover relatively clear statements that conflict with the majority of relatively clear statements, and (iv) includes additional statements that are needed to make the majority of the relatively clear statements more coherent – let them jointly make more sense – than they would be without these additional statements.

Without going into detail, I aver that Plantinga's formulation of the ontological argument in *The Nature of Necessity* (1974, 213–221) is an IaR of St. Anselm's *Proslogion*, chapters 2, 3, and 4, and the texts that constitute the exchange between St. Anselm and Gaunilo. Also, van Inwagen's formulation of McTaggart's argument for the unreality of time in his *Metaphysics* (2009, 81–87) is an IaR of McTaggart's *The Nature of Existence*, sections 303–333.

Justification requires evidence. Relevant evidence in cases like these consists in the reader's ability to coherently explain as many relatively clear statements or passages as possible. The general rule would seem to be this: an IaR is plausible to the degree that it can make sense of parts of the text. If IaR#1 makes more sense of more parts of *T* than IaR#2, then the former is better evidenced and hence more justified than the latter.

In order to grasp the holistic meaning of a text, it is sometimes – and in the case of philosophy and literary studies rather often – needed that we engage in IaR. But surely not always: not in the case of the bee-count newspaper article, nor in the case of Aesop's fable. Nor do we need IaR to get at the holistic meaning of Turner's "Everything." For these texts are not opaque.

Externalist Interpretation

In the accounts of interpretation that I have presented so far, authorial intentions are very important. The allegoresis account,[7] the difficulty

[7] With the exception of allegorical interpretation of texts that were not intended by their authors to be allegories.

account, the IqD account, and the holistic account give pride of place to the author, who could be deemed the expert on the solutions of the difficulties, the proper disambiguations, and the holistic acts, respectively. As I have indicated, however, not all engagements with texts center on authorial intentions – and some of those engagements are often called interpretations as well. This section discusses what I shall call *externalist interpretations* of texts.

Externalist interpretations fit the general account of interpretation in that they are specifications of meaning; more specifically, of indicative (or expressive) meanings. Texts can indicate or express many things that the writer never meant to indicate or express. For example, a text can indicate by its style, formulations, choice of words, or use of imagery and metaphor that the author has a particular kind of background, belongs to a certain class or social group, is familiar with a particular way of life, has a peculiar kind of character, or possesses a special sensitivity, even if the writer never intended to flag any of these facts. This is not unlike what is happening when you hear someone talking and can tell by their accent and intonation that they come from the deep south: the person isn't *telling* you, and doesn't intend to tell you, that they come from the deep south, yet their mode of speech indicates as much. Texts carry more information then what the author intended to convey, express more facts than authorial intentions. Statements of such facts are statements of indicative meaning; hence, they qualify as interpretations on the general account. In this section I make some general remarks about externalist interpretations, provide examples, and discuss epistemological aspects.

The first thing to notice is that whereas some externalist interpretations are theory driven, others are not. Examples of the latter include such statements as that the *Beowulf* manuscript is written in Old English; that Dante's *Divina commedia* reflects the three-storied world picture of the Greeks; that Kant's moral philosophy was deeply influenced by German pietism; that Thomas Reid's antiskeptical commonsense philosophy was in part psychologically occasioned by the fact that he had children and a family life, which functioned as a reality check for his thinking (a check that Hume had to do without); and that John must have been under duress when he wrote that letter. These are *interpretations* because they are statements of meaning – indicative or expressive meaning. They are *externalist* interpretations because they aren't statements about what authors intended to convey. And they are driven, not by anything so exalted as explanatory theories, but by widely accepted commonsensical ideas. In the cases mentioned, these ideas include that authors use language and language forms as they are bequeathed to them; that authors are influenced by others, as people in general are influenced by others; and that one's social position in life, as well as one's psychological condition, influences what one writes.

Interpretations like these are justified to the extent that these common-sensical ideas are justified and to the degree in which they apply to the particular cases at hand.

Other externalist interpretations are driven by theories and by conceptual and normative ideas. Externalist interpretations can be thought of as statements about what happens (what one "sees" epistemically) when one reads a text from the standpoint (that determines the perspective) of a certain theory, or from the standpoint (that determines the perspective) constituted by certain conceptual and normative ideas.

Externalist interpretations can, in principle, be given of texts of all genres. And the possible theories and ideas that determine the perspective of the interpretation are, in principle, legion. In actual fact, however, externalist interpretations are mostly given of literary texts, and the number of theories that determine the interpretative perspectives is not too large. Externalist interpretations that have enjoyed or still enjoy popularity take their point of departure in Marxism, psychoanalysis, feminism, gender studies, and critical race theory. It is impossible to discuss these approaches in any depth and impossible to recount their histories.[8] Instead, I provide examples of such interpretations, no more than sketches really, and only so much as is needed to be able to focus on their epistemological aspects.

Marxist interpreters bring to the interpretation of literary texts ideas about class struggle, about how the economic base structure of a society determines its cultural superstructure, and about ideologies that cause us to misrepresent the world to ourselves. Marxist interpreters of George Eliot's *Middlemarch* (1871–1872) have argued that this novel represents its characters as essentially free and that it thus invites its readers to see themselves as essentially free. But this, the interpreters argue, is an illusion, since alleged free decisions are in fact determined by an economic base structure. Eliot thus perpetuates an ideology that is blind for what really determines human behavior. Marxist interpreters more generally hold that literary works are pervaded by ideologies and are transmitters of them (see, e.g., Macherey 1978). The thesis that *Middlemarch* perpetuates an ideology and blinds us to our real condition is an interpretation, because it is a

[8] Bertens (2014) is a helpful guide here.

statement of meaning – more precisely, a statement of indicative or expressive meaning. *Middlemarch*, this interpretation tells us, expresses a particular ideology. Since the book does so unbeknownst to Eliot herself, the interpretation is of the externalist variety. Marxist interpretations often take the form of a critique of ideology.

The Sherlock Holmes stories by Sir Arthur Conan Doyle present the hero-detective as someone who is gifted with a penetrating mind and who sees his way through the most complex murder mysteries. It has been argued that if one takes a close look at these stories, one cannot help noticing that women and their social position are nowhere depicted or represented in a serious or detailed way. They remain opaque and elusive and receive no voice of their own – in contrast with Holmes and his companion Dr. Watson, whose lives and attitudes are described in interesting and colorful detail. These stories, Catherine Belsey (1980) has argued, are in effect silent with respect to female characters, which reveals that in these stories, a patriarchal ideology is at work in which women are more or less taken for granted. Again, this is an externalist interpretation. We can safely assume that Doyle did not intend to communicate through the Holmes stories anything about patriarchism. Yet from an external perspective, it can be held that this is what Doyle is doing. He may not have endorsed patriarchism, yet his stories express it. Belsey's interpretation can therefore be considered as a statement of the indicative meanings of the Holmes stories.

The novels of D. H. Lawrence have been praised for their open and, as many felt, "liberating" depiction of erotic relations. Kate Millett (1970), however, has argued that the attitudes of the male characters populating Lawrence's books are not so emancipated. The novels, she argues, presume a relation between sex and power that mirrors the distribution of power over men and women in society at large. This approach qualifies on my account as an externalist interpretation. It is *externalist* on the assumption that it was never Lawrence's authorial intent to endorse unemancipated behavior. And it is an *interpretation* because, from the external perspective that takes its departure in feminist theory, the novels do express such a power distribution over the sexes. The approach thus states the expressive or indicative meaning of these works.

Freud's psychoanalytic theory holds that humans have secret unconscious desires and anxieties that can find expression in ways that we are unaware of. There is a plethora of terms figuring in psychoanalysis: the ego, the id, projection, repression, sublimation, Oedipus complex, and more. Psychoanalytic interpretations of literary works take their point of departure in Freud's theory; accordingly, these works are approached as expressions of the secret unconscious desires and anxieties of an author. Psychoanalytic theory is believed to provide a key for decoding information that is supposed to lie hidden in the literary work. By way of example, it has struck readers that the mother figures in Charlotte Brontë's novels are almost always portrayed negatively. Psychoanalytic interpreters hold this to be an expression of Brontë's own unresolved emotions, childhood traumas, and fixations (Dooley 1920). Presumably, Brontë never intended to express any of these, which is why such interpretations are *externalist*. They are *interpretations* because they are specifications of meaning – of indicative meaning.

Let us now turn to epistemology. What is the justifying evidence in these cases? It is rather obvious that in the examples offered, the evidence does not exclusively come from the novels themselves, nor from anything that Eliot, Doyle, Lawrence, and Brontë wrote or said about their works. The crucial evidence for Macherey's interpretation of *Middlemarch* is Marxist theory. But is this really *evidence*? It is impossible to discuss the epistemic status of Marxism here, but we may note in passing that not everybody who has studied Marxism becomes convinced of its epistemic foundations. Marxist interpretations will look epistemically justified to those who are independently convinced of Marxist theory. Hence, it is best to consider Marxist engagements with literature as follows: such engagements take Marxist theory (or parts thereof) as a lens through which readers should look at literary works. If readers look through that lens, particular things strike them. Although the lens is only optional (we aren't forced by the work itself to look through it), it is at the very least permitted by the work. This means that the epistemological status of such interpretations will not look particularly strong to those who aren't convinced of Marxism. Similar things hold for interpretations that look at literary works through other lenses.

Such interpretations may not constitute knowledge or reach the high epistemic status of being beyond reasonable doubt, by which I mean that accepting them is more reasonable than withholding judgment on them. They may have weaker but still positive epistemic statuses. They may, for example, have some presumption in their favor, by which I mean that accepting them is more reasonable than accepting their denials. Or they may be acceptable, by which I mean that withholding judgment on them is not more reasonable than accepting them. In this respect externalist interpretations share the predicament of many scientific theories, for most scientific theories aren't known to be true either; they are not fully certain, since they are underdetermined by the evidence.[9] Although many are beyond reasonable doubt, many more only have some presumption in their favor, and many are at best acceptable.[10] And these statuses may shift over time.

Still, we can say that if there is interpretative knowledge of the externalist variety to be had, it should satisfy a set of conditions that will look familiar by now:

> *S* has externalist IK_A that *p*, that is, *S* knows through externalist interpretation that text *T* expresses *p*, iff
>
> (i) *S* externalistically interprets *T*
> (ii) *T* expresses *p*
> (iii) *S* believes (ii) because of (i)
> (iv) *S*'s interpretation is justified

And (iv) is satisfied when at least either the commonsensical ideas or the conceptual and normative ideas or theories constituting the externalist perspective are justified.

Reader-Response Theories of Interpretation and Common Sense

So far I have been working from a number of commonsense assumptions about reading, meaning, and interpretation. Some of these have been challenged by proponents of reader-response theories of interpretation. In this section, I defend these assumptions against Stanley Fish's attacks. The assumptions I am referring to include the following:

(A1) Texts or text parts are bearers of meanings; meanings are properties of texts or of parts thereof.
(A2) A text's author's meaning doesn't change over time; it is fixed at the time of the production of the text.
(A3) Readers with epistemic interests should not project their own ideas onto the text but yield to the norm of getting at the meanings of texts.
(A4) Texts and readers are, metaphysically speaking, different things.

Assumption (A1) was at work in my application of Dretske's information-theoretic account of knowledge to reading. Texts, I said, are carriers of information, and this independently of whether people actually read the

[9] The underdetermination thesis has received quite a lot of attention in the philosophy of science. One good example is Ladyman (2002, 162–195).

[10] Van den Brink, De Ridder, and Van Woudenberg (2017) make an effort to apply these terms of epistemic appraisal – as Chisholm (1977), from whom we borrowed the terms, calls them – to various parts of evolutionary theory.

texts, or if they do, independently of whether they actually learn something from reading them. The information carried by a text is the *meanings* of the text. And meanings, moreover, are *properties*. I didn't argue for this view but assumed it to be correct. That is, I assumed that it is a property of the word *umbrageous* that it means, among other things, "affording shade"; that it is a property of the sentence "The cat is on the mat" that it means that a certain animal is in a certain spot; that it is a property of the bee-count article that its author's meaning is reporting that the bee count has been extended; and so for all the other types of meaning that I have distinguished: they are properties of texts or of parts thereof. Of course, assuming these things leaves open important questions about the *kind* of properties that meanings are. Are they intrinsic, relational, essential, accidental, or of yet another kind? And we should not assume that all meanings are properties of the same kind. Yet I assumed they are *properties*, and not substances (individual things like leopards and laptops), or modifications (as a knot in a rope is a modification of the rope), or events (like the event of marching to a city), or sets (like the set of European countries).

Assumption (A2) is the commonsense idea that what the author of the bee-count article communicated stays the same, even when later on the meaning of the words that are used take on new meanings, even when the grammatical constructions that are used become unfamiliar, even when it turns out that the journalist was badly misinformed about the counting, and even when the journalist acknowledges that he was badly misinformed – the author's meaning stays the same and is fixed at the time of writing. Nothing can change the author's meaning of a published text, not even the author. Still, the author is responsible for their text's having that kind of meaning. This holds across the genres, so for philosophical books as well as for travel guidebooks, for poems as well as for scientific papers. Assumption (A2) transpired in the factivity conditions in the analyses of RK_A and IK_A.

Assumption (A3), which says we should not project our own ideas on what we're reading, was present in Ruskin's remarks about reading and found expression in the justification and factivity conditions of RK_A and IK_A. The assumption is a normative one: it is about what readers with epistemic interests should and should not do when they read.

Assumption (A4) states that texts and readers are metaphysically different kinds of beings. A reader is not a text, and a text is not a reader. Readers are living beings; texts are not. Readers are not responsible for what texts say, and texts are not responsible for what readers think they mean.

These assumptions I've been working with have come to be denied by reader-response accounts of interpretation; this is the reason I now want to pay attention to Stanley Fish who developed the most famous of such accounts. Fish has developed ideas about reading and interpretation that give pride of place to the reader, and not to the author or the text. In the introduction of his widely read *Is There a Text in This Class?* (1980), he reports how he came to give the reader that central place. I identify three phases in his thinking as he reports it, but the boundaries between them are a bit blurry. I comment on the ideas that he developed in each phase.

Fish tells us that, in the earliest phase reported, he was asking whether the reader or the text is the source of meaning. He notes that this question presupposed the "independence and stability" of both text and reader (1980, 1). He then began to challenge the idea that the text is a "self-sufficient repository of meaning" (1980, 2) and to give prominence to the activities of the reader. Here is what he says (1980, 2–3):

> If meaning is embedded in the text, the reader's responsibilities are limited to the job of getting it out; but if meaning develops, and if it develops in a dynamic relationship with the reader's expectations, projections, conclusions, judgments, and assumptions, these activities (the things the reader *does*) are not merely instrumental, or mechanical, but essential .... [I retained] the text as a stable entity at the same time that I was dislodging it as the privileged container of meaning. The reader was now given joint responsibility for the production of a meaning that was itself redefined as an event rather than an entity. That is, one could not point to this meaning as one could if it were the property of the text; rather, one could observe or follow its gradual emergence in the interaction between the text . . . and the developing response of the reader.
>
> In this formulation, the reader's response is not *to* the meaning; it *is* the meaning, or at least the medium in which what I wanted to call the meaning comes into being.

He furthermore notes that in that phase he had a response to the objection that there are as many reader responses as there are readers. It consisted in "positing a level of experience which all readers share, independently of differences in education and culture" (Fish 1980, 4–5). Diversity in emotive or intellective responses to the same text, he thought at the time, must be explained by superimposing on the basic level of understanding.

These ideas raise critical issues. First, Fish reports that he rejected, in this phase, the idea that meanings are embedded in the text, that they are properties of a text; thus, he rejected (A1). And he rejected that idea because he believed the job of the reader not to be limited to getting the meaning out of the text. He held that meaning develops in a dynamic relationship with the reader's expectations, projections, and so forth; thus, he also rejected (A2). Fish's entailment evaporates, however, when we clearly distinguish between metaphysics and epistemology. We can think of meanings as properties of texts – which is a metaphysical statement – and at the same time acknowledge that getting to know those meanings is a dynamic process in which a reader's expectations, projections, and so forth, play a role – which is an epistemological remark about the process involved. And this is how it should be, for it barely makes sense to say that in the bee-count article, in Aesop's fable, or in Kant's *Critique of Pure Reason*, it is the author's meaning *itself* which develops in a dynamic relationship with reader expectations, projections, and so on. The author's meaning itself doesn't develop – it is the reader's grasp of it that does (if it does).

Second, in the reported phase, Fish held that the response of the reader *is* (i.e., is identical to, is the very same things as) the meaning of the text; the reader's response is not *to* the meaning of the text.[11] This is a glib saying – what does it mean? One problem is that Fish doesn't say what notion of meaning he is using. But the most likely candidate is what I have called author's meaning, or something in the neighborhood. If this is correct, then what he endorsed amounts to the following: the meaning of the article on the bee count is the reader's response to it – not the set of all individual responses, but what is common to them. What *is* common to them? Is it the belief response that a bee count was recently organized in the Netherlands (or something along those lines)? But not everybody will form such a belief (perhaps they have defeating or undercutting information). Is it an action response? But what would be common to all action responses? It is very hard to believe that there is such a common response. Moreover, it is hard to see why, even if there were a common response, this should – or even *could* – be thought of as the meaning of the article. Suppose, just for the sake of argument, that all that is common to the responses is that the readers shrug their shoulders. Then on the approach

[11] Of course, he adds that the response of the reader is the "medium" in which meaning comes into being; but this verges to inconsistency with the thought that the reader's response *is* the meaning. It makes a difference whether we say that the response of a reader *is M* or that it is *the medium in which M* comes into being. It makes a difference whether we say that feeling uplifted (which, I suppose, is a reader's response) *is* the meaning or that it is *the medium in which* meaning comes into being. These are different, and perhaps even incompatible views. Something *M* cannot be identical to the medium in which it comes into being. A fish comes into being in the water (the medium), but it cannot also be identical to the water.

under discussion, the meaning of the article is the shrugging of shoulders. But this just makes no sense.

I conclude that Fish's thoughts in this phase present no serious challenge to the assumptions explicated at the beginning of this section. In the next reported phase, Fish recognized an inconsistency in his earlier thinking. On the one hand, he wanted to free the reader "from the tyranny of the text" in the production of meaning, thus flagging his allegiance to antiformalism (formalism being the view that "the reader's job is to extract the meanings that formal patterns possess prior to, and independently of, his activities" [Fish 1980, 8]). On the other hand, he wished to insist that the text constrains the reader in the production of meaning, thus warding off, as he says, solipsism, anarchy, and subjectivism. In this latter attempt, he now sees, he was still in the grips of another formalist assumption, viz., that subjectivity is a danger. In the new phase, he began looking for a way out of this inconsistency. And the way out, he reports, was to give up his commitment to the assumption that the text and the reader are independent and competing entities. He started to think that "the text and the reader fall together" (1980, 12). Here is a description of the thought (Fish 1980, 12–13):

> The formal features [of the text] ... are the *product* of the interpretive principles for which they are supposedly evidence .... [Formal features are] not discovered by the analytical method but produced by it ....
>
> Formal units are always a function of the interpretive model one brings to bear (they are not "in the text"). Indeed, the text as an entity independent of interpretation and (ideally) responsible for its career drops out and is replaced by the texts that emerge as the consequence of our interpretive activities. There are still formal patterns, but they do not lie innocently in the world: rather, they are themselves constituted by an interpretive act. The facts one points to are still there (in a sense that would not be consoling to an objectivist) but only as a consequence of the interpretive (man-made) model that has called them into being. The relationship between interpretation and text is thus reversed: interpretive strategies are not put into execution after reading; they are the shape of reading, and because they are the shape of reading, they give texts their shape, making them rather than, as is usually assumed, arising from them.

We can easily see that the thoughts here described are fundamentally at odds with the commonsense assumptions (A1)–(A4).

In response, I first note that Fish held texts to be tyrants that somehow take readers into captivity. This is metaphorical language. What proposition does Fish intend it to express? A plausible candidate is the proposition "(A3) is false." That is, Fish's thought is that by observing the norm of getting at the author's meaning, readers become unfree. I can see no merit in this thought whatsoever. It is like saying that by observing the norm of basing one's theories on evidence, scientists become unfree. To be more precise, Fish's thought has no merit if interpretation is thought of as a truth-aimed enterprise. Of course, if you have no veritistic intentions, you're free to do with texts whatever you like. And you're also free to call such dealings "interpretation," if you like. But it is confusing to do so. My point is that if you do so, you're just not talking about the subject matter of this book.

Second, Fish tells us that, in order to overcome the inconsistency in his thinking that he noted, he started to ponder the view that "linguistic and textual facts, rather than being the objects of interpretation, are its products" (1980, 9). This is a very radical thought.[12] To see this, consider the following sentences that state what I take to be linguistic and textual facts:

- This book bears the title *The Epistemology of Reading and Interpretation.*
- One of Shakespeare's sonnets begins with the line "Shall I compare thee to a summer's day?"
- *To procrastinate* means "to put things off."
- Verbs can be conjugated whereas substantives cannot.
- Questions normally begin with a verb.

The view that Fish toyed with entails that these linguistic and textual facts are the products of interpretation. Applied to the earlier examples, this means that the fact that this book bears the title *The Epistemology of Reading and Interpretation* is the product of interpretation; that this fact is, somehow, created through interpretation; and that if no one engaged in interpretative activities, this fact would not be. It also means that the fact that *to procrastinate* means "to put things off" is a product of interpretation: it would not have that meaning if there were no interpreters – indeed, it has its meaning thanks to interpretation. The crucial question here is this: What is *interpretation* as the word is used here by Fish supposed to be? It certainly isn't one of the notions covered by my general account of interpretation. For none of those notions is such that, by engaging in

[12] Fish's view, in a way, mimics Kant's Copernican revolution, which entails, among other things, that the eagle you see drawing lazy circles in the air *an sich* has neither spatial nor temporal properties: such properties as you are inclined to ascribe to the eagle are the products of your perception; space and time are "forms of the intuition." An incisive exposition and criticism of Kant's Copernican revolution is Van Cleve (1999), chapters 1, 3, and 5.

interpretation in that sense, readers can bring it about that Shakespeare's famous sonnet begins with the line "Shall I compare thee to a summer's day?" or can make it a fact that verbs can be conjugated whereas substances cannot. As far as I can see, there just is no sense of *interpretation* that can do such tricks.

Fish's report about the latest phase of his thinking contains the words "what I finally came to see." What he finally came to see, he writes, is that

> there is no single way of reading that is correct or natural, only "ways of reading" that are extensions of community perspectives .... This meant that the business of criticism was not (as I had previously thought) to determine a correct way of reading but to determine from which of a number of possible perspectives reading will proceed. (Fish 1980, 16)

And,

> I now believe that interpretation is a source of texts, facts, authors, and intentions. Or to put it another way, the entities that were once seen as competing for the right to constrain interpretation (text, reader, author) are now all seen to be the *products* of interpretation. (Fish 1980, 16–17)

I raise three issues. First, what Fish reports he came to see really exists, but what he reports he now believes is unbelievable; it is crazy. Let me explain. "There is no single way of reading that is correct" is ambiguous between (a) no way of reading is correct and (b) there is more than one correct reading. I take it that Fish intended to affirm (b) and not (a), and also that a "way of reading" is something like a way of approaching a text, a way of understanding it. As should be clear from what I have been arguing over the last few chapters, I can entirely agree with (b). Texts are carriers of diverse information. They carry information about what the author intended to convey, and about the aims the author wanted to secure through writing the text (in short, about author's meaning). But they also contain information of the sort that externalist interpretations latch onto. These different kinds of interpretation all have their place under the sun; they are compatible in the way that sun and wind are compatible. Of course, a particular statement of the author's meaning of *T* can be false, and so can a particular statement of one of *T*'s indicative meanings. But this does nothing to discard the notions of author's meaning and indicative meanings as such. So, I can use the words that Fish uses to report what he came to see to express what I came to see. I put the point in this somewhat hedging way, for in fact I doubt that when Fish and I use the same words, we use them to express the same proposition. Doubt creeps in when I read what Fish reports that he now believes and which is, he suggests, in important ways related to what he came to see (had Fish not added this suggestion, my doubt would not have arisen). What he now believes is this: texts, readers, and authors are the *products* of interpretation. This is, of course, wholly unbelievable. And it is unbelievable because it entails the denial of the commonsense assumptions mentioned earlier. If *Y* is the product of *X*, then *X* is in some way responsible for the existence of *Y*. What Fish now believes entails that interpretation is responsible for the existence (i) of the text that is John Locke's *Essay concerning Human Understanding*, (ii) of me and many other readers of the *Essay*, and (iii) of the author, John Locke, himself. I take this to be a sufficient reductio ad absurdum of the belief that Fish claims to have now. (It should be clear that vis-à-vis Fish's reader-response theory of interpretation, I find myself in a position analogous to van Inwagen's position vis-à-vis anti-Realism: I am unable to enter into the smallest degree of imaginative sympathy with it. I have a Type II understanding of the view but am entirely lacking a Type III understanding.)

Second, on the view that Fish reports he now believes, it becomes entirely unclear what interpretation is. It is a fully intelligible thing to say that interpretation has objects; for instance, newspaper articles, fables, scientific papers, historical narratives, poems, travel guidebooks, cookbooks, catalogs, manuals – in short, texts. But since Fish now believes that texts are the *products* of interpretation, it becomes entirely mysterious just what interpretation is. Interpretation without objects of interpretation is like playing tennis with no ball. As little as the latter is tennis, as little is the former interpretation. The notion of interpretation that Fish uses is miles removed from the one that figures in the general account of interpretation.

Third and finally, it is, I think, a sound philosophical method to reject theses that conflict with common sense unless one has good arguments for accepting them.[13] A number of the claims that Fish considers and makes fly in the face of common sense: they deny, directly or by implication, (A1)–(A4). Given the methodological principle mentioned, we should therefore be given strong arguments if we are to adopt these claims. But Fish offers no arguments – not for the claim that meaning *is* the response

[13] This methodological principle was developed in the tradition of commonsense philosophy. See Van Woudenberg (2021).

of the reader, nor for the claim that linguistic and textual facts are the products of interpretation, nor for the claim that texts, readers, and authors are the products of interpretation. Without arguments for these very counterintuitive claims, and assuming we've understood them correctly, we are justified in rejecting them.[14]

Interpretation as a Source of Knowledge

In Chapter 8 I argued that we can be reading texts and not be engaged in allegoresis, nor have to overcome difficulties. To this I can now add that we can be reading and not engage in holistic textual act interpretation, nor in interpretation as reconstruction, nor in any manner of externalist interpretation. This means that reading isn't identical to any of these four kinds of interpretation, nor does it have any of these four kinds of interpretation as a constitutive element.

The final question I take up is whether interpretation should be considered as a source of knowledge. Since there are various kinds of interpretation, the question is manifold. But I think we can easily see that all the kinds of interpretation that I have distinguished satisfy the first two conditions of being a source of knowledge. For they are all, as condition (i) requires, processes that only take place "in" subjects. Furthermore, as condition (ii) requires, these processes are triggered or set to work in certain conditions. Allegoresis is triggered in situations in which there is a sense of (or a reason to believe that there is) a deeper or hidden meaning. Difficulty-overcoming interpretations are triggered in conditions where there are difficulties that hamper understanding. Interpretation qua disambiguation is triggered in situations of lexical or other sorts of ambiguity. Holistic textual act interpretations are triggered in situations in which we reflect on what it is that the author wanted to say by the text as a whole, on what the core of the work is. Interpretation as reconstruction is triggered in situations in which one reflects on the overall point that the author is making in a text that is opaque. Externalist interpretations are triggered in circumstances in which we think that certain widely accepted ideas or specific theories or views have made us aware of kinds of meaning that the author themselves most likely was unaware of.

Does interpretation, due to being so triggered, yield knowledge by acquaintance, know-how, and/or beliefs that can, and in the

[14] A delightful, thorough, and critical discussion of the views of Fish and other theorists that assign central importance to reader response is Gaskin (2013, 154–182).

preponderance of cases do, constitute knowledge – in other words, is condition (iii) satisfied? My conclusion, based on what I have argued over the last three chapters, is that it can, in principle, be satisfied for all the kinds of interpretation that I have discussed. Whether it is satisfied in a specific instance, depends on the available evidence.

References

Adams, Robert. 1972. "Must God Create the Best?" *Philosophical Review* 81:317–332.

Alfano, Mark. 2009. "Sensitivity Theory and the Individuation of Belief-Formation Methods." *Erkenntnis* 70:271–281.

Alston, William P. 1964. *Philosophy of Language*. Englewood Cliffs: Prentice-Hall.

1991. *Perceiving God: The Epistemology of Religious Experience*. Ithaca: Cornell University Press.

1993. *The Reliability of Sense Perception*. Ithaca: Cornell University Press.

1996. *A Realist Conception of Truth*. Ithaca: Cornell University Press.

2000. *Illocutionary Acts and Sentence Meaning*. Ithaca: Cornell University Press.

2005. *Beyond "Justification": Dimensions of Epistemic Evaluation*. Ithaca: Cornell University Press.

Anscombe, Elizabeth. 1957. *Intention*. Oxford: Basil Blackwell.

Apel, Karl-Otto. 1984. *Understanding and Explanation*. Cambridge: MIT Press.

Armstrong, David M. 1989. *Universals: An Opiniated Introduction*. Boulder: Westview Press.

Audi, Robert. 1993. *Action, Intention, and Reason*. Ithaca: Cornell University Press.

1994. "Dispositional Beliefs and Dispositions to Believe." *Nous* 28:419–434.

1998. *Epistemology*. London/New York: Routledge.

1999. "Moral Knowledge and Ethical Pluralism." In *The Blackwell Guide to Epistemology*, edited by John Greco and Ernest Sosa, 271–302. Oxford: Blackwell.

2002. "The Sources of Knowledge." In *The Oxford Handbook of Epistemology*, edited by Paul K. Moser, 71–94. Oxford: Oxford University Press.

2010. *Epistemology*. London: Taylor & Francis.

2013. *Moral Perception*. Princeton: Princeton University Press.

Austin, J. L. 1962. *How to Do Things with Words*. Oxford: Oxford University Press.

1970. *Philosophical Papers*. Edited by J. O. Urmson and G. J. Warnock. Oxford: Clarendon.

Baker-Hytch, Max. 2018. "Complexity-Based Beliefs and the Generality Problem for Reliabilism." *Quaestiones Disputatae* 8:19–35.

Bealer, George. 1999. "The Apriori." In *The Blackwell Guide to Epistemology*, edited by John Greco and Ernest Sosa, 243–270. Oxford: Blackwell.

Belsey, Catherine. 1980. *Critical Practice*. London: Methuen.

Benacerraf, Paul. 1973. "Mathematical Knowledge." *The Journal of Philosophy* 70:661–679.

Bertelson, Paul, and Beatrice de Gelder. 2004. "The Psychology of Multimodal Perception." In *Crossmodal Space and Crossmodal Attention*, edited by Charles Spence and Jon Driver, 151–177. Oxford: Oxford University Press.

Bertens, Hans. 2014. *Literary Theory: The Basics*. 3rd ed. London/New York: Routledge.

"Bijentelling enkele dagen verlengd" [Bee count extended by a few days]. 2019. *Trouw*, p. 8, 15 April.

Bleicher, Joseph. 1980. *Contemporary Hermeneutics: Hermeneutics as Method, Philosophy, and Critique*. London: Routledge & Kegan Paul.

Bloomfield, Leonard. 1935. *Language*. London: Allen & Unwin.

Bod, Rens. 2015. *A New History of the Humanities: The Search for Patterns and Principles*. Oxford: Oxford University Press.

BonJour, Laurence. 1985. *The Structure of Empirical Knowledge*. Cambridge: Harvard University Press.

1998. *In Defense of Pure Reason*. Cambridge: Cambridge University Press.

2002. *Epistemology: Classic Problems and Contemporary Responses*. Boulder: Rowman & Littlefield.

Bos, Abraham P. 2003. *The Soul and Its Instrumental Body: A Reinterpretation of Aristotle's Philosophy of Living Nature*. Leiden: Brill.

Bouter, Lex, and Sven Hendrix. 2017. "Both Whistleblowers and the Scientists They Accuse Are Vulnerable and Deserve Protection." *Accountability in Research* 24:359–366.

Bratman, Michael. 1999. *Faces of Intention*. Cambridge: Cambridge University Press.

Broad, C. D. 1969. *Religion, Philosophy, and Psychical Research*. New York: Humanities Press.

Bryson, Bill. 2008. *Shakespeare: The World as a Stage*. London: Harper Collins.

Byers, William. 2007. *How Mathematicians Think: Using Ambiguity, Contradiction, and Paradox to Create Mathematics*. Princeton: Princeton University Press.

Cappelen, Herman, and John Hawthorne. 2009. *Relativism and Monadic Truth*. Oxford: Oxford University Press.

Carter, Adam, and Ted Poston. 2018. *A Critical Introduction to Knowledge-How*. London: Bloomsbury.

Carter, Craig A. 2018. *Interpreting Scripture with the Great Tradition: Recovering the Genius of Premodern Exegesis*. Grand Rapids: Baker Academic.

Cassam, Quassim. 2009. "What Is Knowledge?" In *Epistemology*, edited by Anthony O'Hear, 101–120. Royal Institute of Philosophy Supplement 64. Cambridge: Cambridge University Press.

Chisholm, Roderick. 1957. *Perceiving: A Philosophical Study*. Ithaca: Cornell University Press.
1977. *Theory of Knowledge*. 2nd ed. Englewood Cliffs: Prentice-Hall.
Chladenius, Johann Martin. 1742. *Einleitung zur richtigen Auslegung vernünfftiger Reden und Schriften*. Leipzig: Lanckisch.
Clark, Andy. 2008. *Supersizing the Mind*. Oxford: Oxford University Press.
Clark, Andy, and David Chalmers. 1998. "The Extended Mind." *Analysis* 58:7–19.
Coady, C. A. J. 1992. *Testimony: A Philosophical Study*. Oxford: Clarendon.
Conee, Earl. 1994. "Phenomenal Knowledge." *Australasian Journal of Philosophy* 72:136–150.
Cuneo, Terence. 2007. *The Normative Web*. Oxford: Oxford University Press.
Cuneo, Terence, and Russ Shafer-Landau. 2014. "The Moral Fixed Points: New Directions for Moral Nonnaturalism." *Philosophical Studies* 171:399–443.
Dancy, Jonathan. 1985. *Introduction to Contemporary Epistemology*. Oxford: Blackwell.
2004. *Ethics without Principles*. Oxford: Oxford University Press.
Davidson, Donald. 1984. *Inquiries into Truth and Interpretation*. Oxford: Clarendon.
Dehaene, Stanislas. 2009. *Reading in the Brain*. New York: Viking.
Dennett, Daniel. 1990. "The Interpretation of Texts, People, and Other Artifacts." *Philosophy and Phenomenological Research* 50:177–194.
Dilthey, Wilhelm. 1927. *Gesammelte Schriften*. Vol. 7, *Der Aufbau der geschichtlichen Welt in den Geisteswissenschaften*. Leipzig/Berlin: B. G. Teubner.
Domaradzki, Mikolaj. 2017. "The Beginnings of Greek Allegoresis." *Classical World* 110:299–321.
Donaldson, Sue, and Will Kymlicka. 2011. *Zoopolis: A Political Theory of Animal Rights*. Oxford: Oxford University Press.
Dooley, Lucile. 1920. "Psychoanalysis of Charlotte Brontë, as a Type of the Woman of Genius." *The American Journal of Psychology* 31:221–272.
Dretske, Fred. 1969. *Seeing and Knowing*. Chicago: University of Chicago Press.
1981. *Knowledge and the Flow of Information*. Oxford: Blackwell.
2000. "Simple Seeing." In *Perception, Knowledge, and Belief: Selected Essays*, by Fred Dretske, 97–112. Cambridge: Cambridge University Press.
Dutilh Novaes, Catarina. 2012. *Formal Languages in Logic: A Philosophical and Cognitive Analysis*. Cambridge: Cambridge University Press.
Elgin, Catherine. 1996. *Considered Judgment*. Princeton: Princeton University Press.
Evans, Gareth. 1982. *The Varieties of Reference*. Oxford: Oxford University Press.
Ewing, A. C. 1953. *Ethics*. London: English University Press.
1962. *The Fundamental Questions of Philosophy*. New York: Collier.
Fales, Evan. 1996. *A Defense of the Given*. Lanham: Rowman & Littlefield.
Feldman, Richard. 2003. *Epistemology*. Upper Saddle River: Prentice-Hall.
Fish, Stanley. 1980. *Is There a Text in This Class? The Authority of Interpretative Communities*. Cambridge: Harvard University Press.

Fischer, Steven Roger. 2004. *A History of Writing*. London: Reaktion Books.
Foley, Richard. 2018. *The Geography of Insight: The Humanities, the Sciences, How They Differ, Why They Matter*. Oxford: Oxford University Press.
French, Craig. 2012. "Does Propositional Seeing Entail Propositional Knowing?" *Theoria* 78:115–127.
Freud, Sigmund. (1915) 1979. *Introductory Lectures on Psychoanalysis*. Harmondsworth: Penguin.
Fricker, Elizabeth. 1995. "Telling and Trusting: Reductionism and Anti-Reductionism in the Epistemology of Testimony." *Mind* 104:393–411.
2003. "Understanding and Knowledge of What Is Said." In *Epistemology of Language*, edited by Alex Barber, 325–366. Oxford: Oxford University Press.
Fumerton, Richard. 2001. "Classical Foundationalism." In *Resurrecting Old-Fashioned Foundationalism*, edited by Michael R. DePaul, 3–20. Lanham: Rowman & Littlefield.
Gadamer, Hans-Georg. 1975. *Wahrheit und Methode*. Tubingen: J. C. B. Mohr (Paul Siebeck).
1976. *Philosophical Hermeneutics*. Translated by David E. Linge. Berkeley: University of California Press.
Gaskin, Richard. 2013. *Language, Truth, and Literature: A Defence of Literary Humanism*. Oxford: Oxford University Press.
Gelfert, Axel. 2014. *A Critical Introduction to Testimony*. London: Bloomsbury.
Gendler, Tamar Szabó, and John Hawthorne, eds. 2006. *Perceptual Experience*. New York: Oxford University Press.
Gibson, John. 2007. *Fiction and the Weave of Life*. Oxford: Oxford University Press.
2009. "Literature and Knowledge." In *The Oxford Handbook of Philosophy and Literature*, edited by Richard Eldridge, 467–485. Oxford: Oxford University Press.
Gilovich, Thomas. 1991. *How We Know What Isn't So: The Fallibility of Human Reason in Everyday Life*. New York: Free Press.
Ginet, Carl. 1975. *Knowledge, Perception, and Memory*. Dordrecht: Reidel.
Girard, René. 1965. *Mensonge romantique et vérité romanesque*. Paris: Grasset.
1976. *Deceit, Desire, and the Novel*. Baltimore: Johns Hopkins University Press.
Gisborne, Nikolas. 2010. *The Event Structure of Perception Verbs*. Oxford: Oxford University Press.
Goldman, Alvin. 1979. "What Is Justified Belief?" In *Justification and Knowledge*, edited by George S. Pappas, 1–23. Dordrecht: Reidel.
1986. *Epistemology and Cognition*. Cambridge: Harvard University Press.
1999. *Knowledge in a Social World*. New York: Oxford University Press.
Goldsmith, Oliver. 1973. *Treasury of Aesop's Fables*. Illustrated by Thomas Bewick. New York: Avenel Books.
Goodman, Jeffrey. 2020. "On Reading." *Acta Analytica* 35:51–59. https://doi.org/10.1007/s12136-019-00400-5.
Govier, Trudy. 1976. "Belief, Values, and the Will." *Dialogue* 15:642–663.
Graham, Gordon. 2005. *Philosophy of the Arts*. 3rd ed. London: Routledge.

Grice, Paul. 1989. *Studies in the Way of Words*. Cambridge: Harvard University Press.

Grimm, Stephen R. 2006. "Is Understanding a Species of Knowledge?" *British Journal for the Philosophy of Science* 57:515–535.

2016. "How Understanding People Differs from Understanding the Natural World." *Philosophical Issues* 26:209–225.

2018. "Understanding as an Intellectual Virtue." In *The Routledge Handbook of Virtue Epistemology*, edited by Heather Battaly, 340–351. London: Routledge.

2020. "Transmitting Understanding and Know-How." In *What the Ancients Offer to Contemporary Epistemology*, edited by Stephen Heatherington and Nicholas D. Smith, 124–139. New York: Routledge.

Hamlyn, D. W. 1970. *The Theory of Knowledge*. London: Macmillan.

Haraway, Donna. 2007. *When Species Meet*. Minneapolis: University of Minnesota Press.

Hasan, Ali, and Richard Fumerton. 2017. "Knowledge by Acquaintance vs. Description." In *The Stanford Encyclopedia of Philosophy* (Fall 2017), edited by Edward N. Zalta. https://plato.stanford.edu/archives/fall2017/entries/knowledge-acquaindescrip/.

Hemeren, Goran. 1983. "Interpretation: Types and Criteria." *Grazer Philosophische Studien* 19:131–161.

Jack, Belinda. 2019. *Reading: A Very Short Introduction*. Oxford: Oxford University Press.

Jackson, Frank. 1986. "What Mary Didn't Know." *The Journal of Philosophy* 83:291–295.

Johnson, W. E. 1964. *Logic, Part 1*. New York: Dover Publications.

Johnston, Mark. 2006. "Better Than Mere Knowledge? The Function of Sensory Awareness." In *Perceptual Experience*, edited by Tamar Szabó Gendler and John Hawthorne, 260–290. New York: Oxford University Press.

Kahneman, Daniel. 2011. *Thinking, Fast and Slow*. London: Allen Lane.

Keen, Susan. 2007. *Empathy and the Novel*. Oxford: Oxford University Press.

Kornblith, Hilary, ed. 2001. *Epistemology: Internalism and Externalism*. London: Blackwell.

Krämer, Sybille. 2003. "Writing, Notational Iconicity, Calculus: On Writing as a Cultural Technique." *Modern Languages Notes* 118:518–537.

Kvanvig, Jonathan. 2003. *The Value of Knowledge and the Pursuit of Understanding*. New York: Cambridge University Press.

Lackey, Jennifer. 2008. *Learning from Words: Testimony as a Source of Knowledge*. New York: Oxford University Press.

Ladyman, James. 2002. *Understanding Philosophy of Science*. London: Routledge.

Lamarque, Peter. 2000. "Objects of Interpretation." *Metaphilosophy* 31:96–124.

Lamarque, Peter, and Stein Olsen. 1994. *Truth, Fiction, and Literature*. Oxford: Clarendon.

Lewis, David. 1996. "Elusive Knowledge." *Australasian Journal of Philosophy* 74:549–567.

Lipton, Peter. 2004. *Inference to the Best Explanation*. New York: Routledge.
Locke, John. (1689) 1975. *An Essay Concerning Human Understanding*. Edited by Peter H. Nidditch. Oxford: Clarendon.
Loux, Michael J., and Thomas Crisp. 2017. *Metaphysics*. London: Routledge.
Macherey, Pierre. 1978. *A Theory of Literary Production*. London: Routledge.
Machuca, Diego E., and Baron Reed, eds. 2018. *Skepticism from Antiquity to the Present*. London: Bloomsbury.
Mantzavinos, C. 2016. "Hermeneutics." In *The Stanford Encyclopedia of Philosophy* (Winter 2016), edited by Edward N. Zalta. https://plato.stanford.edu/archives/win2016/entries/hermeneutics/.
McNaughton, David. 1999. *Moral Vision*. Oxford: Blackwell.
Menary, Richard. 2007. "Writing as Thinking." *Language Sciences* 29:621–632.
Millett, Kate. 1970. *Sexual Politics*. Garden City: Doubleday.
Moore, G. E. 1993. "Moore's Paradox." In *Selected Writings*, edited by Thomas Baldwin, 207–212. London: Routledge.
Moser, Paul K. 1989. *Knowledge and Evidence*. Cambridge: Cambridge University Press.
Moser, Paul K., Dwayne Mulder, and J. D. Trout. 1998. *The Theory of Knowledge*. New York: Oxford University Press.
Nietzsche, Friedrich. 1954. *The Portable Nietzsche*. Edited by Walter Kaufmann. New York: Viking Press.
Nozick, Robert. 1981. *Philosophical Explanations*. Cambridge: Harvard University Press.
O'Brien, Lilian. 2015. *Philosophy of Action*. London: Palgrave Macmillan.
O'Callaghan, Casey. 2012. "Perception and Multimodality." In *The Oxford Handbook of Philosophy of Cognitive Science*, edited by Eric Margolis, Richard Samuels, and Stephen Stich, 1–28. Oxford: Oxford University Press.
Peacocke, Christopher. 1983. *Sense and Content: Experience, Thought, and Their Relations*. Oxford: Oxford University Press.
Peels, Rik. 2020. "How Literature Delivers Knowledge and Understanding, Illustrated by Hardy's *Tess of the D'Urbervilles* and Wharton's *Summer*." *The British Journal of Aesthetics* 60:199–222.
Plantinga, Alvin. 1974. *The Nature of Necessity*. Oxford: Clarendon.
1993a. *Warrant and Proper Function*. Oxford: Oxford University Press.
1993b. *Warrant: The Current Debate*. New York: Oxford University Press.
2000. *Warranted Christian Belief*. New York: Oxford University Press.
Popper, Karl R. 1960. "The Sources of Knowledge and Ignorance." *Proceedings of the British Academy* 46:39–71.
1972. *Objective Knowledge: An Evolutionary Approach*. Oxford: Clarendon.
Postma, Marten. 2019. "The Meaning of Word Sense Disambiguation Research." PhD dissertation, Vrije Universiteit Amsterdam.
Pritchard, Duncan. 2005. *Epistemic Luck*. Oxford: Oxford University Press.
2006. *What Is This Thing Called Knowledge?* London/New York: Routledge.
2012. *Epistemological Disjunctivism*. Oxford: Oxford University Press.

Putnam, Hilary. 1987. *The Many Faces of Realism*. LaSalle: Open Court.
Quine, Willard V. O. 1961. "Two Dogmas of Empiricism." In *From a Logical Point of View*, by Willard V. O. Quine, 20–46. 2nd ed. Cambridge: Harvard University Press.
Ranalli, Chris. 2014. "Luck, Propositional Perception, and the Entailment Thesis." *Synthese* 191:1222–1247.
2019. "The Puzzle of Philosophical Testimony." *European Journal of Philosophy* 28:1–22.
Reid, Thomas. (1764) 1997. *An Inquiry into the Human Mind on the Principles of Common Sense*. Edited by Derek Brookes. Edinburgh: Edinburgh University Press.
(1785) 2002. *Essays on the Intellectual Powers of Man*. Edited by Derek Brookes. Edinburgh: Edinburgh University Press.
(1788) 1969. *Essays on the Active Powers of the Human Mind*. Edited by Baruch Brody. Cambridge: MIT Press.
Ricoeur, Paul. 1973. "The Hermeneutical Function of Distanciation." *Philosophy Today* 17:129–141.
Rorty, Richard. 1981. *Philosophy and the Mirror of Nature*. Princeton: Princeton University Press.
Rosenberg, Alex. 2011. *The Atheist's Guide to Reality*. New York: W. W. Norton.
Ruskin, John. (1865) 2002. *Sesame and Lilies*. Edited by Deborah Epstein Nord. New Haven/London: Yale University Press.
Russell, Bertrand. 1948. *The Problems of Philosophy*. Oxford: Oxford University Press.
Ryle, Gilbert. 1949. *The Concept of Mind*. London: Hutchinson.
Schacht, Richard. 1984. "Nietzsche on Philosophy, Interpretation and Truth." *Noûs* 18:75–85.
Schlick, Moritz. 1927. "Vom Sinn des Lebens." *Symposion* 1:331–354.
Schwitzgebel, Eric. 2008. "The Unreliability of Naïve Introspection." *Philosophical Review* 117:245–273.
Searle, John. 1969. *Speech Acts*. Cambridge: Cambridge University Press.
Shope, Robert. 1983. *The Analysis of Knowledge: A Decade of Research*. Princeton: Princeton University Press.
2002. "Conditions and Analyses of Knowledge." In *The Oxford Handbook of Epistemology*, edited by Paul K. Moser, 25–70. Oxford: Oxford University Press.
Singh, Simon. 1997. *Fermat's Last Theorem*. London: HarperCollins.
Skinner, Quentin. 1969. "Meaning and Understanding in the History of Ideas." *History and Theory* 8:3–53.
Sosa, Ernest. 1991. *Knowledge in Perspective*. Cambridge: Cambridge University Press.
2007. *A Virtue Epistemology*. New York: Oxford University Press.
Stampe, Dennis W. 1968. "Toward a Grammar of Meaning." *The Philosophical Review* 77:137–174.

Stolnitz, Jerome. 1992. "On the Cognitive Triviality of Art." *British Journal of Aesthetics* 32:191–200.
Stout, Jeffrey. 1982. "What Is the Meaning of a Text?" *New Literary History* 14:1–12.
Stump, Eleonor. 2001. "Augustine on Free Will." In *The Cambridge Companion to Augustine*, edited by Eleonore Stump and Norman Kretzmann, 124–147. Cambridge: Cambridge University Press.
Swinburne, Richard. 1991. *The Existence of God*. 2nd ed. Oxford: Clarendon.
Thomasius, Christian. 1691. *Einleitung zu der Vernunfft-Lehre*. Halle: Salfeld.
Tomalin, Claire. 2006. *Thomas Hardy: The Time-Torn Man*. London: Viking.
Turner, Steve. 1982. *Up to Date*. London: Hodder and Stoughton.
Turri, John. 2010. "Does Perceiving Entail Knowing?" *Theoria* 76:197–206.
Twardowski, Kazimierz. 1999. "On the Logic of Adjectives." In *On Actions, Products and Other Topics in Philosophy*, by Kazimierz Twardowski, 141–143. Edited by Johannes Brandle and Jan Wolenski. Amsterdam: Rodopi.
Ullmann, Stephen. 1972. *Semantics: An Introduction to the Science of Meaning*. Oxford: Blackwell.
Unger, Peter. 2000. "An Argument for Skepticism." In *Epistemology: An Anthology*, edited by Ernest Sosa and Jaegwon Kim, 42–52. London: Blackwell.
Van Cleve, James. 1999. *Problems from Kant*. Oxford: Oxford University Press.
2015. *Problems from Reid*. Oxford: Oxford University Press.
Van den Brink, Gijsbert, Jeroen de Ridder, and René van Woudenberg. 2017. "The Epistemic Status of Evolutionary Theory." *Theology and Science* 15:454–472.
Van Inwagen, Peter. 1981. "Why I Don't Understand Substitutional Quantification." *Philosophical Studies* 39:281–285.
2009. *Metaphysics*. 3rd ed. Boulder: Westview Press.
Van Woudenberg, René. 2006. "Knowledge through Imagination." *Metaphilosophy* 27:151–161.
2009. "Ignorance and Force: Two Excusing Conditions for False Beliefs." *American Philosophical Quarterly* 46:373–386.
2014. "True Qualifiers for Qualified Truths." *Review of Metaphysics* 68:3–36.
2018a. "An Epistemological Critique of Scientism." In *Scientism: Prospects and Problems*, edited by Jeroen de Ridder, Rik Peels, and René van Woudenberg, 167–189. Oxford: Oxford University Press.
2018b. "The Nature of the Humanities." *Philosophy* 93:109–140.
2021. "The Delineation of Common Sense." In *The Cambridge Companion to Common-Sense Philosophy*, edited by Rik Peels and René van Woudenberg, 161–184. Cambridge: Cambridge University Press.
Van Woudenberg, René, and Rik Peels. 2018. "The Metaphysics of Degrees." *European Journal of Philosophy* 26:46–65.
Walsh, Dorothy. 1969. *Literature and Knowledge*. Middletown: Wesleyan University Press.

Walton, John. 2009. *The Lost World of Genesis One: Ancient Cosmology and the Origins Debate*. Westmont: IVP.
Westphal, Merold. 2009. *Whose Community? Which Interpretation?* Grand Rapids: Baker Academic.
Williams, Bernard. 1973. "Deciding to Believe." In *Problems of the Self*, by Bernard Williams, 136–151. Cambridge: Cambridge University Press.
Williamson, Timothy. 2001. *Knowledge and Its Limits*. Oxford: Oxford University Press.
Wilson, Timothy D. 2002. *Strangers to Ourselves: Discovering the Adaptive Unconscious*. Cambridge: Belknap Press.
Winters, Barbara. 1979. "Believing at Will." *Journal of Philosophy* 76:243–256.
Wittgenstein, Ludwig. 2009. *Philosophical Investigations*. The German text, with an English translation by G. E. M. Anscombe, P. M. S. Hacker, and Joachim Schulte. Rev. 4th ed. London: Wiley-Blackwell.
Wolfe, Jeremy M., Keith R. Kluender, Dennis M. Levi, Linda M. Bartoshuk, Rachel S. Hertz, Roberta L. Klatzky, and Daniel M. Merfeld. 2019. *Sensation and Perception*. International 5th ed. New York: Oxford University Press.
Wolterstorff, Nicholas. 1995. *Divine Discourse: Philosophical Reflections on the Claim that God Speaks*. Cambridge: Cambridge University Press.
1996. *John Locke and the Ethics of Belief*. Cambridge: Cambridge University Press.
2019. *In This World of Wonders: Memoir of a Life in Learning*. Grand Rapids: Eerdmans.
Wynne, Clive D. L., and Monique A. R. Udell. 2013. *Animal Cognition: Evolution, Behavior and Cognition*. London/New York: Palgrave.
Zagzebski, Linda. 2001. "Recovering Understanding." In *Knowledge, Truth, and Duty*, edited by Matthias Steup, 235–251. Oxford: Oxford University Press.
Zimmermann, Jens. 2015. *Hermeneutics: A Very Short Introduction*. Oxford: Oxford University Press.

Index

Nota bene: works and authors mentioned only as examples or for illustrative purposes are not included.

www.ingramcontent.com/pod-product-compliance
Ingram Content Group UK Ltd.
Pitfield, Milton Keynes, MK11 3LW, UK
UKHW020354140625
459647UK00020B/2465